Woman *(Pastel on paper)*

The English Writings of Rabindranath Tagore

The English Writings of Rabindranath Tagore

Volume Six

Essays Lectures Addresses

Introduction by

Mohit K. Ray

ATLANTIC

PUBLISHERS & DISTRIBUTORS (P) LTD

Published by
ATLANTIC
PUBLISHERS & DISTRIBUTORS (P) LTD
B-2, Vishal Enclave, Opp. Rajouri Garden,
New Delhi-110027
Phones : 25413460, 25429987, 25466842

Sales Office
7/22, Ansari Road, Darya Ganj,
New Delhi-110002
Phones : 23273880, 23275880, 23280451
Fax : 91-11-23285873
web : www.atlanticbooks.com
e-mail : info@atlanticbooks.com

ISBN 81-269-0740-1 (Vol. VI)
ISBN 81-269-0666-9 (Set)

Printed in India
at Syndicate Binders, NOIDA (U.P.)

CONTENTS

PREFACE

One distinctive feature of the Volumes V-VIII—a feature that marks them out from the previous volumes—is that these volumes include many writings, speeches and utterances of persons other than Tagore. The exigency of the situation and the special character of these volumes make it obligatory to use others' writings, particularly when publishing conversations, interviews, etc.

The volumes offer a wide spectrum of Tagore's English prose pieces—lectures, essays, letters, speeches, tributes, and conversations and interviews. In range and depth these writings show how myriad-minded Tagore was, and how true is Aldous Huxley's assessment that 'he was at once a great idealist and a practical man of actions'. He was a poet with a soaring imagination reaching unimaginable heights, a thinker of the highest order who could also be equally concerned with the miserable condition of the village farmers and engaged in co-operative movement and rural reconstruction. A lover of children, he would write poems for children, write textbooks for them, and would also make a fine analysis of the crisis of civilization. A man of remarkable courage of conviction, he would not hesitate to renounce his knighthood and yet would have his own views about nationalism and would be critical about it. It may not immediately concern us here but the fact remains that the same man started painting when he was around seventy and left us a legacy of some two thousand doodles and paintings which have been praised highly by connoisseurs. A few specimens used in these volumes will justify the accolades. A singer himself, he has left us a collection of, again, some two thousand songs. These facts do not immediately concern us here but they are relevant in giving us an idea of the mighty stature of Tagore about whom we can always say what Arnold said about

Shakespeare: "Others abide our questions; Thou art free./ We ask and ask, thou smilest and art still, outtopping knowledge." And, unlike Shakespeare who remained confined only to drama and poetry, Tagore traversed all the fields of literary universe and whatever he touched turned into gold. He was not only a 'world poet', 'a great sentinel' or 'a universal man' but also an artist of the highest order.

We begin this set of volumes with the speech that Tagore delivered at Stockholm in 1921. Since Tagore could not attend the Nobel Award Ceremony at Stockholm in 1913, this speech may be regarded as 'the Nobel Prize Acceptance Speech'. The speech very succinctly describes 'the growth of a poet's mind'. We learn about his early exposure to Nature, how he 'used to live in utmost seclusion in the solitude of an obscure Bengal village by the river Ganges in a boat house', his growing love for the children, his translation of the *Gitanjali* 'without having any desire to have them published, being diffident of my mastery of that language', his enthusiastic reception in the West, his faith in the cultural heritage of India, for all its splendours and wisdom and wealth, his identification of the spirit of India as 'the ideal of unity' which he considers as 'the highest aim of our spiritual exertion to be able to penetrate all things with one soul, to comprehend all things as they are, and not to keep out anything in the whole universe—to comprehend all things with sympathy and love'. The speech, in brief, gives us an idea, though in an embryonic form, of the quality and substance of Tagore's vision of man and India. All his writings can be seen as elaborate manifestations of this vision in diverse forms.

ESSAYS

Thoughts from Rabindranath Tagore was first published by Macmillan, New York, in 1921 under the title *Thought Relic,* with 103 pages. The next edition edited by C.F. Andrews came out in 1929 under the title *Thoughts from Tagore* divided into three parts and containing 192 passages. The passages are meditative in nature.

The first edition of *The Religion of Man,* originally delivered as Hibbert Lectures at Manchester College, Oxford, in May

1930, was published by Allen and Unwin in 1930. Tagore made many major corrections in the edition and Macmillan, New York, brought out the second edition, incorporating all these changes, in 1931. The text reproduced here is the second edition. It should, however, be borne in mind, that these lectures are different from Kamala lectures delivered in Calcutta, published as *Mānuṣer Dharma* (Religion of Man) in Bengali, though there is a marked affinity in tone and temper.

Man was originally delivered as a course of three lectures, at Andhra University, in 1933.

Letters to a Friend, a revised and enlarged edition of *Letters from Abroad* (1922), was published by George Allen and Unwin, London, in 1928. The Preface and the first two essays are written by Charles Freer Andrews (1871–1940). These are also reproduced for a proper understanding of the letters. It is for the same reason that Andrews has presented the letters in several chapters with introductory notes. The letter dated 21 April was actually written not to Andrews but to Rothenstein with a copy to Andrews who by mistake included it in the volume.

Mahatmaji and the Depressed Humanity was published by the Visva-Bharati Bookshop, Calcutta, in 1932. The book contains lectures, essays, telegrams, etc., occasioned by Gandhi's decision to 'fast unto death' in protest 'against the communal award by Prime Minister Ramsay MacDonald'.

East and West, containing the letters exchanged between Gilbert Murray (1866–1957) and Tagore, was first published in Paris in 1935. Murray, because of his Greek scholarship and love of liberal values, was a great admirer of the poetry of Tagore.

LECTURES AND ADDRESSES

Race Conflict, originally an address delivered at the Congress of the National Federation of Religious Liberals held at Rochester, New York, in 1912, was published in *The Modern Review* in 1913.

The Spirit of Japan, originally a lecture delivered in Japan in 1915, was first published in *The Modern Review* in June 1917.

The Meeting of the East and the West, a critique of the contemporary political situation in India and originally published in the *Manchester Guardian,* was reprinted in *The Modern Review* in June 1918.

At the Cross Roads, also an essay on the political situation in India, was published in *The Modern Review* in July 1918.

The Message of the Forest, originally a lecture delivered in Bangalore on the occasion of the Festival of Fine Arts in January 1919, was published in its revised and enlarged version in May 1919.

Construction Versus Creation, originally an address delivered at the Gujarat Literary Conference, Ahmedabad, on 2 April 1920, was included in *Letters and Addresses,* edited by Anthony X. Soares and published in 1920.

A Cry for Peace was first published in *The Modern Review* in May 1919.

The Call of Truth, a criticism of Gandhi's non-cooperation movement, was published in *The Modern Review* in October 1921.

The Union of Cultures was published in *The Modern Review* in November 1921. The idea contained in the essay later crystallized in the form of Visva-Bharati, an international university.

A Vision of India's History was first published in *Visva-Bharati Quarterly* in 1923.

The Way to Unity was published in *Visva-Bharati Quarterly* in July 1923.

International Relations, originally a lecture delivered in Japan, was first published in *Visva-Bharati Quarterly* in 1924.

The Indo-Iranians was first published in *Visva-Bharati Quarterly*, Vol. 1, No. 3, October 1922.

Notes and Comments was first published in *Visva-Bharati Quarterly* in January 1924.

The Fourfold Way of India was first published in *The Modern Review* in August 1924.

The Schoolmaster was published in *The Modern Review* in October 1924.

City and Village, originally a lecture delivered in Turin, Italy, was published in *Visva-Bharati Quarterly* in October 1924.

The Voice of Humanity, originally a lecture delivered at Milan, during his first visit to Italy under Mussolini, was published in *Lectures and Addresses* in 1928.

The Indian Ideal of Marriage, based on the Bengali essay *Bhāratīya Bibāher Ādarśa* was published in *Visva-Bharati Quarterly* in July 1925.

The Cult of the Charka was published in *The Modern Review* in September 1995.

Judgment was published in *Visva-Bharati Quarterly* in October 1925.

The Philosophy of Our People, originally delivered as the Presidential Address at the First Indian Philosophical Congress in 1925, was published in *Visva-Bharati Quarterly* in January 1926.

The Rule of the Giant, originally a lecture delivered at Dhaka University, was published in *Visva-Bharati Quarterly* in July 1926.

The Meaning of Art, originally a lecture delivered at Dhaka University, was published in *Visva-Bharati Quarterly* in April 1926.

Notes and Comments, originally published in *Atlantic Monthly,* was reprinted in *Visva-Bharati Quarterly* in April 1927.

The Principle of Literature was first published in *Visva-Bharati Quarterly* in July 1927.

The Function of a Library was published in *Visva-Bharati Bulletin* in January 1929.

On Oriental Culture and Japan's Mission, originally a lecture delivered in Tokyo on 15 May 1929, was published by Indo-Japanese Association, Tokyo.

Ideals of Education, originally an address delivered in Tokyo in 1929, was published in *Visva-Bharati Quarterly* in April-July 1929.

The Philosophy of Leisure, originally an address delivered in Canada, was published in *Visva-Bharati Quarterly* in April-July 1929.

India and Europe was published in *Visva-Bharati Quarterly* in April-July 1929.

Wealth and Welfare was published in *The Modern Review* in February 1930.

The Educational Mission of the Visva-Bharati, originally a lecture broadcast by Radio New York, was published in *The Modern Review* in June 1931.

Meeting of the East and the West, originally an address delivered at a reception in New York in 1930, was published in *Visva-Bharati Quarterly*, Vol. 8, Part-3, 1930-31.

My Pictures was first published in *The Modern Review* in December 1930.

The First and the Last Prophets of Persia, a summary of a speech delivered at New History Society, New York in 1930, was published in *Visva-Bharati Quarterly*, Vol. 8, Part-4, 1931-32.

My School was first published in *The Modern Review* in January 1931.

International Goodwill is a summary of the speech at the All Peoples' Association, London, on 8th January 1931.

Lectures in Iran and Iraq are lectures that Tagore delivered during his visits to Iran and Iraq in 1932.

Asia's Response to the Call of the New Age, originally an address delivered in Teheran, was published in *The Modern Review*, October 1932.

Can Science be Humanised? was published in *Visva-Bharati News*, August 1934.

Rammohun Roy, originally the Presidential Address at Rammohun Roy Death Centenary, was published in *The Modern Review* in March 1933.

To the Youth of Hyderabad, originally a lecture delivered in Hyderabad in 1933, was published in 1963 (with a brief note by Padmaja Naidu).

Women's Place in the World is originally an address delivered at the All-India Women's Conference, Calcutta, in 1933-34 (24 Dec-2 Jan).

Reply to the Madras Corporation Address was first published in *Visva-Bharati News* in November 1934.

The Religion of an Artist was first published in *Visva-Bharati Quarterly* in April 1926 under the title "Meaning of Art", and later a revised version was published in *Contemporary Indian Philosophy* in 1936. It was also published in book form by Visva-Bharati in 1953.

To the Citizens of Delhi was first published in *Visva-Bharati News,* May-June 1936.

The Communal Award, originally the Presidential Address at a Conference held in Calcutta in 1936 to discuss the Communal Award, was first published by Dr Radhakumud Mukherjee.

Address at the Parliament of Religions, originally the Presidential Address at the Sri Ramakrishna Centenary Parliament of Religions, Calcutta, in March 1937, was published in *Visva-Bharati Quarterly* in May 1937.

China and India, originally an address delivered on the occasion of opening the 'Cheena Bhavan' at Santiniketan on 14 April 1937, was published by Prabhat Kumar Mukherjee.

To Subhas Chandra Bose is a translation by Tagore himself of his original Bengali address entitled *Deśañayak* written in May 1939.

Convocation Address at Gurukula Kangri, convocation address to the graduates of Gurukula Kangri, is available in typescript at Rabindra Bhavan, Santiniketan.

Crisis in Civilisation, Tagore's last public address, delivered on 14 April 1941, was published in *Visva-Bharati News,* Vol. 9, No. 2 and in *The Modern Review* in May 1941.

MISCELLANEOUS WRITINGS

A. Open Letters, Speeches, Tributes, etc.

The letter *The Problem of India* was first published in *The Modern Review* August 1910.

The letter *Spiritual Civilisation* was first published in *Visva-Bharati News* in October-November 1933.

National Language of India, Part 1 & 2 were published on 21 January 1918 and 26 March 1937, respectively.

The Object and Subject of a Story was first published in *The Modern Review* in September 1918.

The letter *Vernaculars for the M.A. Degree* was published in *The Modern Review* in November 1918.

The letter *Hindu Intercaste Marriage Validating Bill*, originally sent to the Editor of *Bharat Sevak*, was reprinted in *The Modern Review* in February 1919.

This Youth which Lies Hidden in My Heart was published in *The Modern Review* in February 1919.

On Some Educational Questions, first published in *The Mysore Economic Journal* under the title "Sir Rabindranath Tagore's Views on Some Educational Questions", was reprinted in *The Modern Review* in April 1919.

Poet's Contribution to Your Noble Work is Tagore's response to Gandhi's letter requesting him for a message on the occasion of launching 'Satyagraha' against the 'Rowlatt Act'.

The letter *When Badges of Honour Make Our Shame Glaring* evinces Tagore's reaction to the Jallianwallabagh Massacre.

A Great Crime ... in the Name of Law is Tagore's message to the first memorial meeting of the Jallianwallabagh Massacre, held in Bombay on 13 April 1923.

On British Mentality in Relation to India was published in *The Modern Review* in April 1921.

The Efficacy of Ahimsa was published in *The Bengalee* on 3 February 1922.

Message to the Young was published in *Visva-Bharati News* in July 1934.

Introducing Elmherst appeared on the occasion of Elmherst's arrival at Santiniketan in 1921.

Farewell to Dr. M. Winternitz was reprinted in *Visva-Bharati Quarterly,* October 1923.

To My Ceylon Audience was published in *Visva-Bharati Quarterly* in January 1924.

The *Letter to Lord Lytton* was written on 22 August 1924 in reaction to Lord Lytton's comment on Indian women.

The letter *Birth Control Movement* written on 30 September 1925 to Margaret Sanger, Editor, *Birth Control Review,* was published in *Amrita Bazar Patrika* on 5 January 1926.

Knighthood was published in *The Modern Review* in February 1926.

Deshbandhu Chittaranjan Das is Tagore's message of condolence on the death of Chittaranjan Das on 16 June 1925.

Romain Rolland was written in 1925 and included in *Rolland and Tagore* (1945), edited by Alex Aronson.

Farewell Address to Carlo Formichi was originally delivered in 1925. Later it was published in *Visva-Bharati Quarterly* in 1926.

Philosophy of Fascism was published in *Manchester Guardian* on 5 August 1926.

Fascism Denounced, a rejoinder to Formichi's letter (*Manchester Guardian,* 25 August 1926), was published in *Manchester Guardian* on 15 September 1926.

Protest against the Policy of Repression was published on 3 February 1927.

Henry Barbusse's Appeal: Tagore's Response was published in *Visva-Bharati Bulletin* in July 1927.

Freedom, a letter to J.T. Sunderland (who was writing a book on Indian struggle for independence) was written in February 1927.

Mother India, the first letter registering Tagore's protest against Catherine Mayo's *Mother India*, was first published in *Manchester Guardian* in October 1927; the second letter was addressed to the editor, *Nation,* New York, on 9 December 1927.

Colour Prejudice, a letter—Tagore's protest against colour prejudice—was published in *The Modern Review* in April 1928.

To the World League for Peace was written on 3 September 1928.

At the Immigration Office, originally published in *The Japan Adviser,* Tokyo, was reprinted in *Visva-Bharati Quarterly* in November 1929.

East is East was published in *Visva-Bharati Quarterly* in April-July 1929.

Protest Against the Arrest of Mahatma Gandhi was published in *Manchester Guardian* on 16 May 1930.

India: An Appeal to Idealism was published in *Spectator* on 7 June 1930.

Race and Colour Prejudice was published in *The Friend* on 13 June 1930.

Faith in British Justice was published in *Spectator,* London, on 30 August 1930.

Message to the Quaker Society of Friends was published in *Visva-Bharati Quarterly,* Vol. 8, Part-4.

I am Proud of My People was published in *Natal Witness* on 20 September 1930.

Statement Contradicted was published in *The New York Times* on 10 October 1930.

The Women's International League, originally published in *Pax International,* was reprinted in *The Modern Review* in November 1930.

The Colour Bar was published in *Spectator* on 17 April 1931.

Takagaki: Professor Nokuzo Takagaki was a Japanese expert in *Jujitsu*, and came to Santiniketan in 1929, and stayed for about two years.

India and Britain was published in *The Times* on 16 May 1931, and later in *The Modern Review* in July 1931.

On Proselytism was published in *Indian Social Reformer,* Bombay on 11 July 1931.

Sarnath is the text of the message sent by Tagore on the inauguration of the reconstructed *Vihar* at Sarnath.

Imprisonment of Gandhi is the cable sent by Tagore in protest against government repression.

Message to Iraq Air Force was sent to the Priest of the Iraq Air-Force on 13 April 1932.

The World's Children was published in *The World's Children* in September 1932.

Appeal to America was published in *Dharma,* New York in July-December 1932.

Welcome Address to Professor Davoud is the text of the formal welcome speech of Tagore on 9 January 1933.

On the Centenary of Wilberforce is the text of the message sent to the Centenary Celebration Meeting at Hull in honour of William Wilberforce.

Deshapriya J.M. Sengupta was published in *Visva-Bharati News* in August 1933.

Homage to Islam is the message on Sirat un Nabi that was published in *Forward* on 27 November 1933. The other message was published in *The Peshwa,* Delhi, in February 1936.

Bihar Earthquake and the Mahatma is Tagore's reaction to Mahatma's observations on the calamity on 15 January 1934.

The letter *Protest Against the Nazis* was published in *Israel's Messenger* on 3 August 1934.

My Ideals with regard to the Sreebhavana was published in *Visva-Bharati News* in August 1934.

Communal Award: To Madan Mohan Malviya is statements recording Tagore's position in regard to the Communal Award made by Ramsay McDonald.

Farewell to Abdul Ghafar Khan: Abdul Ghafar Khan came to visit Santiniketan to meet his son who was then a student at Kalabhavan.

My Young Friends was published in *Visva-Bharati News* in December 1934.

A Letter to an English Friend was published in *Visva-Bharati News* in December 1935.

Ishopanishat was published in *Visva-Bharati News* in April 1935.

Ramchandra Sharma Undertakes Fast: Tagore's Appeal was occasioned by Ramchandra Sharma's fast to stop animal sacrifice in the Kalighat temple in September 1935.

A Message of Condolence to Maharajkumari Vidyavati Devi of Kasmunda on the occasion of her personal bereavement.

To Indian National Congress was published in *Visva-Bharati News* in January 1936.

The Rice We Eat was published in *Visva-Bharati News* in January 1936.

Message to World Peace Congress was sent to Brussels on 5 September 1936.

New Education Fellowship was published in *Visva-Bharati News* in February 1936.

The English in India was published in *Manchester Guardian* on 2 October 1936.

Spanish Civil War was published in a pamphlet entitled *Spain* (Calcutta) in March 1937.

Appeal to the United Party of Sind was published in *The Hindu* on 25 April 1937.

In Defence of the Workers on Strike was published in *The Hindu* on 30 April 1937.

On India was published in *Visva-Bharati News* in July 1937.

Appeal for Andaman Prisoners was occasioned by the demand of the release of the Andaman prisoners in August 1937.

In Response to Rasbehari Bose's Appeal was Tagore's response to Rashbehari Bose's cable on the issue of Indo-Japanese friendship.

Vande Mataram was written in response to Jawaharlal Nehru's request to dispel confusions regarding the song.

Appeal to Journalists was published in *The Amrita Bazar Patrika* on 25 December 1937.

Jagadish Chandra Bose was published in *Visva-Bharati News* in December 1937.

The British Constitution in India was published in *Manchester Guardian* on 10 March 1938 and reprinted in *Visva-Bharati News* in April 1938.

To the People of China: Section 1 was published in *Visva-Bharati News* in July 1938 and Section 2 was published in *The Amrita Bazar Patrika* on 26 December 1939.

'Fascism' of the State of Travancore was published in *The Amrita Bazar Patrika* on 6 October 1938.

Letters to Czechoslovakia records Tagore's sympathy for the suffering Czechoslovakians.

Tagore and Noguchi was published in *Visva-Bharati Quarterly* in November 1938 under the title "Poet to Poet".

W.B. Yeats was published in *Hindusthan Standard* on 1 January 1939.

Bihar Cooperative Federation: 21st Conference was published in *Hindusthan Standard* on 22 August 1939.

A Tribute to Mahatma Gandhi was published in the Commemoration Volume, edited by Dr S. Radhakrishnan, on the occasion of the 70th birthday of Mahatma Gandhi in 1939.

European Order and World Order was published in *The Modern Review* in February 1940.

Freedom of Mind was first published in different newspapers on 4 February 1940, and reprinted in *Visva-Bharati News* in February 1940.

Telegram to Roosevelt is Tagore's telegram to Roosevelt on the occasion of the fall of Paris in June 1940.

Bengal's Great Inheritance records Tagore's reaction to the Secondary Education Bill (December 1940).

Man's Lost Heritage was published in *Visva-Bharati News* in November 1940.

Welcome to Xu Beihong was published in *Visva-Bharati News* in February 1940.

Message to 'Forward' was published in *The Modern Review* in February 1941.

Reply to Miss Rathbone records Tagore's reaction to Miss Rathbone's 'Open Letter to Indian', published in June 1941.

B. On Books

Thirty Songs from the Punjab and Kashmir is Tagore's Foreword to the book that was published in February 1913.

To the Nation is an Introduction to the English translation of Paul Richard's book, published in New York in 1917.

The Web of Indian Life is an Introduction to Sister Nivedita's book *The Web of Indian Life*, written on 21 October 1917.

A Great Channel for Communication is a Foreword to the Bengali Book of English Verse, published by Longman's Greene & Co., Bombay, 1918.

The Robbery of the Soil is an Introduction to L.K. Elmherst's book *The Robbery of the Soil.* It was read as lecture on 28 July 1922.

Zoroastrian Hymns is an Introduction, originally published by Macmillan, New York, in 1924.

The Case for India was published in *The Modern Review,* March 1931.

Voiceless India is Foreword to the book published in 1930 from America.

Christ was published in *Visva-Bharati News,* March 1933.

Rebel India is Tagore's review of the book, published in *The Modern Review* in January 1933.

Preface to 'Deliverance' is Preface to Sarat Chandra Chatterjee's *Niskriti* translated by Dilip K. Roy, and published in 1944.

When Peacocks Called is Foreword to Hilde Seligman's *When Peacocks Call* (1940).

CONVERSATIONS AND INTERVIEWS

Marguerite Wilkinson and Tagore was published in *The Touchstone,* New York, in February 1921.

Benedetto Croce and Tagore was published in *Visva-Bharati Quarterly,* October 1936.

Romain Rolland and Tagore was published in *Rolland and Tagore* (Visva-Bharati, 1945).

Salvadori and Tagore was published in *Visva-Bharati Quarterly,* October 1926.

Angelica Balban and Tagore was printed in *My Life as a Rebel,* published in New York (1965).

Interview with F.L. Minigerode was published in *The Weekly Press*, New Zealand, 2 December 1926.

H.G. Wells and Tagore was published in *A Tagore Reader* [Ed. Amiya Chakrabarty], Boston, 1961.

Einstein and Tagore was published in *The New York Times* on 10 August 1930.

Conversations in Russia was published in *The Modern Review* in November-December 1930.

Interview with the 'Jewish Standard': On the Palestinian Problem was published on 28 November 1930 (reprinted in *Rabindra-Bhavana,* autumn, 1990).

Interviews in Persia was originally published in *Parasya-Yatri* in 1933.

Tagore on Films was published in *The Observer,* London, on 8 August 1925.

MOHIT K. RAY

ESSAYS

Letters to a Friend

PREFACE

The letters contained in this volume were written to me by Rabindranath Tagore during the years 1913-1922. Many of them were published in India, in the *Modern Review,* and also in book form, under the title *Letters from Abroad.* The present volume represents an entire revision and enlargement of that book, of which only a few copies reached England. The material has now been divided into chapters, with a brief explanatory summary of the circumstances in which the letters were written.

It is a pleasure to me to thank Mr Ramananda Chatterjee, editor of the *Modern Review,* and Mr S. Ganesan, publisher, Madras, for permission to use the letters included in this volume, which have already appeared in India. I would also thank Messrs Macmillan for leave to quote in full the poem on page 52, and Mr Kelk for his kind help in proof correction.

With the Poet's sanction, this volume has been dedicated to the memory of my own dear friend and fellow-worker at Santiniketan, William Winstanley Pearson. He accompanied me on journeys undertaken with Rabindranath Tagore in different parts of the world, and also was my companion when I travelled with him alone to South Africa, Australia, New Zealand and Fiji. He was with the Poet in Europe and America at the time when many of these letters were written, and is often referred to in them. His death, owing to a railway accident in Italy in 1923—just when he was at the height of his powers of service and love—has made the fellowship between East and West, for which Santiniketan stands, doubly sacred to us all. He had two homes, one in Manchester and one at Santiniketan, both of them very dear to him. In each his memory is still fresh after the lapse of years.

Any profit from this book will be devoted to the Pearson Memorial Hospital at Santiniketan, which is open to our neighbours, the Santal aboriginals, as well as to the members of the Asram. Willie Pearson's great joy at Santiniketan was to visit these Santal villagers along with the boys of the Asram. He built a school and a well for them and did other acts of service. There could be no more suitable way of preserving his memory than such a hospital.

In conclusion, my special thanks are due to Muirhead Bone and Mukul Dey for their kindness in allowing me to use their drypoint etchings, and to William Rothenstein for the facsimile of the Poet's handwriting. They all shared with me the friendship of Willie Pearson, to whose memory this book is dedicated.

October 1928 C.F. Andrews

An Essay on the Bengal Renaissance

I

The course taken by the Bengal Renaissance a hundred years ago was strangely similar to that of Western Europe in the sixteenth century. The result in the history of mankind is likely to be in certain respects the same also. For just as Europe awoke to new life then, so Asia is awakening to-day.

In Europe it was the shock of the Arab civilization and the Faith of Islam which startled the West out of the intellectual torpor of the Dark Ages. Then followed the recovery of the Greek and Latin Classics and a new interpretation of the Christian Scriptures, both of which, acting together, brought the full Reformation and Renaissance.

In Bengal it was the shock of the Western civilization that startled the East into new life and helped forward its wonderful rebirth. Then followed the revival of the Sanskrit Classics and a reformation from within of the old religions. These two forces, acting together, made the Bengal Renaissance a living power in Asia. In Bengal itself the literary and artistic movement came into greatest prominence. Rabindranath Tagore has been its crown.

II

Early in the nineteenth century the burning question in Bengal was whether the spread of the English language should be encouraged or not. Macaulay's famous minute, written in 1835, fixed the English tongue as the medium for higher education. "Never on earth," writes Sir John Seeley, "was a more momentous question discussed." The phrase is an arresting one, and appears a palpable exaggeration until we understand the issues involved, not only for Bengal, but for every country in the East.

Macaulay won the victory. Nevertheless, some of his premises were unsound and his conclusions inaccurate. He poured contempt on the Sanskrit Classics; he treated Bengali literature as useless. In expressing these opinions he committed egregious blunders. Yet, strangely enough, in spite of his narrow outlook, his practical insight was not immediately at fault. The hour for the indigenous revival had not yet come. A full shock from without was needed, and the study of English gave the shock required.

But the new life which first appeared was not altogether healthy. It led immediately to a shaking of old customs and an unsettlement of religious convictions, carried often to a violent and unthinking extreme. The greatest disturbance of all was in the social sphere. A wholesale imitation of purely Western habits led to a painful confusion of ideas. It was a brilliant and precocious age, bubbling over with a new vitality; but wayward and unregulated, like a rudderless ship on a stormy sea.

III

The one outstanding personality, whose presence saved Bengal at this crisis, was the great Raja Ram Mohun Roy. Towering above his contemporaries, solitary and majestic, this extraordinary genius seems to have measured accurately the force of every new current as it flowed quickly past, and to have steered his own course with an almost unerring precision. As practical as Macaulay, he was no mere opportunist. He was a true prophet, and had the prophet's sacred fire of enthusiasm. On the literary side he was one of the most ardent promoters of the new Western learning, and eagerly helped forward Macaulay's programme. But the best energies of his marvelously full life were directed to re-create in the heart of the Bengali people that true reverence for the Indian past which should lead to a revival of their own Sanskrit Classics. Above all, he did not despise his Bengali mother-tongue, but brought it back into full literary use.

IV

Debendranath Tagore, the father of Rabindranath, was the next outstanding figure in the Bengali literary revival. His work and influence lasted for more than half a century. If Ram Mohun Roy may be likened to the root of this tree of literature, planted deep in the soil, Debendranath Tagore may be compared to its strong and vigorous stem, and Rabindranath, his son, to its flower and fruit. Rarely in the history of literature can such a direct succession be traced.

Debendranath's religious character illuminated the age with a moral grandeur of its own. So impressive was his spiritual authority, that he received by universal consent the name of Maharshi, or great saint. During the flood-tide of English fashion he held fast to the ancient moorings and strengthened every bond which kept his country close to its own historic past.

His autobiography, translated by his son, reveals the deep religious spirit of modern Bengal, along with its passion for intellectual truth. The Tagore family had already been attracted within the orbit of Raja Ram Mohun Roy, and the vivid memory of the great reformer was one of the strongest influences in moulding the life of Debendranath as he grew up from boyhood to youth.

By the middle of the nineteenth century, owing to these initial movements, a creative period in Bengali literary history had set in. It represented not merely an awakening of Bengal, but the beginning of a new era for the whole of Asia.

V

This Bengal Renaissance bears on its surface the marks of conflict between the new Western learning and the revived Sanskrit Classics. Toru Dutt, the fairest and frailest flower among the writers, composed her songs only in English; but the fragrance of the Sanskrit past pervades all her works and makes them a national possession. Michael Dutt began by writing English verse; but he abandoned this, while his literary powers were still at their height, and composed his later poems in a wonderfully sonorous and majestic Bengali metre. He has been called the Milton of the Bengal revival. Bankim's novels carry back the mind at every turn to the romance writers in the West.

We can almost feel behind them the zest with which young Bengal explored their new-found treasures.

But the strength of the period consisted in this, that the writers, amid all their passionate and devoted study of English, remained true to the ancient Indian ideal. They remembered the rock from whence they were hewn. They did not despise their own birthright. Not only the language, but also the subjects, of this new literature were brought more in touch with the people. The village life of Bengal, which had tended to fall into the background, gained a new appreciation. The mediaeval as well as the classical times were laid under contribution for subject-matter. The commanding ideal at last rose up before the minds of men, to build a truly national literature and art out of the living stones of indigenous poetry, music and song.

VI

Into this rich heritage of the past the young poet Rabindranath entered, and he has done more than anyone else to make this ideal a living inspiration in Bengal. A friend of mine has described to me the scene that took place when the aged novelist Bankim was being honoured and garlanded. The old man took the garland from off his own neck and placed it on that of a young writer who was seated at his feet—Rabindranath Tagore.

This act of Bankim has now been universally recognized as both generous and just. That which others were struggling to attain, in the midst of insuperable difficulties, Rabindranath has reached with the quick leap and joyful ease of supreme genius. The ideals of art, which were before only dimly discerned, he has seen with open vision. Moreover, in his later works he has carried still further the spiritual mission of his father, and he has clothed his own deepest religious thoughts with a raiment of simplicity and beauty.

His fame has come to the full in recent years, and his poetry has taken on a more prophetic tone. He has passed forward from the subjective period of unbounded delight in Nature, to enter into the mystery of the vast sorrow of the world; to share the heavy burden of the poor; to face death itself unmoved; to look for and attain the unclouded vision of God.

VII

In all this, Rabindranath has remained close to the heart of Bengal. Every day that I was with him, in 1912, his eyes seemed to be straining across the sea, to greet his boys at Santiniketan—longing also to be back among his village people at Shileida, among whom he was a father and a friend.

It is not wonderful, therefore, that Bengal, from whose soil he seems to draw his deepest inspiration, should have been inspired in turn by his music and song with a high consciousness of its own destiny. He has given vital expression, at a supreme moment of history, to the rising hopes of his own people. In that country of music and art and song,

> The prophetic soul of the wide world
> Dreaming of things to come

has found at last its vision in and through his poems. The dreams which Bengal is now dreaming may not all come true.

> The tumult and the shouting dies:
> The captains and the kings depart,

in the pageant of literature as well as that of empire. But song and music are mighty instruments, when the spirit of a rising people is beating high with hope; and to-day men, women, and even little children, are seeing through the eyes of Rabindranath the vision of "Golden Bengal."

That gracious vision is radiant and luminous. And there is not unmixed with it a sacred sense of awe, that God has visited His people.

If this supreme power of music and literature to create a new spirit in a whole people seems somewhat unreal in the West, it must be remembered that India still retains, deep below the surface, her living faith in the Unseen.

An Essay on the Personality of Tagore

I

The Temperament and character of Rabindranath Tagore may best be understood if I attempt to describe one memorable day in London, when he told me in outline the story of his own life in relation to his literary career.

He was lodging in the upper room of a house just outside the entrance to South Kensington Underground Station. The time was a morning in September 1912, and a thick London fog filled the air. He was still weak on account of a very serious illness, which had brought him to the West to undergo an operation, and his face looked pale and worn.

He first told me about his father—how all the household became still and hushed when he was present in the house, as if anxious not to disturb his meditations.

He spoke to me, also, about his mother, who had died when he was quite young. As he saw her face for the last time on earth, calm and beautiful in death, it awakened in him no childish terror, nor even wonder; all seemed so peaceful and natural. It was only later, as he grew older, that he learnt Death's inner meaning.

The account he gave me of his own life in early childhood was as follows:

I was very lonely—that was the chief feature of my childhood—I was very lonely. I saw my father seldom: he was away a great deal, but his presence pervaded the whole house and was one of the deepest influences on my life. I was kept in the charge of servants of the household after my mother died, and I used to sit, day after day, in front of the window and picture to myself what was going on in the outer world.

From the very first time that I can remember, I was passionately fond of Nature. Oh! it used to make me mad with joy when I saw the clouds come up in the sky one by one. I felt, even in those early days, that I was surrounded with a companionship very intense and very intimate, though I did not know how to name it. I had such an exceeding love for Nature, that I cannot think in what way to describe it to you; but she was a kind of loving companion, always with me, and always revealing to me some fresh beauty.

This was how he pictured his childhood to me on that foggy day in London, and a passage in his *Reminiscences* makes the portrait still more vivid:

In the morning of autumn (he writes) I would run into the garden the moment I got up from sleep. A scent of leaves and grass, wet with dew, seemed to embrace me, and the dawn, all tender and fresh with the newly awakened rays of the sun, held out its face to me to greet me beneath the trembling vesture of palm-leaves. Nature shut her hands and laughingly asked every day: "What have I got inside?" and nothing seemed impossible.

II

Rabindranath Tagore went on to tell me that his first literary awakening came from reading the old Bengali poets, Chandidas and Vidyapati. He studied them in a recently published edition, when he was twelve or thirteen, and revelled in their beauty. He went still further, and, with the precocity of youth, imitated their style and published some poems under the name of Bhanu Sinha. Literary Bengal wondered for a time who this Bhanu Sinha could be. He laughed as he told me of this exploit of his boyhood, and went on to say that these and many other juvenile poems were merely conventional and imitative. They followed the old classical style.

When he wrote, however, the poems published later under the name of *Sandhya Sangit* (Evening Songs), he broke away from the classical style altogether and became purely romantic. At first he was derided by the older generation for his new metres; but the younger generation was with him. He chose no

English model; the early Vaishnava religious literature was the source of his inspiration. These religious poems ever afterwards remained intimately endeared to him. Their influence is marked in his own lyrics, and especially in the *Gitanjali* series.

III

The time of his real birth as a poet he dates from a morning in Free School Lane, Calcutta, when with dramatic suddenness the veil seemed to be withdrawn from his eyes and he saw the inner soul of reality.

It was morning (he said to me). I was watching the sunrise from Free School Lane. A veil was suddenly withdrawn and everything became luminous. The whole scene was one perfect music—one marvellous rhythm. The houses in the street, the men moving below, the little children playing, all seemed parts of one luminous whole—inexpressibly glorious. The vision went on for seven or eight days. Everyone, even those who bored me, seemed to lose their outer barrier of personality; and I was full of gladness, full of love, for every person and every tiniest thing. Then I went to the Himalayas, and looked for it there, and I lost it.... That morning in Free School Lane was one of the first things which gave me the inner vision, and I have tried to explain it in my poems. I have felt, ever since, that this was my goal: to express the fullness of life, in its beauty, as perfection—if only the veil were withdrawn.

I copied this account down as the Poet told it on that dark, misty London morning; and I can remember distinctly even now the quiet laugh he gave as he said, "And I lost it," and also the emphasis he laid upon the words "fullness of life." In Rabindranath's own prose writings the same incident is also recorded. It may be well to compare this other record with the picture he gave me in London. They corroborate and explain one another.

Where the Sadar Street ends, trees in the garden of Free School Street are visible. One morning I was standing in the verandah; looking at them. The sun was slowly rising above the screen of their leaves; and as I was watching it, suddenly, in a moment, a veil seemed to be lifted from my eyes. I found the world wrapt in an inexpressible glory with its waves of joy and beauty bursting and breaking on all sides. The thick shroud of sorrow that lay on my heart in many folds was pierced through and through by the light of the world, which was everywhere radiant.

That very day the poem known as *The Fountain Awakened from its Dream* flowed on like a fountain itself. When it was finished, still the curtain did not fall on that strange vision of beauty and joy. There was nothing and no one whom I did not love at that moment.... I stood on the verandah and watched the coolies as they tramped down the road. Their movements, their forms, their countenances seemed to be strangely wonderful to me, as if they were all moving like waves in the great ocean of the world. When one young man placed his hand upon the shoulder of another and passed laughingly by, it was a remarkable event too.... I seemed to witness, in the wholeness of my vision, the movements of the body of all humanity, and to feel the beat of the music and the rhythm of a mystic dance.

For some days I was in this ecstatic mood. My brothers had made up their minds to go to Darjeeling, and I accompanied them. I thought I might have a fuller vision of what I had witnessed in the crowded parts of the Sadar Street, if once I reached the heights of the Himalayas.

But when I reached the Himalayas the vision all departed. That was my mistake. I thought I could get at truth from the outside. But however lofty and imposing the Himalayas might be, they could not put anything real into my hands. But God, the Great Giver, Himself can open the whole Universe to our gaze in the narrow space of a single lane.

IV

The volume of lyrics called *Morning Songs* was the direct outcome of this time of ecstatic early vision. There is a romantic longing to know intimately the secret of the beauty of the world. But as yet he had not the deep-laid basis of practical experience whereon to build. His first lyrics, therefore, are mainly in the realm of imagination, and not closely related to common human experience.

But outer circumstances, as well as his own inner spirit, prevented the young writer from remaining too long in that enchanted garden of the soul. His father, seeing his son's remarkable genius, very wisely insisted that he should leave Calcutta and go down to the banks of the Ganges in order to supervise there the family estate. This work brought him into closest touch with the village life of Bengal. He had to deal each day with the practical affairs of men, and to understand and appreciate the elemental hopes and fears of mankind, stripped of all convention. To his own good fortune, also, as a poet, his joy in communing with Nature found at the same time its fullest and freest expression. During pauses in his active business life he would live all alone on the sand-flats of the Ganges, moving up and down from village to village in his boat.

Sometimes (he told me) I would pass many months absolutely alone without speaking, till my own voice grew thin and weak through lack of use. I used to write from my boat the stories of the village life which I had witnessed in the course of my work, and put into written words the incidents and conversations which I had heard. This was my "short-story" period; and some think these stories better than the lyrics which I had written before.

It was during this long residence at Shileida that the deepest love for Bengal, his motherland, developed. The national movement had not yet come into actual outward shape and form; but the forces which were to break forth later were already acting powerfully in the hearts of leading Bengali thinkers; and Rabindranath's soul caught the flame of patriotism, not in Calcutta itself, but among the villagers. His unshaken faith in the destiny of his country received its strongest confirmation from what he saw in the village life of his own people. He was not unaware of the dangers which threatened that life through its contact with the new social forces from the West. Indeed, this forms the theme of many of his short stories. But he believed, with all his heart, from what he had witnessed, that the stock from which the new national life was to spring forth was sound at the core. He spoke to me, that morning, with the greatest possible warmth and affection of the Bengali villagers, and of the many lessons he owed to them of patience and simplicity, of human kindliness and sympathy.

V

Rabindranath Tagore dated the next stage in his literary life from the time when he went to Santiniketan Asram from Shileida.

He left his father's estate; and there seemed to come to him the strongest impression that a new period of adventure was about to arrive in his life. He anticipated some change, for which these quiet unbroken years in the country had been a preparation.

Slowly there came to him the clear call to give up his life more wholly for is country. He first went to Calcutta in order to found a school, and afterwards to Santiniketan with the same object. On his arrival at Santiniketan, to take up this new work, he was handicapped for want of funds. "I sold my books," he said to me pathetically.

I sold all my books, my copyrights, everything I had, in order to carry on the school. I cannot possibly tell you what a struggle it was, and what difficulties I had to go through. At first the object in view was purely patriotic, but later on it grew more spiritual. Then, in the very midst of all these outer difficulties and trials, there came the greatest change of all, the true *Varsha Sesha*, the change in my own inner life.

He went on to tell me how, when he was forty years old, his wife had died, and almost immediately after his daughter showed signs of consumption. He left the school and went away with his daughter to nurse her and tend her, but after six months of mingled hope and fear she passed away from his arms and left his heart still more desolate. Then came the third overwhelming wave of sorrow. His youngest son, to whom he had learnt to be father and mother in one, was taken suddenly ill with cholera and died in his presence—the child of his love.

As he spoke of these things that morning, the darkness of the London mists rolled away and the light shone through the clouds with a majestic radiance. This outward scene was but a faint symbol of the story that was being told me to quietly in that upper room.

The Poet spoke of the days and hours wherein Death itself became a loved companion—no longer the king of terrors, but altogether transformed into a cherished friend.

You know (he said to me), this death was a great *blessing* to me. I had through it all, day after day, a sense of fulfilment, of completion, as if nothing were lost. I felt that if even an atom in the universe seemed lost, it could never actually perish. It was not mere resignation that came to me, but the sense of a fuller life. I knew then, at last, what Death was. It was perfection.

Through what depth of suffering that peace and joy came out at last triumphant, the lines in his face told me as he spoke these words.

VI

It was during this period that *Gitanjali* was written in his own mother-tongue, Bengali. "I wrote," he said, "those poems for myself. I did not think of publishing them when I was writing."

They mark the great transition in his life, when the Poet's social and national longings became wholly merged in the universal. He has attempted—to use his own words—"to express the fullness of human life, in its beauty, as perfection."

Since that period of sorrow he has fared forth as a voyager, a pilgrim. This is the last phase of all. It was his own health which first compelled him to set out to the West. But here again, as in the former period mentioned, the outward circumstance has brought with it a new spiritual development.

As I crossed the Atlantic (he wrote to me), and spent on board ship the beginning of a new year, I realized that a new stage in my life had come, the stage of a voyager. To the open road! To the emancipation of self! To the realization in love!

In another letter, which he wrote earlier to me, dealing with the meeting of the conflicting races of the world and the removal of colour prejudice, he uses these words:

This meeting of the races affords the greatest of all problems that men have ever been asked to solve. It is, I believe, the one question of the present age, and we must be prepared to go through the martyrdom of suffering and humiliation till the victory of God in man is achieved.

Since *Gitanjali* was written, Rabindranath Tagore has been facing, day by day, these larger international questions and casting aside altogether that narrower nationalism which for one period in his life had affected his own songs. He has attempted, also, to comprehend the inner harmony of his own life's work and to read its deeper meaning. The stage of philosophy has been reached by the Poet. Yet his lyrical powers seem in no way to be diminished. The fountain of song is still sending forth new streams.

VII

When Rabindranath Tagore first landed in London, in 1912, he had placed before his English friends some translations of his Bengali poems. He had offered them with singular diffidence, without at all realizing the value of his great achievement. "I found," he said, "that I had to strip my Bengali verses of all their gaudy ornaments and to clothe them in the simplest English dress."

That English setting has since been acknowledged, by those who are best able to judge, to represent a beautiful and musical prose—a comparatively new form of English, which has enriched the literature of Great Britain. The triumph has been won—a triumph hardly ever before achieved in literary history—of an author translating his own poems into a wholly new language, thus giving his message to two peoples at once in a noble literary form.

This crowning success of Rabindranath Tagore has already brought East and West closer together in a common fellowship and understanding. Where the forces of racial rivalry and religious division are so strong, it is indeed no small blessing to humanity when a generous voice can be clearly heard, above the discordant tumult of the times, which the whole world welcomes as a messenger and revealer of peace and goodwill to mankind.

CHAPTER I

The letters contained in this opening chapter were written to me by the poet Rabindranath Tagore in the early years when my work as teacher at Santiniketan had only just begun. He came back from Europe in September 1913, but I was not able to join him then on account of an attack of malarial fever. Later on it was necessary for me to go out to South Africa along with my friend W.W. Pearson in order to take part in the Passive Resistance struggle which was being carried on against the evils of the indenture system of Indian labour. We both returned to India in April 1914, and were with the Poet until we went out to Fiji together in September 1915.

Some explanation must be given concerning the special series of letters which the Poet sent me each day from Ramgarh, near Nainital, in the latter part of May 1914.

He had gone in good health to the Hills in order to spend there his summer holidays; but he told me afterwards that the mental pain he experienced soon after his arrival was almost equivalent to a death-agony. He had hardly expected to survive it. This was all the more strange because it came upon him quite suddenly at a moment when he was feeling a sense of physical exhilaration in the supreme beauty of the Himalayas and also the delight of the change from the intense heat of the plains. I remember him saying to me that the shock of agony overtook him like a thunderstorm out of a clear, unclouded sky.

This suffering, which is referred to in the letters written in May, entirely passed away. The Poet was in the best of health and spirits all through the month of June, renewing his own full, active work in his schools among his boys after the holidays were over. Indeed, I can remember June 1914 as a singularly happy month.

But early in July the darkness again came down upon his life and seemed once more to overwhelm him. It appeared to have no external source, either in bad health or bad climate; and the school work was progressing wonderfully. But he spoke to me constantly of the mysterious and unbearable weight of mental oppression which drove him into solitude. He went away from the school and lived alone at Surul. For nearly three months this depression continued. There are hardly any letters written during this period; but I have the most vivid and painful recollections of his suffering.

Long before any news reached us about the World War that was impending, and before any hint of it had come to us in the midst of our comparative retirement from the world at Santiniketan, his mind was entirely preoccupied with the foreboding of some disaster which was about to overwhelm humanity. He wrote at this time, and published some weeks before the war began, a very remarkable Bengali poem called *The Destroyer*, in which he spoke of the sudden destruction that was coming upon the earth. It contained the following lines:

Is it the Destroyer who comes?
For the boisterous sea of tears heaves in the flood-tide of pain.
The crimson clouds run wild in the wind, lashed by lightning, and the thundering laughter of the Mad is over the sky.
Life sits in the chariot crowned by Death.
Bring out your tribute to him of all that you have.

Looking back now on that period, when humanity was suddenly torn in pieces by internecine war, it seems certain to me that the Poet's highly sensitive nature had made him feel dimly beforehand the tragedy which was about to happen. In no other way can I account for his intense mental suffering.

London, *August 16th, 1913*

I am so glad to know that you are now in Santiniketan. It is impossible to describe to you my longing to join you there.

The time has come at last when I must leave England; for I find that my work here in the West is getting the better of me. It is taking up too much of my attention and assuming more importance than it actually possesses. Therefore I must, without delay, go back to that obscurity where all living seeds find their true soil for germination.

This morning I am going to take a motor-ride to Rothenstein's country house, and if I delay any longer I may not have time to write to my other correspondents by this mail, so I must close this letter.

Calcutta, *October 11th, 1913*

I have gone through a period of difficulty. My life had appeared to me lonely and burdened with responsibilities too heavy for a single man to bear. Evidently my mind has got into a habit of leaning too much upon my friends whom I had acquired in England, and letting most of its current flow outward. Therefore, coming to my own country, where the contact of humanity is not so close as in the West, I felt suddenly stranded and in a desolation, wherein every individual has to struggle through his own problem unaided. For some length of time, solitariness weighed upon my heart like a heavy load, till I gained my former mental adjustment and felt again the current turn inward from the world outside. Now I feel the flood-tide of life and companionship. It sweeps the burden from off my shoulders and carries me along with it on its joyous course.

In India the range of our lives is narrow and discontinuous. This is the reason why our minds are often beset with provincialism. In our Asram at Santiniketan we must have the widest possible outlook for our boys, and universal human interests. This must come spontaneously—not merely through the reading of books, but through dealings with the wider world.

Santiniketan, *October 11th, 1913*

You must certainly rid your system of this malarial poison before you take up your regular work at Santiniketan.

Is it wholly impossible for you to come down here at once, and stay with us quietly and indulge in absolute rest for some time? Jagadananda had a very bad type of malaria before he joined his work here. His coming to Bolpur has been the saving of his life. Do give our Asram a trial. She will nurse you back to health. Your room shall be fitted with a desk and writing materials and other necessaries. You can start a little gardening in our school grounds and take occasional excursions into our *Sal* grove. Possibly, giving me a Greek lesson now and then will not fatigue you too much, if you feel so inclined.

Just now the singing mood is upon me, and I am turning out fresh songs every day.

Santiniketan, *February 1914*

[*Written to meet me in England after my return from South Africa*]

I send you my love and the translation of a song of mine written about two months ago. We are waiting for you, knowing that you are coming to us with your heart filled with the wisdom of death and the tender strength of sorrow. You know our best love was with you, while you were fighting our cause in South Africa along with Mr Gandhi and others.

My days of turmoil are not yet over. Indeed, I have not yet been able to settle down to my work and to my rest. Interruptions come almost daily to me in various forms. At last I have made up my mind to be rude, and to leave all invitations ignored and letters unanswered.

The mango blossoms have appeared in our Asram. The air is full of music, heard and unheard, and I do not know why we should be callous to the call of the seasons and foolishly behave as if the Spring and the Winter are the same to human beings, with the same round of works to follow, without having the option to be occasionally useless and absurd. However, I am in that mood when one forgets that he has any other obligations to meet than to be good for nothing and glad.

Santiniketan, *March 5th, 1914*

Lately I have been spending some days alone in the solitude of Shileida; for I needed it very greatly, and it has done me good. I feel that I must protect myself from all distractions for some time, so as to be able to add to my inner resources, never considering it a duty to force myself to work merely with the vain intention of doing good, but rather making the work I do living and real.

To try to benefit others, and yet not to have enough of oneself to give others, is a poor affair.

Santiniketan, *May 10th, 1914*

When are you coming to stay with me in the Hills? I am afraid you are passing through a great deal of worry, and you are in need of a good rest. I won't let you work during this vacation. We must have no particular plans for our holidays. Let us agree to waste them utterly, until laziness proves to be a burden to us. Just for a month or so we can afford to be no longer useful members of society. The cultivation of usefulness produces an enormous amount of failure, simply because in our avidity we sow seeds too closely.

Ramgarh, *May 14th, 1914*

Here I feel that I have come to the place that I needed most in all the world. I hated to be disloyal to the plains of Bengal, where the earth lies so meek and unobtrusive, leaving the sky to the undisputed dominion of all the horizons. But happily the poet's heart is inconstant; it is easily won; and to-day I am already bending my knees to Father Himalaya asking pardon for keeping aloof for so long in blind distrust.

The hills all round seem to me like an emerald vessel brimming over with peace and sunshine. The solitude is like a flower spreading its petals of beauty and keeping its honey of wisdom at the core of its heart. My life is full. It is no longer broken and fragmentary.

Ramgarh, *May 15th, 1914*

At last I am supremely happy, not simply because the quiet of this place affords me the needful change from the worries of a crowded life, but because it supplies my mind with its natural food. Directly I come to a place like this I can realize at once that I had been living before on half-rations.

I have found myself since I came here, and I am filled with the wonder that the infinite Power and Joy has become what I am and what this blade of grass is. When we are restless we raise dust all about us and we forget the supreme truth that 'we are.' I cannot tell you the great joy of seeing everything through the sight which comes from within.

Ramgarh, *May 17th, 1914*

To-day is my father's birthday anniversary. We have just had our morning prayer, and my mind is full. It is a stormy morning, dark and threatening, with an occasional burst of pallid light. It seems like the symbol of a spiritual new birth. I have been experiencing the feeling of a great expectation, although it has also its elements of very great suffering. To be born naked in the heart of the eternal Truth; to be able to feel with my entire being the life-throb of the universal heart—that is the cry of my soul. I tell you all this, so that you may understand what I am passing through and may help me when the occasion arrives.

Do take care of yourself and get well, so as to be fit to fight your own battle with renewed strength and hope.

Ramgarh, *May 21st, 1914*

I am struggling on my way through the wilderness. The light from across the summit is clear; but the shadows are slanting and deep on the slope of the dark valley. My feet are bleeding, and I am toiling with panting breath. Wearied, I lie down upon the dust and cry and call upon His name.

I know that I must pass through death. God knows, it is the death-pang that is tearing open my heart. It is hard to part with the old self. One does not know, until the time comes, how far it had spread its roots, and into what unexpected, unconscious depths it had sent its thirsty fibres draining out the precious juice of life.

But the Mother is relentless. She will tear out all the tangled untruths. We must not nourish in our being what is dead. For the dead is death-dealing. 'Through death lead us to deathlessness.' The toll of suffering has to be paid in full.

For we can never enter the realm of white light and pure love until all our debts are cleared and nothing binds us to the dead past. But I know my Mother is with me and before me.

Ramgarh, *May 22nd, 1914*

The spiritual bath is not that of water, but of fire. For the water merely takes away the dirt that is superficial, not the dead matter that clings to life, abusing its hospitality. So we must take our plunge into fire, time after time.

We shrink and tremble at the prospect; but the Mother assures us that it will never touch anything that is true and living.

The fire consumes the sin, but not the soul. Our soul is the last thing that we come to know; for it is dark where the Mother feeds the soul in secret. And we can see that sacred sight in the intense glow of the fire of suffering. Sometimes Death brings the torch to light it, and sometimes a messenger whose face is hidden from us.

The latter is at my door. I ask him questions. He answers not. But the fire is burning fiercely, exposing the hidden corners of my being with all their unsuspected accumulations of untruth and self-deception. Let the fire burn until it has nothing to feed upon. Let nothing be spared that awaits destruction.

Ramgarh, *May 23rd, 1914*

Now I feel that I am emerging once again into the air and light and am breathing freely. It is an unspeakable relief to come out into the open and the normal, to regain the balance of life once more, to be able to take again my natural part in the open fair of the world.

Strenuousness is the open foe of attainment. The strength that wins is calm and has an exhaustless resource in its passive depth. Greed is sure to frustrate itself, even the greed after God.

I had been struggling, during these last few days, in a world where shadows held sway and right proportions were lost. The enemies with whom I was fighting were mostly phantoms. But this experience of the dark has had a great lesson for me.

Untruth when spread thinly over a large area of life is hardly felt and seen. We live in truce with it. Now that I have had its vision, in all its concentrated ugliness, I am called upon to fight it every day of my life.

Ramgarh, *May 24th, 1914*

To-day I feel as sound as these mountain oaks, ready to store my share of light from the sky and joyfully try my strength with the storm when it comes. Again I feel that I must have all my interests alive, grow on all sides, and enter into various relations with the world, keeping my body and mind fully awake.

Harmony is difficult when one's own nature is complicated; when the strings in the *vina* are numerous and each one claims its right to be tuned.

But I know life is simple, however complex the organism may be; and everything goes to pieces when the living truth of the central simplicity is lost.

Ramgarh, *May 25th, 1914*

Morning is simple, though infinitely more varied than night; for it is open and luminous. Night tries to hide and suppress all problems of reality, making the tyranny of dreams absolute. Light bares the heart of truth; and whatever is unformed or struggling, dying or dead is revealed, not merely at the side but at the root of all that is growing in strength and grace.

We see all the contradictions, yet we feel the inner harmony; strife and struggle are everywhere, yet beauty is supreme. This makes Night, with its phantoms of false mystery of exaggeration, slink away in shame when Morning appears in her simple robe of white. Hope and joy come in her wake all the more triumphant, because not a single blade of grass or thorn is hidden. Morning has dawned upon me at last. My wrestlings with the shadows are over. My heart looks out upon the undulating field of life, chequered with the fruitful green and the pallor of the sandy waste, and feels that all is good. It is vast; it is free to all the horizons; and over it from end to end reigns the light of the sky.

CHAPTER II

The period of the next few months was one of increased tension, followed later by a gradual recovery from the mental strain that had been oppressing the Poet for so long.

At the beginning of the European War this strain had become almost unbearable, owing both to the world tragedy of the war itself and the suffering of Belgium, which the Poet felt most acutely. He wrote and published simultaneously in India and England three poems which expressed the inner conflict going on in his own mind. The first of these was called *The Boatman*, and he told me, when he had written it, that the woman in the silent courtyard, 'who sits in the dust and waits,' represented Belgium. The most famous of the three poems was *The Trumpet.* The third poem was named *The Oarsmen.* Its outlook is beyond the war; for it reveals the daring venture of faith that would be needed by humanity if the old world with its dead things were to be left behind and the vast uncharted and tempestuous seas were to be essayed leading to a world that was new.

A fourth poem, which was not published then, but later, was given to me by the Poet towards the end of the year 1914. On Christmas Day that year he delivered in the Asram a very remarkable address to the students and teachers, speaking of Christ, who was called the Prince of Peace, and how the name of Christ was being denied in Europe.

Santiniketan, *October 4th, 1914*

It seems as though I am coming out of the mist once more, and I am trying to throw off my shoulders the burden that has been oppressing me all these days. As my mind feels lighter, I hope I have rightly earned my freedom.

We have all come to Santiniketan from Surul; and this change has done me good. Dr Maitra has sent me a long letter about you. He thinks you will have to be very careful in future about your health, if you are not to get ill again.

Santiniketan, *October 7th, 1914*

My period of darkness is over once again. It has been a time of very great trial to me, and I believe it was absolutely necessary for my emancipation. I know that I am being lifted from the sphere where I was before; and it is the loneliness of the new situation and the cry of the old life that is still troubling me. But I have glimpses of the ineffable light of joy which I am sure will not fail me. Preaching I must give up, and also trying to take up the role of a beneficent angel to others. I am praying to be lighted from within, and not simply to hold a light in my hand.

Darjeeling, *June 12th, 1914*

Real love is always a wonder. We can never take it for granted. Your love for me I accept with joy and thankfulness, and wonder to which account to put it. Perhaps every man has some worth unknown to himself, inspiring love through the cover of his self. It gives one a hope that truth is more than appearance, and that we deserve more than we can claim with apparent reason. Love is for the unlimited in us, not for the one who is loudly evident.

Some say that we idealize him we love; but the fact is that we realize through love the ideal in him—and the ideal is the real, if we know it. We have the eternal contradiction in us, that our worth unfolds itself through our unworthiness, and love can go beyond the process, overtaking the ultimate truth. We could never be certain that we are more in truth than we are in fact, if we were not loved.

Give my love to Mr Rudra. Tell him I am hopelessly lost in the wilderness of correspondence, distributing thanks to all quarters of the globe, till not an atom of gratitude is left in my nature.

Calcutta, *November 12th, 1914*

I know these school financial difficulties are good for us, but I must have strength enough to extract the good. We must have faith in the Truth. But this faith must be active and self-respecting.

The whole Asram must rouse itself from its passive inanity and be ready to meet the danger, never expecting help from outside, but using all its wisdom, self-restraint and resourcefulness.

Our school is a living body. The smallest of us must feel that all its problems are his own; that we must give, in order to gain. Even the little boys should not be kept entirely ignorant of our difficulties. They should be made proud of the fact that they also bear their own share of the responsibility.

Calcutta, *November 15th, 1914*

Critics and detectives are naturally suspicious. They scent allegories and bombs where there are no such abominations. It is difficult to convince them of our innocence.

With regard to the criticism of my play, *The King of the Dark Chamber,* that you mention in your letter, the human soul has its inner drama, which is just the same as anything else that concerns Man, and Sudarshana is not more an abstraction than Lady Macbeth, who might be described as an allegory representing the criminal ambition in man's nature. However, it does not matter what things are, according to the rules of the critics. They are what they are, and therefore difficult of classification.

Ramgarh is said to be not unfavourable for wintering; and this it is that has induced me to try to go there for quiet during the next few months till it becomes decently warm and comfortable. But it is a secret of mine, and you must not let it out. Whatever may happen, I must remain beyond the reach of correspondence. I need to be entirely alone. By going to an inaccessible region, I shall escape anniversary meetings, addresses and conferences, and other evils that the flesh is *not* heir to, but which, all the same, fasten upon it without ceremony. It is wicked of me to be away when you are returning to the Asram after your illness; but I feel that you will have a better opportunity of coming closer to the boys and teachers if I am not there, and that will compensate you for my absence.

Agra, *December 5th, 1914*

I was surprised to read in the *Modern Review* that our Bolpur boys are going without their sugar and ghee in order to open a relief fund. Do you think this is right? In the first place, it is an imitation of your English schoolboys and not their own original idea. In the second place, so long as the boys live in our institution they are not free to give up any portion of their diet which is absolutely necessary for their health. For any English boy, who takes meat and an amount of fat with it, giving up sugar is not injurious. But for our boys in Santiniketan, who can get milk only in small quantities, and whose vegetable meals contain very little fat ingredients, it is mischievous.

Our boys have no right to choose this form of self-sacrifice—just as they are not free to give up buying books for their studies. The best form of self-sacrifice for them would be to do some hard work in order to earn money; let them take up menial work in our school—wash dishes, draw water, dig wells, fill up the tank which is a menace to their health, do the building work. This would be good in both ways. What is more, it would be a real test of their sincerity. Let the boys think out for themselves what particular works they are willing to take up without trying to imitate others.

Allahabad, *December 18th, 1914*

I feel happy to imagine you lost in the sunny blue and the silent green of our Asram, and I am glad that we have had our talk together before you left. I know from my own experience that our Asram will give you the peaceful detachment of mind needed so much for bringing oneself face to face with one's own inner being and the deeper reality of the world.

You must have recognized by this time that I have something elusive in me, which eludes myself not less than others. Because of this element in my nature, I have to keep my environments free and open, fully to make room in my life for the Undreamt-of who is expected every moment. Believe me, I have a strong human sympathy, yet I can never enter into such relations with others as may impede the current of my life, which flows through the darkness of solitude beyond my ken. I can love, but

I have not that which is termed by phrenologists 'adhesiveness'; or to be more accurate, I have a force acting in me, jealous of all attachments, a force that ever tries to win me for itself, for its own hidden purpose.

If this purpose were only moral, it could be more easily tolerated—nay, welcomed; but it is life-purpose—the purpose of growth—and for this very reason it meets with a certain amount of opposition when it crosses with other life-currents. It may seem to be egoistic. But this life-impulse I speak of belongs to a personality which is beyond my ego. I must own this Master in me, who is not a mere abstract moral ideal, but a Person. I must be true to it, even at the cost of what men call happiness, at the risk of being misunderstood, forsaken and hated. I am sociable by nature, and would intensely like to enjoy the company of friends, the pleasures and advantages of friendship. But I am not free to give myself away, even when it seems necessary and good; and the somewhat wide expanse of time and space that I always try to keep in reserve about me is not mine to use as I wish. This loneliness often becomes hard for me to bear, but I have my ample compensation; and I dare say it will bear fruit for those who know what to expect from it.

The human soul is God's flower. It gives its best bloom and scent, not when shut up in eager palms to be squeezed, but when left alone in the immense freedom of light and air. But, very unfortunately,

> The World is too much with us; late and soon
> Getting and spending, we lay waste our powers;
> Little we see in Nature that is ours;
> We have given our hearts away, a sordid boon!

My love is bare and reticent. It was gaudily covered in its youthful flowering season; bulging with gifts in its fruitful maturity; but now that its seed-time has come, it has burst its shell and is abroad in the air; it has thrown away all the extra burden of allurements, carrying in its minute covering the density of its life. So when you come and shake the bough for it, it will not answer; for it is not there. But if you can believe in its silence, and accept it in silence, you will not be disappointed.

The following is the translation of the Bengali poem given to me by the Poet at Christmas, 1914:

JUDGEMENT

When, mad in their mirth, they raised dust to soil thy robe,
O Beautiful, it made my heart sick.
I cried to thee and said: 'Take thy rod of punishment and judge them.' The morning light struck upon those eyes, red with the revel of the night; the place of the white lily greeted their burning breath; the stars through the depth of the sacred dark stared at their carousing—at those that raised dust to soil thy robe, O Beautiful!
Thy judgement-seat was in the flower garden; in the birds' notes in springtime; in the shady river banks, where the trees muttered in answer to the muttering of the wave.

O my Lover, they were pitiless in their passion.
They prowled in the dark to snatch thy ornaments to deck their own desires.
When they had struck thee and thou wert pained, it pierced me to the quick, and I cried to thee and said:
'Take thy sword, O my Lover, and judge them!'
Ah, but thy justice was vigilant.
A mother's tears were shed on their insolence; the imperishable faith of a lover hid their spears of rebellion in its own wounds.
Thy judgement was in the mute pain of sleepless love; in the blush of the chaste; in the tears of the night of the desolate; in the pale morning light of forgiveness.
O Terrible, they in their reckless greed climbed thy gate at night, breaking into thy storehouse to rob thee.
But the weight of their plunder grew immense, too heavy to carry or to remove.
Thereupon I cried to thee and said: 'Forgive them, O Terrible!'
Thy forgiveness burst in storms, throwing them down, scattering their thefts in the dust.
Thy forgiveness was in the thunderstone, in the shower of blood; in the angry red of the sunset.

Calcutta, *January 20th, 1915*

I could feel from your last letters, hastily written, that you were depressed. Your mind is still in that region of phantoms where shadows are exaggerated land the least thing makes one unhappy. I find that your very happiness is a strain to you—it is so jerky and violent—because very often it comes to you in the shape of reaction. It makes me feel far more anxious about you than your bad health.

Calcutta, *January 29th, 1915*

I don't like to frighten you with news of my ill-health, but it must be given to justify my absence from the Asram. I feel that I am on the brink of a breakdown. Therefore I must take flight to the solitude of the Padma. I need rest and the nursing of Nature.

If you ever have a relapse of your illness, do not despair. Try not to fret, or to strain, but to give yourself up to sleep. We must not force ourselves to be too conscious, even of God—our spirit cannot bear it. Depression comes very often from repletion. Our subconscious nature must have sufficient time to store up what our conscious nature requires.

Calcutta, *January 31st, 1915*

I hear that you are really ill. This won't do. Come to Calcutta. Consult some doctor; and if he recommends, come to Shileida, where I am going tomorrow morning. I dare not go to Bolpur. I have reached such a sublime depth of tiredness, that it has conferred a dignity on my selfish isolation; and I don't feel the least ashamed of my flight from all responsibilities. I must be alone, with all my heart and soul.

But you must not delay. We are very anxious about you, and we cannot let you breakdown completely.

Shileida, *February 1st, 1915*

You are right. I had been suffering from a time of deep depression and weariness. But I am sane and sound again, and willing to live another hundred years, if critics would spare me.

At that time I was physically tired; therefore the least hurt assumed a proportion that was perfectly absurd. However, I am glad that there is still the child in me, who has its weakness for the sweets of human approbation. I must not feel myself too far above my critics. I don't want my seat on the dais; let me sit on the same bench with my own audience and try to listen as they do. I am quite willing to know the healthy feeling of disappointment when they don't approve of my things; and when I say 'I don't care!' let nobody believe me.

A great proportion of our humankind is inarticulate. I find I have quite a number of friends among them, and that I need not put any bounds to my estimation of their partiality towards my writings; so that though they do not confirm, neither do they contradict.

I am living in a boat here in a lovely spot. Mukul, Nandalal and another artist are my companions. Their enthusiasm of enjoyment adds to my joy. Every little thing brings to them a sense of surprise, and thus their fresh minds come to my service, bringing to my notice things that I have been getting into the habit of ignoring.

Shileida, *February 3rd, 1915*

Directly I reached here I came to myself, and am now healed. The cure for all the illness of life is stored in the inner depth of life itself, the access to which becomes possible when we are alone. This solitude is a world in itself, full of wonders and resources unthought of. It is so absurdly near, yet so unapproachably distant. But I do not want to talk; please forgive my absence and my silence. I cannot afford to scatter my mind just now.

I do so earnestly hope that you are better.

Calcutta, *February 18th, 1915*

Calcutta will keep me till Sunday. I do not expect to free myself from its clutches before them, though I shall try. Anyhow, Monday will see me in Bolpur, somewhat feeble and worn-out, unfit to be trusted with any responsibility.

I hope that Mahatma and Mrs Gandhi have arrived in Bolpur, and Santiniketan has accorded them such a welcome as befits her and them. I shall convey my love personally to them when we meet.

I am glad that our Asram has given shelter to the persecuted Rajput boy. Let him feel that he has won a home in Santiniketan by being driven from his own place and by his own people.

CHAPTER III

In the middle of the month of May 1915, after repeated illnesses from which I had hardly recovered, an attack of Asiatic cholera came suddenly upon me, which proved very nearly fatal. The Poet himself helped to nurse me, and his care and affection were full of the most sensitive tenderness and sympathy. On my account, he did not go away for a holiday during the worst of the hot weather. He waited near at hand, while I was slowly recovering in a nursing-home in Calcutta. At last, when I was able to be moved to Simla, as a convalescent, his letters began again.

During this year 1915 we were so completely outside the range and area of the war, in our isolation in India itself, that it horrors gradually tended to recede into the background of our minds; but the greater thoughts which had been awakened so painfully during the previous year, owing to the war itself—such as the problem of human suffering; the possibility of complete human brotherhood; the meeting of East and West in common fellowship—these were more present than ever before. Our talks together, while I was in the nursing-home in Calcutta, were continually about these problems. They remained deep in the subconscious mind of the Poet all through this year. At the same time, the whole burden of the school work at Santiniketan fell upon his shoulders and he threw himself into every detail of it with his own characteristic energy and determination.

Through the summer of 1915 the Poet's plans were maturing for a visit to the Far East. His father, Maharshi Debendranath Tagore, had made his Far Eastern journey more than half a century before, and it had formed one of the means by which he had realized so deeply in his own life the universal brotherhood of man. To the Poet, whose thoughts were always in the terms of Humanity rather than in those of any lesser unit, the fratricidal war in the West revealed the dangerously unbalanced condition of the human race. Out of the agony from which he had suffered in the previous year, both before and after the war had begun, the determination had been ever growing in his own mind to enlarge the bounds of his Asram at Santiniketan, which his father, the Maharshi, had founded as a home of religion. He looked more and more to the time when his Asram would pass beyond the school stage and become a centre of world fellowship, wherein students and teachers from the East and West should be equally honoured and welcomed.

These thoughts were brooding in his mind during the year 1915; therefore it became clear to him that a visit to the Far East, in order to win the friendship and co-operation of the leading thinkers of China and Japan, would be necessary if the cycle of his work at Santiniketan was to be completed. He had very nearly made up his mind to start in August, and had actually taken his passage on a Japanese steamer, when a series of circumstances intervened which made the journey impossible.

After these plans for a voyage to the Far East had been entirely abandoned, a sudden crisis arose in India itself with regard to a humanitarian struggle against the indentured system of Indian labour in the colonies. My friend W.W. Pearson and I had fully investigated and condemned this system in Natal, and we were therefore more immediately in touch with the direct problem than other people. The immoral and servile conditions of indentured Indian labour had to be thoroughly exposed. For this reason, after the tour to the Far East had been abandoned, we received the Poet's cordial consent, when we proposed to go out together to Fiji and carry through an independent inquiry into the indenture system of Indian labour in that colony. He felt very keenly indeed that this new journey of ours would be in keeping with his own ideals of universal brotherhood and fellowship, and he gave us his blessing on our departure. Two texts from the Upanishad were his own gift to me when we bade him farewell.

They may be translated as follows:

From Joy all things have their origin: in Joy they subsist, and unto Joy they return.

I meditate upon His glory, who creates the earth, the sky and the stars, and sends into our minds the power of comprehension.

The inspiration which Rabindranath Tagore thus gave to us, by his encouragement and sympathy, carried us through what proved to be the most difficult journey we had ever undertaken. In the end, the inquiry we made very nearly effected its object; and the pledge was given that the whole indenture system of Indian labour would be abolished at the earliest possible moment.

Santineketan, *June 30th, 1915*

Just now I am in Santiniketan. It still has the holiday atmosphere; for only a few boys have come back, and it is not unlikely that some of them have left for good. So our Finance Minister will have a hard time before him with arrears to clear off and the buildings to complete. Do not try to come now, however strong you may feel—for financial difficulties are just as bad as disease germs in their insidious attacks on our health. However, be assured that this bad time will not be thrown away on us altogether, and we shall come out of it with more freedom than ever, if considerably thinner.

As for myself, I have the call of the open road, though most of the roads are closed. I am in a nomadic mood, but it is becoming painful to me for want of freedom. I am carrying, as it were, my tents on my back, instead of living in them.

Possibly my life is on the eve of another bursting of its pods and scattering of its seeds; there is that continual urgency in my blood, the purpose of which is hidden. The conclusion is being forced upon me that poets should never bind themselves to any particular work; for they are the instruments of the world's moods. And after the years of building up all kinds of benevolent schemes, my life is emerging once again upon the open health of irresponsibility, where the sun rises and sets, where there are wild flowers, but no committee meetings.

Calcutta, *July 7th, 1915*

Haven't I confessed elsewhere that renunciation is not for me, and that my freedom is to be moving from bondage to bondage? My mind must realize itself anew. Once I give form to my thought, I must free myself from it. For the time being, it seems to me that I want absolute freedom to create new forms for new ideas. I am sure physical death has the same meaning for us—the creative impulse of our soul must have new forms for its realization. Death can continue to dwell in the same sepulchre, but life must unceasingly outgrow its dwelling-place; otherwise the form gets the upper hand and becomes a prison. Man is immortal; therefore he must die endlessly. For life is a creative idea; it can only find itself in changing forms.

Forms are stupid dumb things that struggle to standstill, until at last they break into pieces.

You will have heard about all my plans from Pearson. I am seeking my freedom by surrendering my ideas into the hands of a new bondage. In Santiniketan, some of my thoughts have become clogged by accumulations of dead matter. I do not believe in lecturing, or in compelling fellow-workers by coercion; for all true ideas must work themselves out through freedom. Only a moral tyrant can think that he has the dreadful power to make his thoughts prevail by means of subjection. It is absurd to imagine that you must create slaves in order to make your ideas free. I would rather see them perish than leave them in the charge of slaves to be nourished. There are men who make idols of their ideas, and sacrifice humanity before their altars. But in my worship of the idea I am not a worshipper of Kali.

So the only course left open to me, when my fellow-workers fall in love with the form and cease to have complete faith in the idea, is to go away and give my idea a new birth and create new possibilities for it. This may not be a practical method, but possibly it is the right one.

Calcutta, *July 11th, 1915*

Conscientious men are comfortable men; they live within the bounds of their duties, and consequently enjoy their fixed proportion of leisure. But I shirk my duties in order to create works that eat up all my time; and then I suddenly leave my work and try to elope with unmitigated indolence.

I shall be floating on the Padma before the next week is out, and shall forget to imagine that my presence in the Council of Creation is imperatively necessary for the betterment of Humanity. I am a born nomad—as I am sure you are—and my work has to be fluid, if it is to be my work. But absolute fluidity in work can only be had at its commencement. Therefore my duty is to start things and then leave them. Unless I leave them and keep at a distance, I cannot help them in maintaining their ideal character. But, this time, it is the fatigue of my body and mind that is driving me into solitude. The kind of work that I can do in a particular scheme requires freshness of mind more than perseverance. Therefore there must be a break before I resume my duties.

It is easy for me to understand the stress of pain that you are feeling now about the wrongs of the world, and especially among the weaker races of mankind, who are oppressed by the strong. Human wrongs are not pitiable, they are terrible. Those who are in power forget every day that it is for their very power's sake that they have to be just. When God's appeal comes from the weak and the poor, then it is full of danger for those who are in power; for then they are apt to think that they can disregard it with impunity, especially if it upsets their office arrangements in the very least degree. They have more faith in their pitiful system and their prestige than in moral providence.

In India, when the upper classes ruled over the lower, they forged their own chains. Europe is closely following Brahmin India, when she looks upon Asia and Africa as her legitimate fields for exploitation. The problem would be simpler if she could altogether denude other continents of their population; but so long as there are alien races, it will be difficult for Europe to realize her moral responsibility with regard to them. The gravest danger is when Europe deceives herself into thinking that she is helping the cause of humanity by helping herself; that men are essentially different, and what is good for her people is not good for others who are inferior. Thus Europe, gradually and imperceptibly, is losing faith in her own ideals and weakening her own moral supports.

But I must not go on weaving truisms; and on our own side I must equally acknowledge this truth, that weakness is heinous because it is a menace to the strong and the surest cause of downfall for others than those who own it. It is a moral duty for every race to cultivate strength, so as to be able to help the world's balance of power to remain even. We are doing England the greatest disservice possible by making it easy for her to despise us and yet to rule; to feel very little sympathy for us and yet to judge us.

Will Europe never understand the genesis of the present war, and realize that the true cause lies in her own growing scepticism towards her own ideals—those ideals that have helped her to be great? She seems to have exhausted the oil that once lighted her lamp. Now she is feeling a distrust against the oil itself, as if it were not at all necessary for her light.

Shileida, *July 16th, 1915*

I wonder whether you got my last letter, which I wrote to you in a railway train, informing you of my proposed visit to Japan.

I am busy floating my dreams, as the children do their paper boats, on this wide expanse of green, gold and blue. This world is wonderfully beautiful, but you cannot help feeling that there is a lurking pain in its heart, which has its own immortal beauty. It is a pearl shell of wonderful tints and design, hiding in its bosom a teardrop, which gives it priceless value. All our payments have to be made in pain; otherwise life and this world would become cheap as dirt.

Shileida, *July 23rd, 1915*

After long years I have come among my tenants; and I feel, and they also, that my presence was needed. It was a great event of my life when I first dwelt among my own people here, for thus I came into contact with the reality of life. For in them you feel the barest touch of humanity. Your attention is not diverted, and then you truly know that Man is very much to man. One is apt to forget them, just as one does not think of the earth on which one walks.

But these men compose the great mass of life, which sustains all civilizations and bears their burdens. They are content barely to live, so that others may prove that man's life is a great deal more than mere existence. They keep steady the level of the minimum, which is enormous quantitatively, so that the maximum may be unhampered by its own development. Thousands of acres of land are tilled, so that a University can be maintained upon one acre. Yet these men are insulted merely because while they are so absolutely necessary, it is their necessity to live that drives them to this position. They are in their place because they cannot help it.

We all hope that here, at this very point, Science in the end will help man. She will make the necessities of life easily accessible to every man, so that humanity will be freed from the tyranny of matter which now humiliates her. This struggling mass of men is great in its pathos, in its latency of infinite power. It is beautiful where it is simple and spontaneous; sublime where it is large, deep and enduring. I must confess that I have been neglecting these people, while I was away from them in Santiniketan; and I am glad that I am now with them once more, so that I may be more actively mindful of them. I am afraid my life at the Asram was at last making me into a teacher, which was unsatisfactory for me, because unnatural. But one has to be a helper to be a real man; for then you share your life with your fellow-beings and not merely your ideas.

Calcutta, *July 29th, 1915*

The Infinite Being is not complete if He remains absolutely infinite. He must realize Himself through the finite; that is, through creation. The impulse to realize comes from the fullness of joy; but the process must be through pain. You cannot ask why it should be—why the Infinite should attain truth by passing through the finitude; why the joy should be the cause of suffering, in order to come back to itself—for it is so. And when our minds are illumined, we feel glad that it is so.

When we fix all our attention to that side of the Infinite where it is pain and death, where it is the process of fufilment, we are overwhelmed. But we must know that there is the positive side; that always there is a completeness along with the incomplete. Otherwise, there would be no pity in us for the suffering; no love in us for the imperfect.

What I am trying to express is this: you saw the monkey dead entangled in the telegraph-wires, while round it was beauty in all its superbness. The incongruity struck you as cruel. That is something. The cruelty would not have been apparent to you if ugliness were absolute. You felt the pity of it, because there is the ideal of perfection. Here, in this ideal, lies our hope and the ultimate solution of our doubts. In creation, joy is always getting the better of pain, otherwise our sympathy for pain would be unmeaning.

Then why should we despair? We cannot fathom the mystery of existence. But this much we have known, that there is a love which is greater in truth than pain and death. Is not that sufficient for us?

Santiniketan, *August 7th, 1915*

Your letter was of great interest to me. I have one principle to guide my thoughts in most things of vital importance. It is this, that the figure which represents creation is not 'one,' but 'two.' In the harmony of two contradictory forces everything rests. Whenever our logic tries to simplify things, by reducing the troublesome 'two' into 'one,' it goes wrong. Some philosophies say that motion is all *maya* and truth is static; others are of the opinion that truth is fluid and it is only *maya* that represents truth to us as static.

But truth is beyond logic; it is the everlasting miracle; it is static and dynamic at the same time; it is ideal and real; it is finite and infinite.

The principle of war and that of peace both make truth. They are contradictory; they seem to hurt each other, like the finger and the strings; but this very contradiction produces music. When only one predominates, there is the sterility of silence. Our problem is not only whether we should have war or peace but how to harmonize them perfectly.

So long as there is such a thing as force, we cannot say that we must not use force, but rather that we must not abuse it, as we are prone to do when we make it the sole standard and ignore love. When love and force do not go together, then love is mere weakness and force is brutal. Peace becomes death when it is alone. War becomes a demon when it destroys its mate.

Of course, we must not think for a moment that killing one another is a necessary form of war. Man is pre-eminently on a moral plane, and his weapons should be moral weapons.

Santiniketan, *September 23rd, 1915*

[*Written on the eve of our departure to Fiji.*]

The golden bell of the autumn sun tolls silently and the period for migration has come. You and Pearson are the first of our brood who have left their nest for the passage across the seas; and I can hardly control my wings. Things round us have their weight, and they gradually sink into our soul without our knowing it, till one day we are oppressed with a burden whose nature we hardly know. Movement is the only cure when life becomes heavy with *débris*.

My heart at this moment is like a leaky boat, full of water, that can just keep itself afloat, but the least burden of responsibility becomes too much for it. I must go to the wilderness and take upon myself the severe discipline of freedom. I want to say 'No' emphatically to all the importunities of the world; to all the moral and social obligations. But in spite of my protestations, I am afraid that I shall have to end my days as an ascetic—with certain modifications.

I am going on with the rehearsal, and rather like it. For it gives me opportunity to come close to the little boys, who are a perpetual source of pleasure to me.

CHAPTER IV

After our return from Fiji, at the end of January 1916, the longings of the Poet to go out to the Far East became insistent. He took W.W. Pearson, Mukul Dey the artist and myself with him on this voyage. We sailed from Calcutta on the *Tosa Maru*. In the Bay of Bengal our vessel passed through a terrible cyclone and had great difficulty in weathering the storm. Our stay in China was very short, because the people of Japan were impatiently waiting for the Poet's arrival in their own country. They received him with enthusiasm at first, as one who had brought honour to Asia.

But when he spoke out strongly against the militant imperialism which he saw on every side in Japan and set forward in contrast to his own ideal picture of the true meeting of East and West, with its vista of world brotherhood, the hint went abroad that such 'pacifist' teaching was a danger in wartime, and that the Indian Poet represented a defeated nation. Therefore, almost as rapidly as the enthusiasm had arisen, it subsided. In the end, he was almost isolated, and the object for which he had come to the Far East remained unfulfilled. It was at this time that he wrote his poem called *The Song of the Defeated*, which begins:

> My Master bids me, while I stand at the wayside, to sing the song of defeat.
> For that is the bride whom He woos in secret.

These summer months in Japan, at a time when the fever of militarism was at its height, were filled with disappointment. The mental suffering which had appeared at the beginning of the war returned. The Poet's whole inner nature was in revolt against the violently aggressive spirit of the age. All this is brought out in his book called *Nationalism*, the first chapters of which were written in Japan at a white heat. These lectures, delivered in Japan, were reprinted in Europe. They were translated into French in Switzerland by Romain Rolland towards the end of the year 1916. It needs to be added that at a later visit to Japan, in 1924, these earlier impressions, formed in war-time, were considerably modified. He found then in Japan, as also in China, those who were eager to appreciate his universal message.

The Poet went from Japan to America, accompanied by W.W. Pearson and Mukul Dey, while I returned to the Asram. His stay in America was crowded with engagements. He made new friends and received great kindness at their hands. In many ways he was satisfied with his visit, and felt that it had been a success. But he fell ill there, and after a short time came back home by way of the Pacific, only staying between steamers in Japan and China.

Shortly after his arrival at the Asram it became necessary for me to go out again to Fiji, in order to obtain the final and complete abolition of the indenture system of Indian labour. The years 1917 and 1918 were fully taken up by the Poet with quiet fruitful work at Santiniketan. All the while, his plans for widening the scope and aim of his educational enterprise, after the war was over, were slowly shaping themselves in his mind. These will come forward as the main subject in the succeeding chapters in this book; for they began to absorb his whole attention.

After returning from Fiji, early in the year 1918, I was free to remain at the Asram. Since I was constantly with the Poet from that time onwards, I received no letters from him, but some which he sent to W.W. Pearson in England may serve to keep touch with his thoughts up to the close of this period.

Srinagar, Kashmir, *October 12th, 1915*

I am technically in Kashmir, but still have not entered its gate. I am passing through the purgatory of public receptions and friendly solicitations; but Paradise is in sight. Now I feel I am coming nearer myself; the intruder in me, who always fusses about arranging and dusting his absurd store of knicknacks, is, I hope, shut out at least for a few weeks. It is becoming easier for me to feel that it is I who bloom in flowers, spread in the grass, flow in the water, scintillate in the stars, live in the lives of men of all ages.

When I sit in the morning outside on the deck of my boat, before the majestic purple of the mountains, crowned with the morning light, I know that I am eternal, that I am *ananda-rupam.*[1] My true form is not that of flesh or blood, but of joy. In the world where we habitually live, the self is so predominant that everything in it is of our own making and we starve because we have to feed upon ourselves. To know truth is to become true; there is no other way. When we live the life of self, it is not possible for us to realize truth.

'Come out, come away.' This is the urgent cry we have in our soul—the cry in the blood of the chick, living in its shell. It is not merely truth that frees us, but freedom that gives us truth. That is why Buddha dwelt on the importance of freeing our lives from trammels of self; for then Truth comes of itself.

Now I understand at last that the restlessness that has been so persistent with me is of this nature—I must come out from the life of habit, the life of compromise, the life of self. I think the first step towards it is going to the solitude.

My coming to Kashmir has helped me to know clearly what I want. It is likely that it will become obscured again when I go back to my usual routine; but these occasional detachments of life from the usual round of customary thoughts and occupations lead to the final freedom—the Santam, Sivam, Advaitam. The first stage towards freedom is the Santam, the true peace, which can be attained by subduing self; the next stage is the Sivam, the true goodness, which is the activity of the soul when self is subdued; and then the Advaitam, the love, the oneness with all and with God.

Of course this division is merely logical; these stages, like rays of light, may be simultaneous or divided according to the circumstances, and their order may be altered, such as the Sivam leading the Santam. But all we must know is that the Santam, Sivam, Advaitam, is the only goal for which we live and struggle.

---

1. Literally, "Joy-Form". This is a part of a famous Sanskrit text.

Shileida, *February 3, 1916*

Coming away from Calcutta, I have come to myself. Every time it is a new discovery to me. In the town, life is so crowded that one loses the true perspective. After a while it makes me feel weary of everything, simply because the truth of our own self is lost sight of. We have our Lover waiting in the depth of our being. Unless we come to him, time after time, the tyranny of things grows intolerable. We must know that our greatest resource of all is lying hidden in our heart. We have to be assured of it in order to be cured of our miserliness.

Shileida, *February 5th, 1916*

You know the English translation of my poem about 'taking truth simply.' Last night, while reading it in *The Gardener* along with others, it seemed to me strangely incongruous in its semi-metrical form. It was like meeting a woman dressed in tights in the midst of others dressed in simple *saris.* So I tried to divest it of its metrical disguise, though it is difficult to exorcise altogether the ghost of the old metre.

Whatever may come, my heart, take truth simply,
Though there be some who can love you, there must be others who never can, and if you must know the cause, it is as much in you as in them, and in all things around.
Some doors are closed against your knocks, while your doors are not open always and to all comers.
Such has been and shall be for evermore; and yet if you must have peace, my heart, take truth simply.
There is no need to be abusive if your boat founders by the shore, though it sailed through the storm.
Keep yourself afloat by all means; but if it is impossible to do so, then be good enough to sink without noise.
It is a commonplace fact that things may or may not fit you and events happen without asking for your leave.
Yet if you must have peace, my heart, take truth simply.
You press and are pressed hard in the crowd, but space there is enough and to spare in this world.
When you have counted your losses to the last farthing, your sky remains as blue as ever.

You find, when suddenly tested, that to live is sweeter than to die.

You may miss this and that and the other thing, but if you must have peace, my heart, take truth simply.

Must you stand with your back to the rising sun and watch your shadow lengthened before you?

Must you take pleasure in finding fault with your destiny and thus tease your soul to death?

Then for mercy's sake be quick and have done with it; for if, with the evening stars, you must light your lamp, my heart, take truth simply.

Shileida, *February 24th, 1916*

Where are you? Seven fathoms deep in your report-writing? When are you going to float up into the sun and sail on, dancing with all surface-drifts of existence?

I have my work here, but it is play as well. It does not savour of office and officials; it has its humour and some amount of pathos. It is almost like painting a picture.

Pearson has succeeded in getting ill and joining me on my trip.

Santiniketan, *July 9th, 1917*

This is the first time that you have given me your address in your letter since your departure for Fiji. We have been feeling very anxious since we learnt about your accident and injury to your back and leg.

The boys have begun their agriculture in right earnest under the leadership of Santosh Mitra; and I believe it is not going to be like the road—the brilliant work of Nepal Babu—which suddenly stops, with a sublime futility, at the brink of Nowhere. The artist Surendranath Kar has joined our school, and his presence is very much appreciated by the boys and the teachers. Our former student and a veteran of Calcutta football fields, Gora, has taken up the work of a mathematical teacher, and I am sure he will prove to be a valuable acquisition to us.

The rainy season this year, like a great many of our boys, did not wait until the vacation was over, but made its appearance before the time and has been very seriously attending to its business ever since. I have taken my seat of indolence at the window of my second storey—in the middle region between the extravagant pageantry of the clouds and the immense spread of the exuberant green of the earth.

There was a time when my life seemed to be an overflow of spendthriftness in a reckless Universe, before Purposefulness crept into the Eden Garden of my youth and changed the naked felicity of existence into the draped decency of a fashionable cut. I am waiting to regain that Lost Paradise of mind, to forget that I must be of any use to anybody, and to know that the true purpose of my life is the great purpose in me of All-time and All-world, urging me to be fully what I am.

And am I not a poet? What business have I to be anything else? But unfortunately I am like an inn, where the poet lodger has to accommodate strange bedfellows by his side. Yet is it not high time for me to retire from this none too lucrative business of the innkeeper? Anyway, I am feeling tired, and my duty to my numerous lodgers is in imminent danger of being shamefully neglected.

Shileida, *July 20th, 1917*

The accompanying letter is from Pearson. I am glad that he has come out of his seclusion feeling better in mind and body.

After a separation of nearly a year and a half, I have come once more to my Padma and have renewed my courtship. She is unchanged in her changeableness. She is shifting her course and leaving the side of Shileida. She is showing a decided preference for Pabna. My only consolation is that she cannot remain constant for long.

It is a beautiful day to-day. The sunshine is coming out after the fitful showers of rain, like a boy emerging from his dive in the sea with his naked limbs glowing and glistening.

[*The letters that follow were written to W.W. Pearson.*]

Calcutta, *March 6th, 1918*

Each one of us in this unfortunate country is looked upon with suspicion, and our British rulers cannot see us clearly through the dust which they themselves raise. Humiliation follows us at every step and in each good work we try to do.

All blind methods are easy methods at the beginning. But such cheap methods as these do not pay in the end. For, after all, mere bullying is stupidity; it assumes frightfulness only because it does not know its way. What is radically wrong with our rulers is this: they are fully aware that they do not know us, and yet they do not *care* to know us. And, in consequence, thorny hedges are springing up of unscrupulous intermediaries between the rulers and the ruled, giving rise to conditions which are not only miserable, but unspeakably vulgar.

I have just received a letter from Thadani, complaining of the insults and harassments which only Indian British subjects have to go through in British ports. These have the effect of making them feel ashamed of the Government under which they live. Such invidious treatment is sinking deeply into the memory of my people, and the moral providence of history cannot altogether ignore such an accumulated burden of indignities loaded upon humanity.

Santiniketan, *March 10th, 1918*

I can guess from your letter that some questions are troubling your mind about the best way of self-realization. There can be no single path for all individuals; for we vastly differ in our natures and habits. But all great masters agree in their teaching on one cardinal point, saying that we must forget our personal self in order to attain our spiritual freedom. Buddha and Christ have both of them said that this self-abnegation is not something which is negative—its positive aspect is love.

We can only love that which is profoundly real to us. The larger number of men have the most intense feeling of reality only for themselves; and they can never get out of the limits of their self-love. The rest of mankind can be divided into two classes—those who have their love for persons and those who have their love for ideas.

Generally speaking, women fall into the first category and men into the second. In India this fact has been recognized. Therefore our teachers have pointed out two different paths for the two different sexes.

It has been said that women can attain their emancipation by sublimating their personal relationships into the realm of the ideal. If, in spite of all obvious contradictions, a woman can realize in her husband something which transcends his personal limitations, then through her devotion to him she touches the Infinite and thus is freed from the bondage of self. Through the luminous intensity of her love, her husband and her child reveal to her the ultimate Truth which is divine. For biological reasons, men's natures have had comparative freedom from the attachment to persons, and therefore it has become easier for them to find direct access to those ideas, lying behind the screen of things, which they have ever been pursuing in all their knowledge and creative activities. Once you become conscious of the idea, as the inner spirit of reality, the joy becomes so unbounded that your self becomes obliterated, and you can easily lay aside all that you have for its sake.

But we must keep in mind that love of persons and love of ideas can both be terribly egoistic, and therefore may lead to bondage instead of setting us free.

It is only constant sacrifice in service which can loosen the shackles. We must not merely enjoy our love (whether personal or ideal) by contemplating its beauty and truth, but rather make it fruitful giving expression to it in our life's work. Our life is the material whereby we have to build the image of the ideal of Truth that we have in our mind. But life, like all other materials, contains an obstinate antagonism to the idea to which it must give shape. Only through the active process of creation can such antagonism be discovered at every step and chiselled away at every stroke.

Look at the aboriginal Santal women around our Asram. In them the ideal of physical life finds perfect development only because they are ever active in giving it expression in work. Their figures and their movements attain their beautiful harmony because they are always being tuned by life's activities. The one thing which I am never tired of admiring is the vigorous cleanliness of their limbs, which never get soiled even by the constant contact with dirt. Our ladies, with their soaps and scents, only give an artificial polish to the superficial body; but the cleanliness which is induced by the body's own current of movement, coming from the completeness of physical health, can never be theirs.

The same happens with regard to our spiritual body. It is not by meticulous care in avoiding all contaminations that we can keep our spirit clean and give it grace, but by urging it to give vigorous expression to its inner life in the very midst of all the dust and heat.

But I must stop to find out if I have given in what I have written any answer to the original question you have put to me. It may be that I have not; for it is difficult to know exactly what you want of me. You have spoken of impersonal love and impersonal work, and you ask me which I consider to be the greater. To me, they appear as one, like the sun and the light; for love's expression is in work. Where love has no work, there is a dead world.

Santiniketan, *October 6th, 1918*

All through this last session in the Asram, I have been taking school classes in the morning and spending the rest of the day in writing text-books. It is a kind of work apparently unsuitable for a man of my temperament. Yet I have found it not only interesting but restful. The mind has its own burden, which can be lightened when it is floated on a stream of work. Some engrossing ideas also help us in the same way. But ideas are unreliable; they run according to no time-table whatever; and the hours and days you spend in waiting for them grow heavy.

Lately I have come to that state of mind when I could not afford to wait for inspiration of ideas; so I surrendered myself to some work which was not capricious, but had its daily supply of coal to keep it running. However, this teaching was not a monotonous piece of drudgery for me; for I have been treating my students as living organisms; and any dealing with life can never be dull.

Unfortunately, poets cannot be expected to enjoy lucid intervals for long. Directly some new subject takes possession of their minds, they become useless for all decent purposes. They are intellectual gypsies; vagrancy is in their blood; and already I feel the call of the irresponsible vagabondage, a kind of passion for extravagant idleness. The schoolmaster in me is perilously near being lured away by the mischievous imps of truancy.

I am going to move away from this place in a day or two, with the ostensible reason of visiting South India, from where invitations have been pouring in upon me for a long time; but I tell you in confidence, it is the lapse of reason—my frequent visitor—the Spirit of Truancy, that is beckoning me, ready to escort me over all lines of proscribed works. I long to discover some fairy-land of holidays—not a lotus-land—not a world where all weekdays are Sundays—but where Sundays are not at all needed, where all works carry their rest in themselves, where all duties look delightfully undutiful, like clouds bearing rain, appearing perfectly inconsequential.

Sa̋ntiniketan, *December 11th, 1918*

Yesterday I had a letter from the University of Sydney asking me if it was true that I would not visit Australia, even if I was wanted there. I have written, in answer, that it would be wrong on my part if I refused to accept any invitation sent in the right spirit. Pride of patriotism is not for me. I earnestly hope that I shall find my home anywhere in the world, before I leave it. We have to fight against wrongs, and suffer for the cause of righteousness; but we should have no petty jealousies or quarrels with our neighbours merely because we have different names.

The barrier of Self is *maya*. When it is dispelled, then we in our suffering have tasted the draught of sorrow that wells up from the heart of creation, flowing out to be merged and transformed into the sea of endless joy.

When we do not see ourselves in the Infinite, when we imagine our sorrow to be our very own, then life becomes untrue and its burden becomes heavy. I understand more and more the truth of Buddha's teaching, that the root of all our miseries is this self-consciousness. We have to realize the consciousness of the All before we can solve the mystery of pain and be free.

Our emancipation lies through the path of suffering. We must unlock the gate of joy by the key of pain. Our heart is like a fountain. So long as it is driven through the narrow channel of self it is full of fear and doubt and sorrow; for then it is dark and does not know its end. But when it comes out into the open, on the bosom of the All, then it glistens in the light and sings in the joy of freedom.

CHAPTER V

The letters that now remain to be quoted form an almost uninterrupted series, though I have continued to divide them into chapters. They were written by the Poet during a long tour, in Europe and America, in which he was accompanied by his friend W.W. Pearson.

Out of the misery and darkness of the Great War, Rabindranath Tagore had been led, step by step to the one fixed purpose of gradually forming at Santiniketan Asram a home of brotherhood and peace, where East and West might meet in a common fellowship of study and work.

At first his design had been to gather together at his Asram the scattered religious cultures of Asia in order to present them in a united manner to the rest of the world. But his comprehensive vision could not stop at any horizon that was less wide than humanity. During the years 1918 and 1919 he took me with him on many tours, while he wandered up and down India, seeking to find a seed-ground in which his thoughts concerning human progress might take root in the soil and afterwards bear fruit. I was able to watch in these tours this one central purpose that I have mentioned taking concrete shape. He pictured to himself Santiniketan opening its doors to the whole world, and inviting those who were lovers of peace and goodwill, in East and West alike, to come together there, on equal terms, without distinction of caste or race or creed.

He named the institution which should offer such world-hospitality Visva-bharati. 'Visva' in Sanskrit means 'world,'—in its universal aspect. 'Bharati' is more difficult to translate, but implies knowledge, wisdom, culture. Visva-bharati was to be a House of Learning for all peoples and all religions.

The Poet traced back his whole conception to the Upanishads and had in his mind those forest Asrams, or religious retreats, of ancient India, which were freely open to all who came to them, and made their guests welcome with the fullness of fellowship and love. One of the most celebrated of his lectures was called

'The Religion of the Forest.' In a noble passage from another lecture he concludes with the following words:

> Our forefathers spread a single pure white carpet, whereon all the world was cordially invited to take its seat in amity and good-fellowship. No quarrel could have arisen there; for He in whose name the invitation went forth, for all time to come, was Santam, Sivam, Advaitam—the Peaceful, in the heart of all conflicts; the Good, who is revealed through all losses and sufferings; the One, in all diversities of creation. And in His name was this eternal truth declared in Ancient India:
>
> He alone sees truly who sees all beings as himself.

For the fulfilment of his central purpose it was necessary for him to go once more to Europe and America in order to gain the support of the West and to invite the West to his Asram. But at the very time when he was beginning to prepare for his journey certain disturbances occurred in the Punjab which for a time threw everything else into the background. Riots had occurred and reprisals had been taken. At the critical moment when the news came about Amritsar I happened to be with him in Calcutta, and it will be impossible for me ever to forget the torture of his mind. Night after night was passed sleeplessly. At last some relief came to him by renunciation of his knighthood as a protest against what had been done. For a time it seemed as though 'Amritsar' had shattered all his hopes and aims.

But while he felt such intense sensitiveness, as a poet, at the wrong which had been done to humanity in Jallianwalla Bagh, he took his stand at once against any memorial being erected upon the spot as a permanent record of the deed of blood. In the same way, on an earlier occasion, when asked in Japan to celebrate, by means of a short poem, to be engraved on a rock, a tragic story concerning a blood-feud, he wrote:—

> They hated and killed, and men praised them,
> But God in shame hastened to hide its memory under the green grass.

I have mentioned these facts because they belong essentially to the period covered by the letters which follow. They reveal the inner spirit of the Poet as at last, after long absence, he approached Europe in the year 1920. With a great effort he had recovered his serenity of mind. His faith in the generous spirit of the West had passed through its ordeal of fire. Deep down in his subconscious nature he had been wounded at heart by the events of the previous year in the Punjab. Therefore it was with great anxiety that I watched his vessel depart from Bombay, and went back to the Asram.

Red Sea, *May 24th, 1920*

We shall reach Suez this evening. It is already beginning to grow cold, and now I feel that we have reached a truly foreign part of the world tinder the rule of different gods than ours. Our hearts are strangers in this region and even the atmosphere of this place looks askance at us. The people here want us to fight their battle and supply them with our raw materials, but they keep us standing outside their doors, over which is written on the notice-board: 'Trespassers from Asia will be prosecuted.' When I think of all this, my thoughts shiver with cold and I feel home-sick for the sunny corner in my Santiniketan bungalow.

To-day is Monday, and next Sunday morning our steamer will reach Marseilles. But I am already counting the days for my return journey; and I know the sight of the bare rocks of Aden will give a thrill of delight to my heart while pointing with lifted fingers the way to India.

London, *June 17th, 1920*

Time is scarce, and sugar, and butter, and a quiet place where I can gather thoughts and recognize myself. Do not expect long letters from me, or indeed anything else. The fury of social engagements is on me. It is a thing on which one might compose an Ode like that on the West Wind. I am willing to try, if only it would allow me some time to do it. The poet Hafiz was willing to exchange the wealth of Samarkand and Bokhara for a mole on the cheek of his beloved. I am willing to give the whole of London away for my corner in Santiniketan. But London is not mine to dispose of; neither was the wealth of Samarkand and Bokhara the Persian poet's. So our extravagance does not cost us anything, nor does it bring us any help.

I am going to Oxford to-morrow. Then I shall be knocking about in different places. Just at this moment I am starting for a tea-party given in my honour, from which I cannot absent myself on any pretext, unless I can manage to be run over by a motor-car in the London streets. It is a matter of eternal wonder to me that this does not happen to me four times a day. You won't believe in my scarcity of time if I go on to the end of the note-paper. So I hastily bid you farewell.

London, *July 8th, 1920*

Everyday I have been wishing to write you a letter—but the flesh is weak. My days have become solid like cannon-balls, heavy with engagements. It is not true that I have no leisure at all, but unfortunately I cannot utilize interrupted leisure for any work whatever. Therefore those intervals are lost doing nothing.

I am sure you know it, better than anybody else, that doing nothing is a burden hard to bear. But if you look at my exterior, you will find no trace of damage there—for my health is absurdly good.

I hope Pearson is regularly furnishing you with all the news. He has been of very great help to me, as you can well imagine, and I find that the arduous responsibility of looking after a poet suits him wonderfully well. He is looking the very picture of health, and on the whole his dreams are felicitous. For instance, last night he dreamt that he had been buying strawberries as large as gourds. It proves the magnificent vitality of his dreams.

I know our school vacation is over. The boys are back at school and the Asram is resounding with laughter and song. The advent of the rains is also contributing its portion to the general rejoicing. How I wish I had wings! Give my love to all the children, and my blessings.

London, *July 12th, 1920*

It gave me great joy, and a feeling of relief, when your sister came to see me yesterday and gave me reassuring news about your other sister. She repeatedly asked me to tell you that there was not the least cause for anxiety on account of them, and that they were comfortably settled in their new home. I gave her all the news about you, but unfortunately could not assure her that you were careful of your own health.

Invitations are pouring in from the continental countries, and I feel sure that a hearty welcome is awaiting me in these places. When I am weary and feel a longing to go back, it gives me strength to think that the migratory flock of my thoughts have found their nest on these shores, and with genuine love and wonder these enormously busy people have listened to a voice from the distant East.

This is a constant surprise to me. However, there is no question that one only truly and fully lives where one's thoughts and works find their medium of responsive life. When I am in the West, I feel more strongly than ever that I am received in a living world of mind. I miss here my sky and light and leisure, but I am in touch with those who feel and express their need of me and to whom I can offer myself.

It is not unlikely that some time hence my thoughts will no longer be necessary to them and my personality will lose its flavour; but does it matter? The tree sheds its leaves, but the fact is that so long as these were living they brought sunshine into the heart of the tree and their voice was the voice of the forest; and my communication with Western humanity has been a communication of life. Even when it ceases, the fact remains that it brought some rays of light there, which have been transformed into the living stuff of their minds. Our span of life is short and opportunities are rare, so let us sow our seeds of thought where the soul claims them and where the harvest will ripen.

London, *July 22nd, 1920*

The result of the Dyer debates in both Houses of Parliament makes painfully evident the attitude of mind of the ruling classes of this country towards India. It shows that no outrage, however monstrous, committed against us by agents of their Government, can arouse feelings of indignation in the hearts of those from whom our governors are chosen.

The unashamed condonation of brutality expressed in their speeches and echoed in their newspapers is ugly in its frightfulness. The feeling of humiliation about our position under the Anglo-Indian domination had been growing stronger every day for the last fifty years or more; but the one consolation we had was our faith in the love of justice in the English people, whose soul had not been poisoned by that fatal dose of power which could only be available in a Dependency where the manhood of the entire population had been crushed down into helplessness.

Yet the poison has gone further than we expected, and it has attacked the vital organs of the British nation. I feel that our appeal to their higher nature will meet with less and less response every day. I only hope that our countrymen will not lose heart at this, but employ all their energies in the service of their country with a spirit of indomitable courage and determination.

The late events have conclusively proved that our true salvation lies in our own hands; that a nation's greatness can never find its foundation in half-hearted concessions of contemptuous niggardliness.

It is the sign of a feeble character to seek for a short-cut to fulfilment through the favour of those whose interest lies in keeping it barred—the one path to fulfilment is the difficult path of suffering and self-sacrifice. All great boons come to us through the power of the immortal spirit we have within us, and that spirit only proves itself by its defiance of danger and loss.

London, *August 1st, 1920*

We live on the topmost floor of this house far away from the surging life of the town. Only the crest of the swell of the London street-noise reaches me, gently undulating like those clustering tree-tops of Kensington Gardens that I watch from my window. The long and persistent spell of bad weather seems to have exhausted its spite, and the mellow light of the morning sun from behind the fleecy clouds is greeting me like the smile of a child whose eyes are still heavy with sleep. It is nearly seven o'clock, and every one of our party, including Pearson, is fast asleep within shut doors and behind drawn blinds. To-day is our last day in London, and I am not sorry to leave it. I wish it were the day for sailing home, but that day looks hazily distant and my heart aches.

London, *August 4th, 1920*

Owing to a change of plans, we are still detained in London. We hope to leave it the day after to-morrow. Now that people believe that we are away, and since your London weather has ceased to persecute me, these last two days have been very restful for me. I wonder if you know that at the last moment we decided not to start on our tour to Norway, though our tickets were bought. I am sure you are ready to ascribe this to the inconstancy of mind!

P.S.—I have just written this about Dr Geddes:

What so strongly attracted me in Dr Patrick Geddes when I came to know him in India was not his scientific achievement but, on the contrary, the rare fact of the fullness of his personality rising far above his science. Whatever he has studied and mastered has become vitally one with his humanity. He has the precision of the scientist, and at the same time the vision of the prophet. He has also the power of an artist to make his ideas visible through the language of symbol. His love of man has given him the insight to see the truth of man and imagination to realize in the world not merely the mechanical aspect but also the infinite mystery of life.

Paris, *August 13th, 1920*

I have come to Paris, not stay here, but to decide where to go. The sun is shining bright and the spirit of exhilaration is in the atmosphere. Sudhir Rudra received me at the station and made all arrangements for us. Pearson has gone to stay with his mother for some weeks before we start for America. Therefore I am in the hands of Sudhir just at present and he is taking proper care of me. Paris is empty, and there is no chance of our meeting the people whom I should like to meet. Our stay in England has been wasted. Your Parliament debates about Dyerism in the Punjab and other symptoms of an arrogant spirit of contempt and callousness about India have deeply grieved me, and it was with a feeling of relief that I left England.

Near Paris, *August 20th, 1920*

We are in a delightful country, in a delightful place in France, meeting with people who are so human.

I feel clearly that the ultimate reality for man's life is his life in the world of ideas, where he is emancipated from the gravitational pull of the dust and he realizes that he is spirit. We, in India, live in a narrow cage of petty interests; we do not believe that we have wings, for we have lost our sky; we chatter and hop and peck at one another within the small range of our obstructed opportunities. It is difficult to achieve greatness of mind and character where our responsibility is diminutive and fragmentary, where our whole life occupies and affects an extremely limited area.

And yet through the cracks and chinks of our walls are must send out our starved branches to the sunlight and air, and the roots of our life must pierce the upper strata of our soil of desert sands till they reach down to the spring of water which is exhaustless. Our most difficult problem is how to gain our freedom of soul in spite of the cramped condition of our outward circumstances; how to ignore the perpetual insult of our destiny, so as to be able to uphold the dignity of man.

Santiniketan is for this *tapasya* of India. We who have come there often forget the greatness of our mission, mostly because of the obscurity and insignificance with which the humanity of India seems to be obliterated. We have not the proper light and perspective in our surroundings to be able to realize that our soul is great; and therefore we behave as if we were doomed to be small for all time.

Ardennes, *August 21st, 1920*

Here we are in a most beautiful part of France. But of what avail is the beauty of Nature when you have lost your trunks which contained all your clothes? I could have been in perfect sympathy with the trees surrounding me if, like them, I were not dependent upon tailors for maintaining self-respect. The most important event for me in this world at present is not what is happening in Poland, or Ireland, or Mesopotamia, but the fact that all the trunks belonging to our party have disappeared from the goods-van in their transit from Paris to this place!

And therefore, though the sea is singing its hymns to the rising and setting sun and to the starlit silence of the night, and though the forest round me is standing tiptoe on the rock, like an ancient Druid, raising its arms to the sky, chanting its incantation of primeval life, we have to hasten back to Paris to be restored to respectability at the hands of tailors and washermen!

I have just received your letter, and for some time I have felt myself held tight in the bosom of our Asram. I cannot tell you how I feel about the prolonged separation from it which is before me; but at the same time I know that unless my relationship with the wide world of humanity grows in truth and love, my relationship with the Asram will not be perfect.

Paris, *September 7th, 1920*

Your letters always bring the atmosphere of Santiniketan round my mind, with all its colour and sounds and movements; and my love for my boys, like a migratory bird, crosses back over the sea, seeking its own dear nest in the Asram. Your letters are great gifts to me—I have not the power to repay them in kind. For now my mind faces the West, and all that it has to give naturally flows towards it. Therefore, for the time being, my direct communication with you has become thin, like the stream of the Kopai River in the summer. But I know Santiniketan will not bring forth its fullness of flower and fruit if, through me, it does not send its roots into the Western soil. Stung by the insult of cruel injustice, we try to repudiate Europe, but by doing so we insult ourselves. Let us have the dignity not to quarrel or retaliate; not to pay back smallness by being small ourselves. This is the time when we should dedicate all our resources of emotion, thought and character to the service of our country in a positive direction of duty. We are suffering because of our offences against Shivam, against Advaitam. We spend all our energy in quarrelling with the punishment and nothing of it is left for the reparation of wrongs we have done and are doing. When we have performed our part of the duties, we shall have the fullest right and power and time to bring others to book for their transgressions.

Let us forget the Punjab affairs—but never forget that we shall go on deserving such humiliation over and over again until we set our house in order. Do not mind the waves of the sea, but mind the leaks in your vessel. Politics in our country is extremely petty. It has a pair of legs, one of which has shrunk and shrivelled and become paralytic and therefore feebly waits for the other one to drag it on. There is no harmony between the two, and our politics, in its hoppings and totterings and falls, is comic and undignified. The entreaty and anger, which alternately are struggling to find expression in the ludicrously lame member of this tragic partnership, both belong to our abject feebleness. When Non-co-operation comes naturally as our final moral protest against the unnaturalness of our political situation, then it will be glorious, because true; but when it is only another form of begging, then let us reject it.

The establishment of perfect co-operation of life and mind among ourselves must come first through sacrifice and self-dedication, and then will come in its natural course the non-cooperation. When the fruit completely ripens, it finds its freedom through its own fulfilment of truth.

Our country is crying to her own children for their co-operation in the removal of obstacles in our social life which for centuries have been hampering us in our self-realization. We need co-operation in the sacrifice of love, more than anything else, to prove to our country that she is ours; and then we shall have the moral right to say to others: 'we have nothing to do with you in our affairs.' And for this, all the moral fervour which the life of Mahatma Gandhi represents, and which he, of all men in the world, can call up, is needed.

That such a precious treasure of power should be put into the mean and frail vessel of our politics, allowing it to sail across endless waves of angry recrimination, is terribly unfortunate for our country, when our mission is to revive the dead with the fire of the soul. The external waste of our resources of life is great owing to external circumstances; but that the waste of our spiritual resources should also be allowed to happen on adventures that are wrong from the point of view of moral truth is heartbreaking. It is criminal to turn moral force into a blind force.

Our time to go to Holland is drawing near. I have numerous invitations from over there to lecture, but I am not yet fully ready. Just now I am busy writing. My subject is the Meeting of the East and West. I hope it will be finished before I leave Paris.

Paris, *September 12th, 1920*

I had invitations from Germany and decided to go. But travelling from one country to another has become so difficult nowadays that I had to give it up. Specially, going from France to Germany is beset with obstacles. On my way back from Holland, I shall try my best at least to visit Hamburg. Germany needs sympathy, and I hope I shall have the opportunity to go there and offer it to her.

A short time ago I was taken to Rheims and other devastated regions of France in a motor-car. It was a most saddening sight. It will take a tremendous effort and also an immense lapse of time to make this a thing of the past. When the spiritual ideal is lost, when the human relationship is completely broken up, then individuals freed from the creative bond of wholeness find a fearful joy in destruction.

In such catastrophes, one can realize what a stupendous force of annihilation is not only kept in check in our society, but made into multitudinous manifestations of beauty and fruitfulness. Then we know that evils are like meteors, stray fragments, wreckage of a broken-up wholeness, which need the attraction of a great planet of life's ideal to be assimilated into the peace of creation.

Only spiritual ideals have that great power of attraction that can transmute these rebellious fractions into a perfect roundness. The evil forces are literally outlaws. They only need the control and cadence of creative laws to change them into good. Our Shiva[1] is the Lord of terrible spirits, who are spirits of death; and he is also Shivam, the Good. True goodness lies not in the negation of badness, but in the mastery of it. It is the miracle that turns the tumult of chaos into the dance of beauty. True education is that power of miracle, that ideal of creation. Punishments and disciplines imposed from outside are negative. The Teacher is Shiva. He has the divine power of destroying the destructiveness; of sucking out the poison. If France had the Shiva in her heart, she could transform evil into good, she could forgive. And that forgiveness could prove her own immortality, and truly save her from the hurt which was inflicted upon her.

This is difficult, but it is the one way of salvation. Only the creative ideal can completely get over the acts of destruction. It is the spiritual ideal, it is love, it is forgiveness. God is perpetually exercising it, and thus the creation is ever kept sweet.

In the heart of death, life has its ceaseless play of joy.

Do we not know this in our individual life? Have we our own right to exist in this wonderful world? Would we not burn it, destroy it? Has not God's creative power given us our place in His universe? Must we forget that, when we judge and deal with our own fellow-beings?

Paris, *September 18th, 1920*

I find our countrymen are furiously excited about Non-co-operation. It will grow into something like our Swadeshi movement in Bengal. Such an emotional outbreak should have

1. The God Shiva in Indian mythology is regarded as the Lord of Terrors. But the name 'Shivam' indicates beneficence; and thus Shiva is also the God of Goodness. He swallows the deadly poison without harm.

been taken advantage of in starting independent organizations all over India for serving our country.

Let Mahatma Gandhi be the true leader in this; let him send his call for positive service, ask for homage in sacrifice, which has its end in love and creation. I shall be willing to sit at his feet and do his bidding if he commands me to co-operate with my countrymen in service and love. I refuse to waste my manhood in lighting fires of anger and spreading it from house to house.

It is not that I do not feel anger in my heart for injustice and insult heaped upon my motherland. But this anger of mine should be turned into the fire of love for lighting the lamp of worship to be dedicated through my country to my God.

It would be an insult to humanity if I use the sacred energy of my moral indignation for the purpose of spreading a blind passion all over my country. It would be like using the fire from the altar of sacrifice for the purpose of incendiarism.

Antwerp, *October 3rd, 1920*

I have spent about a fortnight in Holland. This fortnight has been most generous in its gifts to me. Of one thing you may be sure, that a communication of heart has been opened up between this little country and Santiniketan; and it remains with us to widen it and make use of it for the interchange of spiritual wealth. Altogether, Europe has come closer to us by this visit of ours. I only wish that all my friends in Santiniketan could realize how true this is and what a wealth it represents. Now I know more clearly than ever before that Santiniketan belongs to the world and we have to be worthy of this great fact. It is extremely difficult for us Indians to forget all the irritations that ever keep our consciousness concentrated on our own daily annoyances. But emancipation of consciousness is both the means and end of spiritual life. Therefore Santiniketan must be saved from the whirlwind of our dusty politics.

I am writing this letter from Antwerp, where I came yesterday morning; and I am getting ready to go to Brussels, where I have an invitation. And then I go to Paris.

London, *October 18th, 1920*

Our vision of truth varies according to its perspective. I feel certain that this perspective has become narrow in India owing to the density of mental atmosphere caused by political unrest. There are politicians who must make hasty decisions and act without delay. It is their function to take short cuts to immediate success and dash through blunders with their lumbering 'tanks' of political organizations. But there are needs that belong to all mankind and to all time. Those have to be satisfied through the rise and fall of empires. We all know that there is a vast difference between journalism and literature. Journalism is necessary and there are multitudes of men eager to carry it out. But if it suppresses the light of literature, then it will produce the London fog of November, which substitutes gaslight for the sunlight.

Santiniketan is there for giving expression to the Eternal Man—*asato ma sad gamaya,*[1] the prayer that will ring clearer as the ages roll on, even when the geographical names of all countries are changed and lose their meaning. If I give way to the passion of the moment and the claims of the crowd, then it will be like speculating with my Master's money for a purpose which is not His own.

I know that my countrymen will clamour to borrow from this capital entrusted to me and exploit it for the needs that they believe to be more urgent than anything else. But all the same, you must know that I have to be true to my trust. Santiniketan must treasure in all circumstances that *santi* which is in the bosom of the Infinite. With begging and scrambling we find very little, but with being true to ourselves we find a great deal more than we desire. The best reward that I have gained in my life is through the spontaneous and disinterested expression of truth in me, and never through straining for a result, whatever high-sounding name it may have carried.

1. Literally, 'Lead me from Untruth to Truth.'

CHAPTER VI

The journey undertaken to America, described in the letters contained in this chapter, was directly for the purpose of obtaining sympathy and support for the Poet's Visva-bharati ideal. His earlier visits to America in 1913 and 1916 had given him the hope that the young heart of the New World would respond to him more definitely than the peoples of Europe, who were still involved in their national prejudices and their narrow provincial boundaries.

Since the Poet's conception of Visva-bharati lies in the background in all the letters which he wrote to me from America, it may be well as an introduction to this chapter to give his own explanation of his purpose, as he presented it during his lecture tours in India before he started for the West. The following passages from these lectures appear to me to explain the Poet best:

> The age has come when all artificial fences are breaking down. Only that will survive which is basically consistent with the universal; while that which seeks safety in the out-of-the-way hole of the special will perish. The nursery of the infant should be secluded, its cradle safe. But the same seclusion, if continued after the infant has grown up, makes it weak in mind and body.
>
> There was a time when China, Egypt, Greece and Rome had, each of them, to nurture its civilization in comparative seclusion. The greatness of the universal, however, which was more or less in each, grew strong within its protecting sheath of individuality. Now has come the age for co-ordination and co-operation. The seedlings that were reared within their enclosures must now be transplanted into the open fields. They must pass the test of the world-market if their maximum value is to be obtained.
>
> So we must prepare the grand field for the co-ordination of all the cultures of the world, where each will give to and

take from the other; where each will have to be studied through the growth of its stages in history. This adjustment of knowledge through comparative study, this progress in intellectual co-operation, is to be the key-note of the coming age. We may hug our holy aloofness from some imagined security of a corner, but the world will prove stronger than our corner, and it is our corner that will have to give way, receding and pressing against its walls till they burst on all sides.

But before we in India are in a position to stand a comparison with the other cultures of the world, or truly to co-operate with them, we must base our structure on a synthesis of all the different cultures we have. When taking our stand at such a centre we turn towards the West, our gaze shall no longer be timid and dazed; our heads shall remain erect, safe from insult. For then we shall be able to take our own views of truth from the standpoint of our own vantage-ground, thus opening out a new vista of thought before a grateful world.

All great countries have their vital centres for intellectual life, where a high standard of learning is maintained, where the minds of the people are naturally attracted to find their genial atmosphere, to prove their worth, to contribute their share to the country's culture, and thus to kindle on some common altar of the land a great sacrificial fire of intellect which may radiate the sacred light in all directions.

Athens was such a centre in Greece, Rome in Italy, and Paris is such to-day in France. Benares has been, and still continues to be, the centre of our Sanskrit culture. But Sanskrit learning does not exhaust all the elements of culture that exist in the present-day India.... That is why the inner spirit of India is calling to us to establish in this land great centres, where all her intellectual forces will gather for the purpose of creation, and all her resources of knowledge and thought, Eastern and Western, will unite in perfect harmony. She is seeking for the glorious opportunity to know her own mind and give her mind to the world, to help it in its progress; when she will be released from the chaos of scattered powers and the inertness of borrowed acquisitions.

Let me state clearly that I have no distrust of any culture because of its foreign character. On the contrary, I believe that the shock of such forces is necessary for the vitality of our intellectual nature. It is admitted that much of the spirit of Christianity runs counter, not only to the Classical culture of Europe, but to the European temperament altogether. And yet this alien movement of idea, constantly running against the natural mental current of Europe, has been the most important factor in strengthening and enriching her civilization on account of the very antagonism of its direction. In fact, the European vernaculars first woke up to life and fruitful vigour owing to the impact of this foreign thought-power with all its Oriental forms and feelings. The same thing is happening in India. European culture has come to us, not only with its knowledge, but with its velocity. Though our assimilation of it is imperfect and the consequent aberrations numerous, still it is rousing our intellectual life from its inertia of former habits into growing consciousness by the very contradiction it offers to our mental traditions.

What I object to is the artificial arrangement by which this foreign education tends to occupy all the space of our national mind and thus kills, or hampers, the great opportunity for the creation of a new thought-power by a new combination of truths. It is this which makes me urge that all the elements in our own culture have to be strengthened, not to resist Western culture, but truly to accept and assimilate it; to use it for our food and not as our burden; to get mastery over this culture, and not to live at its outskirts as the hewers of texts and the drawers of book-learning.

Rabindranath Tagore suffered from illness during his visit to America, and this brought with it depression of mind. The response to his appeal for co-operation in his work of international fellowship was not at first as direct and full as he had expected. His longing to go back became at last intense.

The letters which he wrote to me during these months were often full of gloom. Those that follow are some of the most important of them dealing with his ideal of a centre of international fellowship at Santiniketan.

New York, *October 28th, 1920*

Our steamer has arrived in port—too late for us to land to-night. Between one shore and the other there are tossings on the angry waves and menaces of the shrieking winds, but peace comes at the end and shelter when the desolation that divides the world appears unreal and is forgotten. This crossing of the sea has not yet been completed by those who are voyagers from one age to another. Storms have raged and the moaning of the salt sea has haunted their days and nights. But the haven is not very far distant and the new continent of time is ready with its greeting of light and life and its invitation to the unexplored. Already I feel the breath of that future and see birds from the shore bringing songs of hope.

You must know that our Santiniketan belongs to that future. We have not yet reached it. We need stronger faith and clearer vision to direct our course towards its hill of sunlight. There are chains which still keep our boat clinging to the sheltered cove of the past. We must leave it behind. Our loyalty must not be for any land of a limited geography. It should be for the nationality of the common idea, to which are born individuals belonging to various nations, who are carrying their gifts of sacrifice to the one great shrine of Humanity.

New York, *November 4th, 1920*

There is one thing about which I wish to speak to you. Keep Santiniketan away from the turmoils of politics. I know that the political problem is growing in intensity in India and its encroachment is difficult to resist. But all the same, we must never forget that our mission is not political. Where I have my politics, I do not belong to Santiniketan.

I do not mean to say that there is anything wrong in politics, but only that it is out of harmony with our Asram.

We must clearly realize this fact, that the name of Santiniketan has a meaning for us, and this name will have to be made true. I am anxious and afraid lest the surrounding forces may become too strong for us and we succumb to the onslaught of the present time. Because the time is troubled and the minds of men distracted, all the more must we, through our Asram, maintain our faith in Shantam, Shivam, Advaitam.

New York, *November 25th, 1920*

A friend of mine, who is actively interested in my cause, is a Quaker, and he takes me every Sunday morning to the Quakers' meetings. There, in the silence of meditation, I am able to find the eternal perspective of truth, where the vision of outward success dwindles away to its infinitesimal minuteness. What is needed of me is sacrifice. Our payment is for success, but our sacrifice is for truth. If the spirit of sacrifice is pure in quality, then its reward will be more than can be counted and proved, and let my gift to my country and to the world be a life of sacrifice.

But my earnest request to you is to keep your mind high above politics. The problem of this new age is to help to build the world anew. Let us accept this great task. Santiniketan is to make accommodation for the workers from all parts of the world. All other things can wait. We must make room for Man, the guest of this age, and let not the Nation obstruct his path. I am afraid lest the cry of our own sufferings and humiliations should drown the announcement of His coming. For His sake we shall set aside our grievances and shall say: 'Whatever may happen to us, let His cause triumph; for the future is His.'

New York, *November 30th, 1920*

I am often reminded of my *Gitanjali* poem in which the woman tells how she found God's sword when she had been seeking for a petal from God's flower-garden. All through my life I have been seeking for such a petal, and I stand puzzled at the sight of the gift waiting for me. This gift has not been my choice, but my God has chosen for me this gift. And now I say to myself that we prove our worthiness for God's gift of responsibility by acceptance of it and not by success or anything else.

The past has been for men, the future is for Man. These *men* are still fighting for the possession of the world: the din and the clash are deafening; the air is obscured with the dust rising from the trampled earth. Standing in the heart of this struggle, we have to build a seat for the one God revealed to all human races. We may be mocked and pushed away by the crowd, but the fact will remain and invisibly grow into truth that we have believed.

I was born a poet, and it is difficult for me to suffer myself to be rudely hustled in my path by busy men who have no leisure for ideas. I am not an athlete. I do not belong to the arena. The stare of the curious crowd scorches my soul. And yet I, of all persons, am called upon to force my way into the thick of the Western public with a mission for which I have never been trained. Truth fashions its own arrows out of reeds that are light and frail.

New York, *December 13th, 1920*

Our Seventh Paus Festival at the Asram is near at hand. I cannot tell you how my heart is thirsting to join you in your festival. I am trying to console myself with the thought that something very big and great is going to be the outcome of the effort I am making. But deep in my heart I know that simplicity of life and endeavour makes for real happiness. When we realize in some measure our ideal of perfection in our work, it matters very little what its dimensions are. Our trust in bigness very often betrays our want of faith in truth. The kingdom of the earth boasts of the magnitude of its possessions, but the Kingdom of Heaven is content with the depth of its self-realization. There are certain institutions which have for their object some external success. But Santiniketan is there for giving us opportunity to realize ourselves in truth. This can never be done through big funds, but through dedication of our life in love.

In this country I live in the dungeon of the Castle of Bigness. My heart is starved. Day and night I dream of Santiniketan, which blossoms like a flower in the atmosphere of the unbounded freedom of simplicity. I know how truly great Santiniketan is, when I view it from this land. Here I feel every day what a terrible nightmare it is for the human soul to bear this burden of the monster Arithmetic. It incessantly drives it victims and yet leads them nowhere. It raises storms of battle which are for sowing broadcast the seeds of future conflict.

The giant reptiles of the primitive earth were proud of their hypertrophied tails, which did not save them from the doom of destruction. I long to leave all this, totally reject this unreality, take the next steamer I can get, and run back to my Santiniketan and serve it with my life and love.

That life which I dedicate to it, if it is true, will make it live. The true wisdom is there, which can spurn the greed for result and is only concerned with the expression of truth. This wisdom found its utterance in India. But there is imminent danger of its being drowned in the flood of noise which the votaries of success are bellowing forth in the prosperous West. My prayer is growing every day more and more intense, to get away from the dark tower of unreality, from this dance of death trampling sweet flowers of life under its tread.

New York, *December 17th, 1920*

When all my thoughts were furiously revolving, like dead leaves, in a whirlwind of desire for raising funds, a picture came to my hand; it was that of Sujata offering a cup of milk to Buddha. Its message went deep into my heart. It said to me: 'The cup of milk comes to you unasked when you have gone through your *tapasya*. It is offered to you with love, and only love can bring its homage to truth.'

Then your figure at once came to my mind. The milk has been sent to me through you. It is infinitely more than anything that can come from the cheque-book of the rich. I had become famished in the wilderness of solitude for lack of sympathy and comradeship, when you brought your cup of love to me, which is the true life-giving food freely offered by life. And as the poet Morris says, 'Love is enough.' That voice of love calls me away from the lure of dollars—the voice that comes to nestle in my heart from across the sea, from the shady avenue of *sal* trees resonant with laughter and songs of simple joy.

The mischief is that ambition does not fully believe in love. It believes in power. It leaves the limpid and singing water of everlasting life for the wine of success. Everyday I seem to be growing afraid of the very vision of this success. It had been said in the Upanishad, 'Happiness is in greatness.' Ambition points out bigness and calls it greatness, and our track is hopelessly lost. When I look at the picture of Buddha, I cry for the great peace of inner fulfilment. My longing grows painfully intense as my mind becomes distracted at the stupendous unmeaningness of monstrosity in things around me. Every morning I sit by my window and say to myself: 'I must not bow my head to this ugly idol worshipped by the West with daily human sacrifice.' I remember that morning at Shileida when the Vaishnava woman came to me and said: 'When are you coming down from your three-storied building to meet your love under the shade of the trees?'

Just now, I am on the top storey of the skyscraper to which the tallest of trees dare not send its whisper; but love silently comes to me saying: "When are you coming down to meet me on the green grass under the rustling leaves, where you have the freedom of the sky and of sunlight and the tender touch of life's simplicity?' I try to say something about money, but it sounds so ludicrous and yet so tragic, that my words grow ashamed of themselves and they stop.

New York, *December 19th, 1920*

When Life began her first experiments, she was mightily proud of the hugeness of her animal specimens. The bigger the bodies were, the more extravagantly large the armour had to be made for their protection. The ludicrous creatures, in order to maintain their balance, had to carry a tail which was absurdly disproportionate to the rest of their bodies. It went on like this till life became a burden to itself and to the exchequer of creation. It was uneconomical, and therefore not only harmful but ungainly. True economy is the principle of beauty in practical arithmetic. Driven to bewilderment, life began to seek for a pause in her insanity of endless multiplication.

All forms of ambitious powers are obsessed by this delirium of multiplication. All its steps are steps towards augmentation and not completeness. But ambitions, that rely solely upon the suggestion of their tails and armour, are condemned to carry their own obstruction till they have to stop.

In its early history, Life, after its orgies of megalomania, had at last to think of disarmament. But how did she effect it? By boldly relinquishing the ambition to produce bigness—and man was born helplessly naked and small. All of a sudden he was disinherited of the enormity of flesh, when apparently he was most in need of it. But this prodigious loss gained for him his freedom and victory.

Then began the reign of Mind. It brought its predecessor of gigantic bulk under subjection. But, as often happens, the master became the parasite of the slave, and mind also tried to achieve greatness by the bigness of materials. The dynasty of mind followed the dynasty of flesh, but employed this flesh as its prime minister.

Our history is waiting for the dynasty of Spirit. The human succeeded the brutal; and now comes the turn of the Divine.

In our mythology we have often heard of a man taking the side of the Gods and saving Paradise from the dominion of Giants. But in our history we often notice man holding alliance with Giants and trying to defeat the Gods. His guns and ships of huge power and proportion are turned out from the arsenal of the Giant. In the fight of bigness against goodness, man has joined the former, counting the coins of his reward in number and not in quality—in lead and not in gold.

Those who are in possession of material resources have become slaves of their own instruments. Fortunately for us, in India, these resources are beyond all immediate possibility of realization. We are disarmed, and therefore we have no option but to seek for other and higher sources of power. The men who believe in the reality of brute force have made enormous sacrifices in order to maintain it. Let us, in India, have faith in the moral power in man and be ready to sacrifice for it all we have. Let us do our best to prove that Man has not been the greatest mistake in Creation. Let it not be said that, for the sake of peace and happiness in the world, the physical brutes were preferable to the intellectual brutes who boast of their factory-made teeth and nails and poison fangs.

New York, *December 20th, 1920*

In every age and in every country facts are given to us in order that we may provide with them some special expression of Truth. Facts are like atoms in gases: they fight with, or else fly away from, one another. But when they are united into a drop of dew they attain beauty and reality. Man must have that creative magic to bring the facts of his time into some unity of creation. In Christ and in Buddha this creative ideal tried to unite men who were divided because of their formalism in religious faith.

Formalism in religion is like nationalism in politics: it breeds sectarian arrogance, mutual misunderstanding and a spirit of persecution. Our Indian mediaeval saints, through their light of love and inner perception of truth, could realize the spiritual unity of man. For them, the innumerable barriers of formalism had no existence. Therefore the mutually antagonistic creeds of Hindus and Mahomedans, irreconcilable as they seemed, did not baffle them. Our faith in truth has its trial in the apparent difficulty of its realization.

The most important of all facts in the present age is that the East and West have met. So long as it remains a mere fact, it will give rise to interminable conflicts; it will even hurt man's soul. It is the mission of all men of faith to raise this fact into truth. The worldly-rise will shake their heads and say it is not possible—that there is a radical difference between the East and the West and that only physical power will have its sway in their relationship.

But physical power is not creative. Whatever laws and organizations it may produce, it will never satisfy spiritual humanity. Ram Mohun Roy was the first great man in our age who had the profound faith and large vision to feel in his heart the unity of soul between the East and West. I follow him, though he is practically rejected by my countrymen.

I only wish you had been with me in Europe! You would know at once what was the purpose of the modern age; what is the cry of man, which the politicians never hear. There were politicians in the courts of the Moghul Emperors. They have left nothing behind them but ruins. But Kabir and Nanak! They have bequeathed to us their imperishable faith in the unity of man through God's love.

New York, *December 21st, 1920*

All about me is a desert of crowds, a monotony of multitude. Man is drowned in his own deluge of desultoriness. It is an unceasing struggle in me to have to pass through this—especially when I carry in myself such a heavy load of helplessness. Every moment I am made conscious of it, and I am tired. When we have the banner of an idea to carry against obstacles of indifference, the burden of our personal self should be extremely light. But I am so awkwardly cumbersome with my ineptitude.

I remember, when I was young, how a blind old beggar used to come to our door every morning led by a boy. It was a tragic sight; the blindness of the old man robbed the boy of his freedom. The boy looked so wistful and eager for release. Our incapacity is a fetter with which we tie others to our limitations. Consciousness of this, every day adds to my feeling of weariness. But this depression of spirit is likely to do me a service. It has led me to the brink of a discovery that a great measure of one's impotence is *maya*.

Latterly I have been constantly giving myself a shaking, trying to arouse myself from this stupor of self-delusion. During the greater part of my life my mind has been made accustomed to travel the inner paths of dreams, till it has lost all confidence in its power to thread its way through the zigzags of the outer world. In fact, its attention has never been trained to accept the miscellaneous responsibilities of the clamorous surface life of society. Therefore the West is not my world.

And yet I have received the gift of love from the West, and my heart acknowledges her claims to my service and I must unreservedly offer myself to her before I die. I do not belong to the present age, the age of conflicting politics. Nevertheless I cannot repudiate the age which has given me birth. I suffer and struggle. I crave for freedom and yet am held back. I must share the life of the present world, though I do not believe in its cry. I sit at its table, and while it fills its cup with wine to slake its unnatural thirst, I try to listen, through the noisy carousal, to the murmur of the stream carrying its limpid waters to the sea.

New York, *December 22nd, 1920*

To-day is the seventh of Paus. I wish it were allowed to me to stand among you and mingle my voice with yours in uttering our prayer. It is real starvation of my heart to be deprived of this great privilege. To-day I realize more than ever before that nothing can be truer for me than to be with my dear children and friends, this beautiful sunny morning of December, and bow my head to my Father and dedicate my service to Him. By that dedication our works become great, and not by extension of external resources.

Oh, how simple is truth and how full of light and happiness! Not to be distracted by the curiosity of crowds, only to be rewarded by the approval of Him who knows our heart, in the fulfilment of our endeavour. I only hope that what I am doing here is in response to the call of the Shantam, that my lonely celebration of seventh Paus in this hotel room finds its harmony with your festival. Let our faith in the real be not overcome by the lure of the unreal. Let come to us what is good and not what we desire. Let us bow our heads to the Good, to the supreme Good.[1]

I have often felt the desire that you were with me in my adventure. And yet I am deeply thankful that you could remain at the Asram while I was away. For you understand me with the understanding of love, and therefore through you I seem to

1. These sentences are a free translation of the prayer repeated together in the *mandir* (or chapel) at Santiniketan.

dwell in Santiniketan. I know that I am in your mind today and you know that my heart is with you. Is it not a great good fortune that there is a spot in this world where all that is best in us can meet in truth and love? Can anything be greater than that? Please give my blessings to all my boys and girls, and my greetings of love to my friends.

Near New York, *December 25th, 1920*

To-day is Christmas Day. We are about forty-five guests gathered in this inn from different parts of the United States. It is a beautiful house, nestling in the heart of a wooded hill, with an invitation floating in the air of a brook broadening into a lake in the valley. It is a glorious morning, full of peace and sunlight, of the silence of the leafless forest untouched by bird songs or humming of bees.

But where is the spirit of Christmas in human hearts? The men and women are feeding themselves with extra dishes and laughing extra loud. But there is not the least touch of the eternal in the heart of their merriment, no luminous serenity of joy, no depth of devotion. How immensely different from the religious festivals of our country! These Western people have made their money but killed their poetry of life. Here life is like a river, that has heaped up gravel and sand and choked the perennial current of water that flows from an eternal source on the snowy height of an ancient hill. I have learnt since I came here to prize more than ever the infinite worth of the frugal life and simple faith. These Western people believe in their wealth, which can only multiply itself and attain nothing.

How to convince them of the utter vanity of their pursuits! They do not have the time to realize that they are not happy. They try to smother their leisure with rubbish of dissipation, lest they discover that they are the unhappiest of mortals. They deceive their souls with counterfeits, and then, in order to hide that fact from themselves, they artificially keep up the value of those false coins by an unceasing series of self-deceptions.

My heart feels like a wild-duck from the Himalayan lake lost in the endless desert of Sahara, where sands glitter with a fatal brilliance but the soul withers for want of the life-giving spring of water.

New York, *January 8th, 1921*

There are a large number of ideas about which we do not even know that they are inaccessible to us, only because we have grown too familiar with their names.

Such is our idea of God. We do not have to realize it in order to be made aware of it. This is why it requires a great deal of spiritual sensitiveness to be able to feel the life-throb of God's reality behind the vulgar callosity of words. Things that are small naturally come to their limits for us, when they are familiar. But the truth which is great should reveal its infinity all the more vastly when it is near to us. Unfortunately, words that represent truth have not the same immensity of life as truth itself. Therefore the words (and with them our attention and interest) become inert by constant handling, obscuring our faith underneath them without our being conscious of that tragic fact.

This is the reason why men who are obviously religious are frequently more irreligious, in reality, than those who openly ignore religion. Preachers and ministers of religion have made it their business to deal with God at every moment. They cannot afford to wait until they come in touch with Him. They dare not acknowledge the fact that they have not done so. Therefore they have to strain their minds into a constant attitude of God-Knowingness. They have to delude themselves, in order to fulfil the expectations of others, or what they consider to be their duty.

And yet the consciousness of God, like that of all other ideas, comes to us only with intense moments of illumination, of inspiration. If we do not have the patience to wait for it, we only choke the path of inspiration with the *débris* of our conscious efforts. Those who make it their business to preach God, preach creeds. They lose their sense of distinction between these two. Therefore their religion does not bring peace into this world, but conflict. They do not hesitate to make use even of their religion for the propaganda of national self-seeking and boastfulness.

You may wonder, in your mind, as to the reason of my bringing up this topic in my present letter. It is in connection with the same endless conflict within me between the poet and the preacher, one of whom depends for his mission upon inspiration and the other upon conscious endeavour. Straining of consciousness leads to insensitiveness, of which I am more afraid than anything else. The preacher is the professional dealer in particular ideas. His customers come at all hours of the day and put questions to him. The answers, which he gets into the habit of producing, gradually lose their living quality, and his faith in his ideas runs the risk of being smothered under the deadness of his words. I believe that such a tragedy is more common than people suspect, especially with those who are good and therefore are ever ready to sign their cheque of benefit for others without waiting to see if the cash has had time to accumulate in the bank.

This makes me think that it is safe to be nothing better than a mere poet. For poets have to be true to their best moments and not to other peoples' requirements.

New York, *January 14th, 1921*

Even when I was very young my mind ever sought for all experiences in an environment of completeness. That is to say, fact indicated some truth to me, even though I did not clearly understand it. That is why my mind was constantly struck with things that in themselves were commonplace.

When I watched, from over the wall of the terrace of the inner apartments of our Jorashanko house, the coconut-trees and the tank surrounded by the huts of the milk vendors, they came before me with a more-than-themness that could not be exhausted. That faculty—though subsequently mingled with reasoning and self-analysis—has still continued in my life. It is the sense and craving for wholeness. Constantly it has been the cause of my separation from others and also their misunderstanding of my motives.

Swadeshi, Swarajism, ordinarily produce intense excitement in the minds of my countrymen, because they carry in them some fervour of passion generated by the exclusiveness of their range. It cannot be said that I am untouched by this heat and movement. But somehow, by my temperament as a poet, I am incapable of accepting these objects as final. They claim from us a great deal more than is their due. After a certain point is reached, I find myself obliged to separate myself from my own people, with whom I have been working, and my soul cries out: 'The complete man must never be sacrificed to the patriotic man, or even to the merely moral man.'

To me humanity is rich and large and many-sided. Therefore I feel deeply hurt when I find that, for some material gain, man's personality is mutilated in the Western world and he is reduced to a machine.

The same process of repression and curtailment of humanity is often advocated in our country under the name of patriotism. Such deliberate impoverishment of our nature seems to me a crime. It is a cultivation of callousness, which is a form of sacrilege. For God's purpose is to lead man into perfection of growth, which is the attainment of a unity comprehending an immense manifoldness. But when I find man, for some purpose of his own, imposing upon his society a mutilation of mind, a niggardliness of culture, a puritanism which is spiritual penury, it makes me inexpressibly sad.

I have been reading a book by a Frenchman on Japan. The sensitiveness to the ideal of beauty, which has been made universal in Japan, is not only the source of her strength, but of her heroic spirit of renunciation. For true renunciation blossoms on the vigorous soil of beauty and joy—the soil which supplies positive food to our souls.

But the negative process of making the soil poor produces a ghastly form of renunciation which belongs to the nihilism of life. An emancipation of human nature has already been going on for a long time in India. Let us not add to it by creating a mania for self-immolation. Our life to-day needs more colour, more expansion, more nourishment, for all the variety of its famished functions. Whatever may be the case in other countries, we need in India more fullness of life, and not asceticism.

Deadness of life, in all forms, gives rise to impurities, by enfeebling our reason, narrowing our vision, creating fanaticism, owing to our will-power being forced into abnormal channels. Life carries its own purification when its sap finds the passage unbarred through all ramifications.

New York, *January 23rd, 1921*

I have just come back from Greenwich, a suburban part of New York, where last night I had a reception and a speech and a dinner and a discussion, till I felt empty, like a burst balloon with no gas left in it!

At the far-distant end of the wilderness of such trials as this what do I see? But what matters it? Results of our efforts delude us by appearing as final. They raise expectation of fulfilment and draw us on. But they are not final. They are roadside inns where we change our horses for a farther journey. An ideal is different. It carries its own progress within itself. Each stage is not a mere approach to the goal, but carries with it its own meaning and purpose.

Trees proceed on their upward career, not along a railway track constructed by engineers. We, who have been dreamers, should never employ coolies to build railway lines of social service. We must solely deal with living ideas, and have faith in life. Otherwise we are punished, not necessarily with bankruptcy, but with success—behind which sits the Mephistopheles of worldliness, chuckling at the sight of an idealist dragged through the dust by the chariot of the prosperous.

What has made us love Santiniketan so deeply is the ideal of perfection, which we have tasted all through its growth. It has not been made by money, but by our love, our life. With it we need not strain for any result; it is fulfilment itself—the life which forms round it, the service which we daily render it. Now I realize, more than ever before, how precious and how beautiful is the simplicity of our Asram, which can reveal itself all the more luminously because of its background of material poverty and want.

New York, *February 2nd, 1921*

After a break of three weeks and a sultriness of weary waiting, your letters have come in a downpour; and I cannot possibly tell you how refreshing they are! I seem to be travelling across a desert, and your letters are like weekly provisions dropped by some air-service from cloud-land. They are expected; and yet they have the element of surprise. I hungrily attack them and fall upon extra portions supplied from your letters written to others.

Your letters are delightful, because you have your interest in details that are generally overlooked. The world is made beautiful by the unimportant things. They furnish this great world-picture with all its modulations of shades and tints. The important things are like the sunshine. They come from a great source. But the unimportant compose the atmosphere of our life. They scatter the sun's rays, break the atmosphere into colours, and coax it into tenderness.

You have asked for my permission to abolish the matriculation class from our school. Let it go. I have no tenderness for it. In our classical literature it was the strict rule to give all dramas a happy ending. Our matriculation class has ever been the fifth act in our Asram, ending in a tragedy. Let us drop the scene, before that disaster gathers its forest!

I am enclosing with this a translation, which runs thus:

WOMAN

The fight is ended.
Shrill cries of loss trouble the air,
The gains, soiled and shattered, are a burden too heavy to carry home.
Come, woman, bring thy breath of life.
Close all cracks with kisses of tender green,
Nurse the trampled dust into fruitfulness.

The morning wears on;
The stranger sits homeless by the roadside, playing on his reed.
Come, woman, bring thy magic of love!

Make infinite the corner between walls,
There to build a world for him,—
Thine eyes its stars, thy voice its music.

The gate-door creaks in the wind.
The time is for leave-taking at the day's end.
Come woman, bring thy tears!
Let thy tremulous touch call out its last lyric
From the moment of parting.
Let the shadow of thy sad gaze
Haunt the road across the hills.

The night deepens;
The house is empty; its loneliness aches with silence.
Come, woman, bring thy lamp of vigil!
Enter thy secret chamber of sorrow.
Make the dark hours quiver with the agony of thy prayer.
Till the day dawns in the East.

New York, *February 5th, 1921*

Civilization in the West is a magnifying glass. It makes the most ordinary things hugely big. Its buildings, business, amusements, are exaggerations. The spirit of the West loves it high-heeled boots, whose heels are much bigger than itself.

Since I came to this continent my arithmetic has become absurdly bloated. It refuses to be compressed within decent limits. But I can assure you that to carry such a burden even in my imagination is wearisome.

Yesterday some Santiniketan photographs came by chance into my hands. I felt as if I was suddenly wakened up from a Brobdingnagian nightmare. I say to myself, This is our Santiniketan. It is ours, because it is not manufactured by a machine. Truth is beautiful—like woman in our own country. She never strains to add to her inches by carrying extravagances under her feet. Happiness is not in success, not in bigness, but in truth.

What makes me feel so sad, in this country, is the fact that people here do not know that they are not happy. They are proud, like the sandy desert, which is proud of its glitter. This Sahara is mightily big; but my mind turns its back upon it, and sings:

> I will arise and go now, and go to Innisfree,
> And a small cabin build there, of clay and wattles made;
> Nine bean rows will I have there, a hive for the honey-bee,
> And live alone in the bee-loud glade.

In the modern age, with all its facilities of communication, the access to Innisfree has become most difficult. Central Africa opens its secret to the inquisitive man, and also the North and South Pole—but the road to Innisfree lies in an eternal mystery.

Yet I belong to that 'Isle of Innisfree': its true name is Santiniketan. But when I leave it, and cross over to the western shore, I feel occasionally frightened lest I should lose my path back to it.

Oh! But how sweet is our *Sal* avenue, the breath of autumn in our *Shiuli* groves, the rainy evening resonant with music in Dinu's absurd little room!

> And I shall have some peace there, for peace comes dropping slow,
> Dropping from the veils of the morning to where the cricket sings;
> There midnight's all a glimmer and noon a purple glow,
> And evening full of the linnet's wings.

CHAPTER VII

During the months of February and March 1921 the Non-co-operation movement reached its height in India. The appeal made to boycott the Government Schools and Colleges stirred the hearts of the students of Calcutta and some thousands of them came out. The atmosphere was electrical and the spirit of sacrifice was in the very air we breathed. My letters to the Poet were full of these things, and I myself was carried away in the enthusiasm of the moment. It is necessary to understand that the letters which the Poet wrote to me at this time were, in part at least, his own reaction to this news which reached him, week by week, from me. Gradually, as his health improved, his stay in America became brighter, and he wrote more cheerfully. He was specially delighted with his first visit to the Southern States, and deeply appreciated the warmth of heart he found among every class of people in those regions. With this very brief note of explanation, the letters that follow tell their own story and are easily intelligible.

On the voyage to Europe the Poet wrote, day after day, a separate letter to me. He did the same on his later journey from Europe to India and with some amusement gave me the whole series from his own letter-case on arrival at Santiniketan. This will account for the different letters written on board ship which are reproduced in this volume.

New York, *February 8th, 1921*

I have just read a letter published in *Prabasi* by one who is at the Asram, and it has deeply hurt me. This is the ugliest side of patriotism. For in small minds, patriotism dissociates itself from the higher ideal of humanity. It becomes the magnification of self, on a stupendous scale—magnifying our vulgarity, cruelty, greed; dethroning God, to put up this bloated self in its place.

The whole world is suffering from this cult of Devil-worship in the present age, and I cannot tell you how deeply I am suffering, being surrounded in this country by endless ceremonials of this hideously profane cult. Everywhere there is an antipathy against Asia vented by a widespread campaign of calumny. Negroes are burnt alive, sometimes merely because they tried to exercise their right to vote, given to them by law. Germans are reviled. Conditions in Russia are deliberately misrepresented. They are furiously busy building their towers of political civilization upon the quagmire of mob psychology, spreading over it a crust of deliberate lies. They have to subsist upon a continual supply of hatred, contempt, jealousy, and lies and lies!

I am afraid I shall be rejected by my own people when I go back to India. My solitary cell is awaiting me in my motherland. In their present state of mind, my countrymen will have no patience with me, who believe God to be higher than my country.

I know such spiritual faith may not lead us to political success, but I say to myself, as India has ever said: 'Even then—what?'

The more I live in this country the more I understand the true meaning of emancipation.

It is for India to keep her breast supplied with the *Amrita*[1] of wisdom, with which to feed the new-born age and nourish it into a mighty future.

The ideas to which politicians still cling belong to a past that is doomed. It is a wreck rushing towards annihilation. The West is beginning to have doubts about its shelter, but its habit of mind is preventing it from leaving the old shelter for a new one. But we unfortunate creatures are getting ready to jump into the stream and swim across to the sinking ship and fight for our place in its corner. Yet I know that our huts are safer than that doomed and drifting monster.

I long to live in the heart of Peace. I have done my work, and I hope that my Master will grant me leave to sit by Him, not to talk, but to listen to His own great silence.

---

1. *Amrita* is the divine nectar which gives immortal life.

Houston, Texas, *February 23rd, 1921*

Tied to the chariot-wheel of Karma we flit from one birth to another. What that means to the individual soul I have been made to realize in these last few days. It is my tyrant Karma which is dragging me from one hotel to another. Between my two hotel incarnations I usually have my sleep in a Pullman car, the very name of which suggests the agency of death. I am ever dreaming of the day when I shall attain my Nirvana, freed from this chain of hotel lives, and reach utter peace in Uttarayana.[1]

I have not written to you for some time. For I am tired to the profound depth of my being.

Yet, since coming to Texas, I have felt as it were a sudden coming of Spring into my life through a breach in the ice castle of Winter. It has come to me like a revelation that all these days my soul had been thirsting for the draught of sunshine poured from the beaker of infinite space. The sky has embraced me, and the warmth of its caress thrills me with joy.

Chicago, *February 24th, 1921*

We have engaged our passage in a Dutch steamer, which will sail from New York on the 19th of March. My days in this country have not given me much pleasure—the simple course would have been for me to go straight back home.

Why did I not do so? No fool can say why he has been foolish. I have often dreamed of the time when my wayward youth took me to the loneliness of the sandbanks of the Padma, wandering in the neighbourhood of the wild-ducks under the gaze of the evening star. Certainly, that was not the life of the sane, but it fitted me like a fool's cap lined with dreams.

The fool who is content to do nothing whatever is at any rate free from care; but the one who tries in vain to change the face of the world knows no peace. I long to go back to my ducks, and yet I madly whirl round these manufacturing towns like a breath of the wild south breeze stirring the leaves of the documents of an attorney's office. Does it not know that these

1. The Poet's cottage at Santiniketan.

leaves do not shelter the flowers that wait for its whisper of love? Why should I be anything else but a poet? Was I not born a music-maker?

Chicago, *February 26th, 1921*

I have often wondered in my mind whether my path is the path of the good. When I came to this world I had nothing but a reed given to me, which was to find its only value in producing music. I left my school, I neglected my work, but I had my reed and I played on it 'in mere idle sport.' All along I had my one playmate, who also in His play produced music, among leaves, in rushing water, in silence of stars, in tears and laughter rippling into lights and shadows in the stream of human life. While my companion was this eternal Piper, this Spirit of play, I was nearest to the heart of the world. I knew its mother-tongue, and what I sang was caught up by the chorus of the wind and water and the dance-master of life.

But now came the schoolmaster in the midst of my dream-world, and I was foolish enough to accept his guidance. I laid aside my reed, I left my playground, where the Infinite Child is spending his eternity 'in mere idle sport.' In a moment I became old and carried the burden of wisdom on my back, hawking truths from door to door.

Why have I been made to carry this burden, I ask myself over and over again, shouting myself hoarse in this noisy world where everybody is crying up his own wares? Pushing the wheelbarrows of propaganda from continent to continent—is this going to be the climax of a poet's life? It seems to me like an evil dream, from which I occasionally wake up in the dead of night and grope about in the bed asking myself in consternation: 'Where is my music?'

It is lost, but I had no right to lose it, for I did not earn it with the sweat of my brow; it was a gift to me, which I could deserve if I knew how to love it. You know I have said somewhere that 'God praises me when I do good; but God loves me when I sing.' Praise is reward; it can be measured against the work you render; but love is above all rewards; it is measureless.

The poet who is true to his mission reaps his harvest of love; but the poet who strays into the path of the good is dismissed with applause. So I founded my International University—a great work! But I lose my little song—which loss can never be made up to me. How I wish I could find my reed again and be contemptuously ignored by the busy and the wise as a hopeless ne'er-do-well!

When I know for certain that I shall never be able to go back to that sweet obscurity which is the birthplace of flowers and songs, I feel home-sick. It is a world which is so near and yet so far away; so easy of access and yet so immensely difficult. Happiness we go on missing in our life, because it is so simple.

Chicago, *March 2nd, 1921*

Your last letter gives wonderful news about our students in Calcutta.[1] I hope that this spirit of sacrifice and willingness to suffer will grow in strength; for to achieve this is an end in itself. This is the true freedom! Nothing is of higher value—be it national wealth or independence—than disinterested faith in ideals, in the moral greatness of man.

The West has its unshakable faith in material strength and prosperity; and therefore, however loud grows the cry for peace and disarmament, its ferocity growls louder, gnashing its teeth and lashing its tail in impatience. It is like a fish, hurt by the pressure of the flood, planning to fly in the air. Certainly the idea is brilliant, but it is not possible for a fish to realize. We, in India, have to show the world what is that truth which not only makes disarmament possible but turns it into strength.

The truth that moral force is a higher power than brute force will be proved by the people who are unarmed. Life, in its higher development, has thrown off its tremendous burden of armour and a prodigious quantity of flesh, till man has become the conqueror of the brute world. The day is sure to come when the frail man of spirit, completely unhampered by air-fleets and dread-noughts, will prove that the meek are to inherit the earth.

1. Referring to the boycott of schools and colleges by thousands of students.

It is in the fitness of things that Mahatma Gandhi, frail in body and devoid of all material resources, should call up the immense power of the meek that has been waiting in the heart of the destitute and insulted humanity of India. The destiny of India has chosen for its ally the power of soul, and not that of muscle. And she is to raise the history of man from the muddy level of physical conflict to the higher moral altitude.

What is Swaraj! It is *maya;* it is like a mist that will vanish, leaving no stain on the radiance of the Eternal. However we may delude ourselves with the phrases learnt from the West, Swaraj is not our objective. Our fight is a spiritual fight—it is for Man. We are to emancipate Man from the meshes that he himself has woven round him—these organizations of national egoism. The butterfly will have to be persuaded that the freedom of the sky is of higher value than the shelter of the cocoon. If we can defy the strong, the armed, the wealthy—revealing to the world the power of the immortal spirit—the whole castle of the Giant Flesh will vanish in the void. And then Man will find his Swaraj.

We, the famished ragged ragamuffins of the East, are to win freedom for all humanity. We have no word for 'Nation' in our language. When we borrow this word from other people, it never fits us. For we are to make our league with *Narayan*,[1] and our triumph will not give us anything but victory itself: victory for God's world. I have seen the West; I covet not the unholy feast in which she revels every moment, growing more and more bloated and red and dangerously delirious. Not for us is this mad orgy of midnight, with lighted torches, but awakenment in the serene light of the morning.

Chicago, *March 5th, 1921*

Lately I have been receiving more and more news and newspaper cuttings from India, giving rise in my mind to a painful struggle that presages a period of suffering which is waiting for me. I am striving with all my power to tune my mood of mind to be in accord with the great feeling of

1. The godlike element in man.

excitement sweeping across my country. But, deep in my being, why is there this spirit of resistance maintaining its place in spite of my strong desire to remove it? I fail to find a clear answer; and through my gloom of dejection breaks out a smile and a voice saying: 'Your place is on "the sea-shore of worlds," with children; there is your peace, and I am with you there.'

This is why lately I have been playing with inventing new metres. These are merest nothings that are content to be borne away by the current of time, dancing in the sun and laughing as they disappear. But while I play, the whole creation is amused, for are not flowers and leaves never-ending experiments in metres? Is not my God an eternal waster of time? He flings stars and planets in the whirlwind of changes, he floats paper-boats of ages, filled with his fancies, on the rushing stream of appearance. When I tease him and beg him to allow me to remain his little follower and accept a few trifles of mine as the cargo of his play-boat, he smiles and I trot behind him catching the hem of his robe.

But where am I among the crowd, pushed from behind, pressed from all sides? And what is this noise about me? If it is a song, then my own *sitar* can catch the tune and I can join in the chorus; for I am a singer. But if it is a shout, then my voice is wrecked, and I am lost in bewilderment. I have been trying all these days to find in it a melody, straining my ear, but the idea of non-cooperation, with its mighty volume of sound, does not sing to me; its congregated menace of negation shouts. And I say to myself: 'If you cannot keep step with your countrymen at this great crisis of their history, never say that you are right and the rest of them wrong; only, give up your rôle as a soldier, go back to your corner as a poet, be ready to accept popular derision and disgrace.'

R—, in support of the present movement, has often said to me that passion for rejection is a stronger power in the beginning than the acceptance of an ideal. Though I know this to be a fact, I cannot take it as a truth. We must choose our allies once for all; for they stick to us even when we might be glad to be rid of them. If we once claim strength from intoxication, then in the time of reaction our normal strength is bankrupt, and we go back again and again to the demon that lends us resources in a vessel whose bottom it takes away.

Brahma-vidya, the cult of Brahma, the Infinite Being, has for its object *mukti,* emancipation; while Buddhism has *nirvana,* extinction. It may be argued that both have the same ideas in different names. But names represent attitudes of mind and emphasize particular aspects of truth. *Mukti* draws our attention to the positive, and *nirvana* to the negative side of truth. Buddha kept silence through his teachings about the truth of the *Om,* the Everlasting Yes, his implication being that by the negative path, destroying the self, we naturally reach that truth. Therefore he emphasized the fact of *dukkha,* misery, which had to be avoided. But *Brahma-vidya* emphasized the fact of *ananda,* joy, which had to be attained. The latter cult also needs for its fulfilment the discipline of self-abnegation; yet it holds before its view the idea of Brahma, not only at the end, but all through the process of realization.

Therefore the idea of life's training was different in the Vedic period from that of the Buddhistic. In the former it was the purification of life's joy; in the latter it was the eradication of it. The abnormal type of asceticism, to which Buddhism gave rise in India, revelled in celibacy and mutilation of life in all different forms. The forest life of the Brahman was not antagonistic to the social life of man, but harmonious with it. It was like our musical instrument, the *támbura,* whose duty is to supply the fundamental notes to the music to save it from straying into discordance. It believed in the music of the soul, and its own simplicity was not to kill it, but to guide it.

The idea of non-co-operation is political asceticism. Our students are bringing their offering of sacrifices to what? Not to a fuller education, but to non-education. It has at its back a fierce joy of annihilation, which at its best is asceticism, and at its worst that orgy of frightfulness in which human nature, losing faith in the basic reality of normal life, finds a disinterested delight in an unmeaning devastation, as has been shown in the late war and on other occasions which came nearer to us. 'No,' in its passive moral form, is asceticism, and in its active moral form violence. The desert is as much a form of *himsa,* violence, as is the raging sea in storm; they are both against life.

I remember the day, during the Swadeshi movement in Bengal, when a crowd of young students came to see me in the first floor of our Vichitra[1] house. They said to me that if I would order them to leave their schools and colleges they would instantly obey. I was emphatic in my refusal to do so, and they went away angry, doubting the sincerity of my love for my motherland. And yet long before this popular ebullition of excitement, I myself had given a thousand rupees, when I had not five rupees to call my own, to open a Swadeshi store and courted banter and bankruptcy.

The reason of my refusal to advise those students to leave their schools was because the anarchy of mere emptiness never tempts me, even when it is resorted to as a temporary measure. I am frightened at an abstraction which is ready to ignore living reality. These students were no mere plantoms to me. Their life was a great fact to them and to the All. I could not lightly take upon myself the tremendous responsibility of a mere negative programme for them which would uproot their life from its soil, however thin and poor that soil might be. The great injury and injustice which had been done to those boys, who were tempted away from their career before any real provision was made, could never be made good to them. Of course, that is nothing from the point of view of an abstraction, which can ignore the infinite value even of the smallest fraction of reality. I wish I were the little creature Jack, whose one mission is to kill the Giant Abstraction, which is claiming the sacrifice of individuals all over the world under highly painted masks of delusion.

I say again and again that I am a poet; that I am not a fighter by nature. I would give everything to be one with my surroundings.

I love my fellow-beings and prize their love. Yet I have been chosen by destiny to ply my boat at that spot where the current is against me. What irony of fate is this, that I should be preaching co-operation of cultures between East and West on

1. The Poet's hall of music in Calcutta.

this side of the sea just at the moment when the doctrine of non-co-operation is preached on the other side!

You know that I do not believe in the material civilization of the West, just as I do not believe the physical body to be the highest truth in man. But I believe still less in the destruction of the physical body, and the ignoring of the material necessities of life. What is needed is the establishment of harmony between the physical and spiritual nature of man, the maintaining of balance between the foundation and superstructure. I believe in the true meeting of East and West. Love is the ultimate truth of soul. We should do all we cannot to outrage that truth, but to carry its banner against all opposition. The idea of non-co-operation unnecessarily hurts that truth. It is not our hearth-fire, but the fire that burns out our hearth and home.

New York, *March 13th, 1921*

Things that are stationary have no responsibility and need no law. For death, even the tombstone is a useless luxury. But for a world, which is in ever-moving multitude advancing towards an idea, all its laws must have one principle of harmony. This is the law of creation.

Man became great when he found out this law for himself, the law of cooperation. It helped him to move together, to utilize the rhythm and impetus of the world march. He at once felt that this moving together was not mechanical, not an external regulation for the sake of some convenience. It was what the metre is in poetry—not a mere system of enclosure for keeping ideas from running away in disorder, but for vitalizing them, making them indivisible in a unity of creation.

So far this idea of co-operation has developed itself into individual communities, within the boundaries of which peace has been maintained and varied wealth of life produced. But outside these boundaries the law of cooperation has not been realized. Consequently the great world of man is suffering from ceaseless discordance. We are beginning to discover that our problem is worldwide, and no one people of the earth can work out its salvation by detaching itself from others. Either we shall be saved together or drawn together into destruction.

This truth has ever been recognized by all the great personalities of the world. They had in themselves the perfect consciousness of the undivided spirit of man. Their teachings were against tribal exclusiveness, and thus we find that Buddha's India transcended geographical India and Christ's religion broke through the bonds of Judaism.

To-day, at this critical moment of the world's history, cannot India rise above her limitations and offer the great ideal to the world that will work towards harmony and co-operation between the different peoples of the earth? Men of feeble faith will say that India requires to be strong and rich before she can raise her voice for the sake of the whole world. But I refuse to believe it. That the measure of man's greatness is in his material resources is a gigantic illusion casting its shadow over the present-day world—it is an insult to man. It lies in the power of the materially weak to save the world from this illusion; and India, in spite of her penury and humiliation, can afford to come to the rescue of humanity.

The freedom of unrestrained egoism in the individual is licence and not true freedom. For his truth is in that which is universal in him. Individual human races also attain true freedom when they have the freedom of perfect revelation of Man and not that of their aggressive racial egoism. The idea of freedom which prevails in modern civilization is superficial and materialistic. Our revolution in India will be a true one when its forces are directed against this crude idea of liberty.

The sunlight of love has the freedom that ripens the wisdom of immortal life; but passion's fire can only forge fetters for ourselves. The Spiritual Man has been struggling for its emergence into perfection, and every true cry of freedom is for this emancipation. Erecting barricades of fierce separateness, in the name of national necessity, is offering hindrance to it. Therefore in the long run it is building a prison for the nation itself. For the only path of deliverance for nations is in the ideal humanity.

Creation is an endless activity of God's freedom; it is an end in itself. Freedom is true when it is a revelation of truth. Man's freedom is for the revelation of the truth of Man, which is struggling to express itself. We have not yet fully realized it. But those people who have faith in its greatness, who acknowledge its sovereignty, and have the instinctive urging in the heart to break down obstructions, are paving the way for its coming.

India has ever nourished faith in the truth of the Spiritual Man, for whose realization she has made in the past innumerable experiments, sacrifices and penances, some verging on the grotesque and the abnormal. But the fact is she has never ceased in her attempt to find it, even though at the tremendous cost of losing material success. Therefore I feel that the true India is an idea, and not a mere geographical fact. I have come into touch with this idea in far-away places of Europe, and my loyalty was drawn to it in persons who belonged to countries different from mine. India will be victorious when this idea wins the victory—the idea of 'Purusham mahantam adityavarnam tamasah parastat'—'The Infinite Personality, whose Light reveals itself through the obstruction of Darkness.' Our fight is against this Darkness. Our object is the revealment of the Light of this Infinite Personality of Man. This is not to be achieved in single individuals, but in one grand harmony of all human races. The darkness of egoism which will have to be destroyed is the egoism of the Nation. The idea of India is against the intense consciousness of the separateness of one's own people from others, which inevitably leads to ceaseless conflicts. Therefore my own prayer is, let India stand for the co-operation of all peoples of the world.

The spirit of rejection finds its support in the consciousness of separateness; the spirit of acceptance finds its base in the consciousness of unity. India has ever declared that Unity is Truth, and separateness is *maya.* This unity is not a zero; it is that which comprehends all, and therefore can never be reached through the path of negation.

Our present struggle to alienate our heart and mind from the West is an attempt at spiritual suicide. If, in the spirit of national vainglory, we shout from our housetops that the West has produced nothing that has an infinite value for man, then we only create a serious cause of doubt about the worth of any product of the Eastern mind. For it is the mind of Man, in the

East and West, which is ever approaching Truth in her different aspects from different angles of vision. If it can be true that the standpoint of the West has betrayed it into an utter misdirection, then we can never be sure of the standpoint of the East. Let us be rid of all false pride and rejoice at any lamp being lit in any corner of the world, knowing that it is a part of the common illumination of our house.

The other day I was invited to the house of a distinguished art-critic of America who is a great admirer of old Italian Art. I questioned him if he knew anything of our Indian pictures, and he brusquely said that most probably he would hate them. I suspected he had seen some of them and hated them already. In retaliation I could have said something in the same language about Western Art. But I am proud to say it was not possible for me to do so. For I always try to understand Western Art and never to hate it.

Whatever we understand and enjoy in human products instantly becomes ours, wherever they might have their origin. I am proud of my humanity, when I can acknowledge the poets and artists of other countries as my own. Let me feel with unalloyed gladness that all the great glories of man are mine. Therefore it hurts me deeply when the cry of rejection rings loud against the West in my country with the clamour that Western education can only injure us.

It cannot be true. What has caused the mischief is the fact that for a long time we have been out of touch with our own culture and therefore Western culture has not found its true perspective in our life. Very often its perspective is wrong, giving our mental eye a squint. When we have intellectual capital of our own, the commerce of thought with the outer world becomes natural and fully profitable. But to say that such commerce is inherently wrong is to encourage the worst form of provincialism, productive of nothing but intellectual indigence.

The West has misunderstood the East. This is at the root of the disharmony that prevails between them. But will it mend matters if the East in her turn tries to misunderstand the West? The present age has been powerfully possessed by the West; it has only become possible because to her is given some great mission for man. We, from the East, have come to her to learn whatever she has to teach us; for by doing so we hasten the fulfilment of this age. We know that the East also has her lessons to give, and she has her own responsibility of not allowing her light to be extinguished. The time will come when the West will find leisure to realize that she has a home of hers in the East where her food is and her rest.

New York, *March 18th, 1921*

I wish that I could be released from this mission. For such missions are like a mist that envelops our soul—they seem to shut us off from the direct touch of God's world. And yet I have such an immense hunger for this touch. The springtime has come—the sky is overflowing with sunshine. I long to be one with the birds and trees and the green earth. The call comes to me from the air to sing, but, wretched creature that I am, I lecture—and by doing it I ostracize myself from this great world of songs to which I was born. Manu, the Indian lawgiver, enjoins us not to cross the sea. But I have done so; I have sailed away from my native universe—from the birthplace of those morning jasmines, from the lotus lake of Saraswati, which greeted me when I was a child even as the finger-touch of my own mother. Now, when occasionally I come back to them, I am made to feel that I have lost my caste; and though they call me by my name and speak to me, they keep themselves apart.

I know that my own river Padma, who has so often answered to my music with an amused gleam of tender tolerance in her face, will separate herself from me behind an invisible veil when I come to her. She will say to me in a sad voice: 'Thou hast crossed the sea!'

The losing of Paradise is enacted over and over again by the children of Adam and Eve. We clothe our souls with messages and doctrines and lose the touch of the great life in the naked breast of Nature. This letter of mine, carrying the cry of a banished soul, will sound utterly strange to you in the present-day India.

We hold our mathematical classes in Santiniketan under the *madhavi*[1] bower. Is it not good for the students and others that, even in the busiest time of lessons, the branches overhead do not break out into a shower of geometrical propositions? Is it not good for the world that poets should forget all about the resolutions carried at monster meetings? Is it not right that God's own regiment of the useless should never be conscripted for any military contingency of the useful?

When the touch of spring is in the air, I suddenly wake up from my nightmare of giving 'messages' and remember that I belong to the eternal band of good-for-nothings; I hasten to join in their vagabond chorus. But I hear the whisper round me: 'This man has crossed the sea,' and my voice is choked.

We are leaving Europe to-morrow and my days of exile are coming to an end. Very likely my letters will be fewer in number from now, but I shall make up for this when I meet you in person under the shadow of the rain-clouds of July.

Pearson is busy seeking health and happiness, making himself ready for the time when he will join us in India in the cold season.

S.S. 'Rhyndam'

The very fact that we have turned our face towards the East fills my heart with joy. For me my East is the poet's East, not that of a politician or scholar. It is the East of the magnanimous sky and exuberant sunlight, where once upon a time a boy found himself straying in the dim twilight of child-consciousness peopled with dreams. The child has grown, but never grown out of his childhood.

I realize it all the more strongly when some problem, political or otherwise, becomes clamorous and insistent, trying to exact its answer from me. I rouse myself, strain my mind, raise my voice for prophetic utterances, and try in every way to be worthy of the occasion, but in my heart of hearts I feel exceedingly small and, to my utter dismay, discover I am not a leader, not a teacher, and farthest of all away from being a prophet.

1. White jasmine.

The fact becomes fully evident to me, that I had forgotten to grow. It comes of an incorrigible absentmindedness. My mind has ever wandered away from those things that mature one into wisdom and old age. I have neglected my lessons. And this utter want of training makes me such a wretchedly bad reader of journals dealing with the practical questions of the day! But I am afraid the present time is a tremendously difficult one in India for the child, the poet. It is no use protesting that he is lacking in understanding—that he is congenitally incapable of paying attention to anything urgent and serious. No, he must attend meetings or write editorials; cultivate cotton-fields, or accept some responsibility of grave and national importance, in order to make a fool of himself.

And yet my heart is aching and longing to meet, with proper ceremony, the first day of the rainy season, or fill every pore of my mind with the smell of mango blossoms. Is that allowable at the present moment? Does our south breeze still enjoy all the frivolities of spring days? Have our sunset hours taken the vow of discarding all traces of colours from their cloud turbans?

But what is the use of complaining? The poets are too primitive for this age. If they had not ignominiously been discarded by the law of evolution, they would long ago have grown into their career as politicians. But the mischief is—they have been left behind in a world which has stopped growing, where things are still important which have no use or market value. The more the call for action grows loud from across the sea, the more I feel conscious of something in me that cries: 'I am of no use—leave me alone to my utter inutility.'

But I know, when I reach India, the Poet will be defeated; and I shall piously study the newspapers—every paragraph of them. But for the present even poetry is at a disadvantage—for the sea is rough, my head is swimming, and the English language is extremely difficult to manage in a rolling ship.

S.S. 'Rhyndam'

Sometimes it amuses me to see the struggle for supremacy that is going on between the different persons within me. In the present condition of India, when the call is sure to come to me to take some part, in some manner or other, in some political affairs, the Poet at once feels nervous, thinking that his claims are likely to be ignored, simply because he is the most useless member in the confederacy of my personality. He fully anticipates that argument against him, and takes special pains to glorify his deficiency even before any complaint has been submitted by anybody on this point. He has proudly begun to assert: 'I belong to the great brotherhood of the supremely useless. I am the cup-bearer of the Gods. I share the common privilege with all divinities to be misunderstood. My purpose is to reveal Purposelessness to the children of the Immortal. I have nothing to do with committee meetings or laying of foundation-stones for structures that stand against the passage of time and are sure to be trampled to dust. I am to ply the ferry-boat that keeps open the traffic between this shore and the shore of Paradise—this is our King's mail-boat for the communication of messages, and not for carrying cargo to the markets.'

I say to him: 'Yes, I fully agree with you; but, at the same time, take my warning, that your mail-boat may have to be commandeered for other urgent purposes, wholly unconnected with the Celestial Postal Department.' His cheeks grow pale; his eyes become bemisted; his frail body shivers like a cypress at the first breath of winter, and he says to me: 'Do I deserve to be treated like this? Have you lost all your love for me, that you can talk of putting me under martial law? Did you not drink your first cup of Amrita from my hand, and has not the Citizenship of the Sphere of Music been conferred upon you through my persuasion?'

I sit dumb, and muse and sigh, when sheaves of newspaper-cuttings are poured upon my table, and a leer is spread upon the face of the Practical man; he winks at the Patriotic man sitting solemnly by his side; and the man who is Good thinks it his painful duty to oppose the Poet, whom he is ready to treat with some indulgence within proper limits.

As for me who am the President of this *Panchayat*,[1] I have my deepest sentiment of tenderness for this Poet, possibly

1. Committee.

because he is so utterly good-for-nothing and always the first to be ignored in the time of emergency. The timid Poet avoiding the observation of the Practical and the Good comes to my side and whispers: 'Sir, you are not a man made for the time of emergency—but for the time that transcends it on all sides.'

The rascal knows well how to flatter, and generally wins his case with me—especially when others are too certain of the result of their appeal; and I jump up from my judgement-seat and, holding the Poet by the hand, dance a jig and sing: 'I shall join you, Comrade, and be drunk and gloriously useless.' Ah, my evil luck! I know why the chairmen of meetings hate me, newspaper editors revile me, and the virile call me effeminate! So I try to take shelter among the children, who have the gift of being glad with things and men that have no value.

S.S. 'Rhyndam'

My difficulty is that when, in my environment, some intense feeling of pride or resentment concentrates its red light within a certain limited area, I lose my true perspective of life and the world, and it hurts deeply my nature. It is not true that I do not have any special love for my own country, but when it is in its normal state it does not obstruct outside reality; on the contrary, it offers a standpoint and helps me in my natural relationship with others. But when that standpoint itself becomes a barricade, then something in me asserts that my place is somewhere else.

I have not yet attained that spiritual altitude from which I can say, with perfect assurance, that such barricading is wrong, or even unnecessary; but some instinct in me says that there is a great deal of unreality in it, as there is in all passions that are generated through contraction of consciousness, through rejection of a great part of truth.

I remember your wondering why Christ gave no expression to His patriotism, which was so intense in the Jewish people. It was because the great truth of man, which He realized, through His love of God, would only be cramped and crushed within that enclosure. I have a great deal of the patriot and politician in me, and therefore I am frightened of them; and I have an inner struggle against submitting myself to their sway.

But I must not be misunderstood. There is such a thing as a moral standard of judgement. When India suffers from injustice, it is right that we should stand against it; and the responsibility is ours to right the wrong, not as Indians, but as human beings. There your position is higher than most of our countrymen's. You have accepted the cause of India for the sake of humanity. But I know that most of our people will accept your help as a matter of course and yet reject your lesson. You are fighting against that patriotism whereby the West has humiliated the East—the patriotism which is national egoism. This is a comparatively later growth in European history and a far greater cause of misery and injustice in the human world than the bloodthirsty ferocity, the nomadic savagery, in the primitive history of man. The Pathans came to India, and the Moghuls, and they perpetrated misdeeds in their heedlessness; but because they had no taint of patriotism they did not attack India at the very root of her life, keeping themselves superciliously aloof. Gradually they were growing one with us; and just as the Normans and Saxons combined into one people, our Muhammadan invaders would ultimately have lost their line of separateness and contributed to the richness and strength of Indian civilization.

We must remember that Hinduism is not the original Aryanism; in fact, a great portion of it is non-Aryan. Another great mixture had been awaiting us, the mixture with the Muhammadans. I know that there were difficulties in its way. But the greatest of all difficulties was lacking—the idolatry of Geography. Just see what hideous crimes are being committed by British patriotism in Ireland! It is a python which refuses to disgorge this living creature which struggles to live its separate life. For patriotism is proud of its bulk, and in order to hold in a bond of unity the units that have their own distinct individualities it is ever ready to use means that are inhuman. Our own patriots would do just the same thing, if the occasion arose. When a minority of our population claimed its right of inter-caste marriage, the majority cruelly refused to allow it that freedom. It would not acknowledge a difference which was natural and real, but was willing to perpetrate a moral torture far more reprehensible than a physical one. Why? Because power lies in number and in extension. Power, whether in the patriotic or in any other form, is no lover of freedom. It talks of unity, but forgets that true unity is that of freedom. Uniformity is unity of bondage.

Suppose, in our Swaraj, the anti-Brahmin community refuses to join hands with us; suppose, for the sake of its self-respect and self-expression, it tries to keep an absolute independence—patriotism will try to coerce it into an unholy union. For patriotism has its passion of power; and power builds its castle upon arithmetic. I love India, but my India is an Idea and not a geographical expression. Therefore I am *not* a patriot—I shall ever seek my compatriots all over the world. You are one of them, and I am sure there are many others.

S.S. 'Rhyndam'

Plato threatened to banish all poets from his Republic. Was it in pity or in anger, I wonder? Will our Indian Swaraj, when it comes to exist, pass a deportation order against all feckless creatures who are pursuers of phantoms and fashioners of dreams, who neither dig nor sow, bake nor boil, spin nor darn, neither move nor support resolutions?

I have often tried to imagine the banished hordes of poets establishing their own Republic in the near neighbourhood of that of Plato. Naturally, as an act of reprisal, His Excellency the Poet President is sure to banish from the Rhymers' Republic all philosophers and politicians. Just think of the endless possibilities arising from feuds and truces of these rival Republics—peace conferences, deputations of representatives, institutions with busy secretaries and permanent funds having for their object the bridging of the gulf between the two adversaries. Then think of a trivial accident, through which a hapless young man and a melancholy maiden, coming from the opposite territories, meet at the frontier, and owing to the influence of the conjunction of their respective planets fall in love with each other.

There is no harm in supposing that the young man is the son of the President of the Philosophers' Republic, while the maiden is the daughter of that of the Poets'. The immediate consequence is the secret smuggling of forbidden love-lyrics by the desperate youth into the very heart of the commentaries and controversies of the two contradictory schools of Philosophy—the one professed by the yellow-turbaned sages, proclaiming that *one* is truth and *two* is an illusion, and the other, which is the doctrine of the green-turbaned sages, asserting that *two* is truth and *one* is an illusion.

Then came the day of the great meeting, presided over by the Philosopher President, when the pandits of the two factions met to fight their dialectic duels finally to decide the truth. The din of debates grew into a tumultuous hubbub; the supporters of both parties threatened violence and the throne of truth was usurped by shouts. When these shouts were about to be transmuted into blows, there appeared in the arena the pair of lovers who, on the night of the full moon of April, were secretly wedded, though such intermarriage was against the law. When they stood in the open partition between the two parties, a sudden hush fell upon the assembly.

How this unexpected and yet ever-to-be-expected event, mixed with texts liberally quoted from the proscribed love-lyrics, ultimately helped to reconcile the hopeless contradiction in logic is a long story. It is well known to those who have had the privilege to pursue the subsequent verdict of the judges that both doctrines are held to be undoubtedly true: that *one* in *two,* and therefore *two* must find itself in *one*. The acknowledgment of this principle helped to make the intermarriage valid, and since then the two Republics have successfully carried out their disarmament, having discovered for the first time that the gulf between them was imaginary.

Such a simple and happy ending of this drama has caused widespread unemployment and consequent feeling of disgust among the vast number of secretaries and missionaries belonging to the institutions maintained, with the help of permanent funds, for the preaching of Union—those organizations which were so enormously perfect in their machinery that they could well afford to ignore the insignificant fact of their barrenness of result. A large number of these individuals gifted with an ineradicable passion for doing good are joining the opposite organizations, which have their permanent funds, in order to help them to prove and to preach that two is two and never the twain shall meet.

That the above story is a true one will, I am sure, be borne out by the testimony of even the august shade of Plato himself. This episode of the game of hide-and-seek of one in two should be sung by some poet; and therefore I request you to give it, with my blessing, to Satyendranath Datta,[1] that he may set it in those inimitable verse forms of which he is a master, and make it ring with the music of his happy laughter.

S.S. 'Rhyndam'

The sea has been exceedingly rough. The wild east wind, playing its snake-charmer's bagpipe, has made a myriad of hissing waves raise their hoods to the sky. The rude handling by the sea does not affect me much, but the gloom and unrest and the tremendous rise and fall of the waves, like a giant's beating of the breast in despair, depress my mind.

The sad thought very often comes to me, with an imaginary supposition, that I may never reach the Indian shore; and my heart aches with longing to see the arms of my motherland extended into the sea with the palm-leaves rustling in the air. It is the land where I gazed into the eyes of my first great sweetheart—my muse—who made me love the sunlight, touching the top of the coconut row through a pale mist of the serene autumn morning, and the storm-laden rain-clouds rolling up from some abyss behind the horizon, carrying in their dark folds a thrilling expectation of a mad outburst of showers.

But where is this sweetheart of mine, who was almost the only companion of my boyhood, and with whom I spent my idle days of youth exploring the mysteries of dreamland? She, my Queen, has died; and my world has shut against me the door of that inner apartment of beauty which gives the real taste of freedom. I feel like Shah-Jehan when his beloved Mumtaz was dead. Now I have left to me my own progeny—a magnificent

1. A young poet of Bengal, greatly admired by Rabindranath Tagore. He has since, unfortunately, died.

plan of an International University. But it will be like Aurangzeb, who will keep me imprisoned and become my lord and master to the end of my days. Every day my fear and distrust against it are growing in strength. For it has been acquiring power from outside my own resources, and it is material power.

Santiniketan has been the playground of my own spirit. What I created on its soil was made of my own dream-stuff. Its materials are few; its regulations are elastic; its freedom has the inner restraint of beauty. But the International University will be stupendous in weight and rigid in construction; and if we try to move it, it will crack. It will grow up into a bully of a brother, and browbeat its sweet elder sister into a cowering state of subjection. Beware of organization, my friend! They say organization is necessary in order to give a thing its permanence, but it may be the permanence of a tombstone.

This letter of mine will seem to you pessimistic. The reason is I am unwell and utterly home-sick; and the vision of home which haunts my mind night and day is 'Amader Santiniketan.'[1] But the big towers of the International University obstruct its view. I am tired, to the marrow of my bones, trying all these months for a purpose and working in a direction which is against the natural current of my inner being.

S.S. 'Rhyndam'

You, who are given a stable and solid surface on which to work out your problems of daily life, cannot fully realize what a trial it has been for us, these two days, to be tossed upon a wild sea every moment of our existence. I do not feel sea-sick, but the great fact for us is, that we are the children of the land. This is an immovable fact—and yet, when this fact begins to move, it is not only misery, but also an affront to us. The whole sea seems to laugh loud at the conceited creatures who only have a pair of tottering legs and not even a fraction of a fin.

Every moment the dignity of man is outraged by making him helplessly tumble about in an infinite variety of awkwardness.

1. Referring to a song which the boys sing at the Asram, whose retrain is 'Amader Santiniketan,' meaning 'Our Santiniketan.'

He is compelled to take part in a very broad farce; and nothing can be more humiliating for him than to exhibit a comic appearance in his very sufferings. It is like making the audience roar with laughter by having the clown kicked into all manners of helpless absurdities. While sitting, walking, taking meals, we are constantly being hurled about into unexpected postures which are shamefully inconvenient.

When Gods try to become funny in their sublime manner of perpetrating jokes we mortal creatures find ourselves at a terrible disadvantage; for their huge laughter, carried by the millions of roaring waves in flashing foam, keeps its divine dignity unimpaired, while we, on our side, find our self-respect knocked to pieces. I am the only individual in this steamer who is vying with the Gods by fashioning my misery into laughing words and refusing to be the mere passive instrument of an elemental foolery. A laughter which is tyranny has to be answered by another laughter of rebellion. And this letter of mine carries the laughter of defiance. I had no other object in sitting down to write this morning; I had nothing particular to say to you, and to try to think when the ship is rolling in such an insane manner is like trying to carry a full vessel of water while one is drunk; the greater part of the contents is spilt. And yet I must write this letter, merely to show that, though at the present moment I cannot stand erect on my legs, I can write. This is to assert, in the face of the ironical clapping of hands of the mighty Atlantic, that my mind not only can stand up straight in its world of language, but can run, and even dance. This is my triumph.

To-day is Tuesday; on the morning of Thursday we are expected to reach Plymouth. Your letters have helped me more than anything else during these extremely trying months of my exile—they have been like food and water to a soldier who is dragging his wounded and weary limbs, counting every step, across a difficult and doubtful road back to his camp-fire. However, I am coming to my journey's end and intensely hoping to see you when I reach home. What I have suffered God only knows.—I am longing for rest.

CHAPTER VIII

The few days spent in England on the Poet's return from America were on the whole happier and brighter than those of the previous year when the Dyer Debate in the House of Lords had poisoned the air. But he did not stay long enough to meet all those who were eagerly waiting his arrival. He had received invitations from every part of the Continent, and his time was short; for he had determined to get back to India at the earliest possible moment. In the letters from the Continent which follow in this chapter only a very slight portion of what actually happened is told. Many of his letters to me, at his own special request, have not been published; for in his self-diffidence he was almost ashamed, afterwards, to allow any record of the scenes of enthusiasm that greeted him everywhere to appear in print. Very rarely in history has a poet received such a welcome.

What touched him most deeply was the spiritual longing that was behind it all—the earnest hope, especially in the regions of Europe recently devastated by the war, that some light might come from the East to illumine the darkness. The ideal of Visva-bharati, which had become somewhat vague and nebulous before, now took on a more definite concrete shape. At the same time, he could not help but feel sadly that the cries of non-co-operation, which were so strident in India, would lead to his rejection by his own countrymen on his return.

Such a rejection did not take place, because in the heart of the national movement, under the leadership of Mahatma Gandhi, there was a common centre in the universal principle of Ahimsa, or Non-violence, which Mahatma Gandhi professed. No one admired more than the Poet Mahatma Gandhi's spiritual appeal against brute force and his passionate devotion to the service of the poor.

London, *April 10th, 1921*

I am glad to be in England again. One of the first men whom I happened to meet here was H.W. Nevinson; I felt that man's soul was alive in this country, which had produced such a man as that!

A land should be judged by its best products, and I have no hesitation in saying that the best Englishmen are the best specimens of humanity in the world.

With all our grievances against the English nation, I cannot help loving your country, which has given me some of my dearest friends. I am intensely glad of this fact, for it is hateful to hate. Just as a general tries, for his tactics, to attract a whole army of men into a *cul-de-sac,* in order to demolish them, our feeling of anger generalizes the whole people of a country, in order mentally to give them a crushing blow on a tremendously big scale.

Things that are happening in Ireland are ugly. The political lies that are accompanying them are stupendous and in retaliation our anger seeks a victim adequately big; and we readily incriminate the whole people of England, though we know that a great number of Englishmen feel shame and sorrow for these brutalities quite as keenly as any disinterested outsiders.

The fact that such a great proportion of people here—whose interest in keeping Ireland tied to the British Empire is so vital—can feel so keenly the tyranny inflicted on the Irish people, proves the inherent love of justice that thrives in the heart of this country in spite of all aberrations. The saving of a people depends upon the noble personalities holding up the moral tradition high above the floods of iniquity that occasionally deluge the land.

Edmund Burke proves the greatness of Great Britain in spite of Warren Hastings; and we are grateful to Mahatma Gandhi for giving India the opportunity to prove that her faith in the Divine Spirit in man is alive still—in spite of a great deal of materialism in our religions, as they are practised, and a spirit of exclusiveness in our social system.

The fact is that the best people in all countries find their affinity with one another. The fuel displays its differences, but the fire is one. When the fire comes before my vision in this country I recognize it as the same thing which lights our path in

India and illuminates our house. Let us seek that fire and know that wherever the spirit of separation is supreme there reigns darkness. But with the realization of unity comes truth and light. When we ignite our lamps, we at once send response to the eternal lights of heaven. You yourself are a bearer of a lamp from your own land, and let me in response light my own lamp with love for the great humanity revealed in your country.

[*The following letter (a copy of which he enclosed) was in answer to a lady who had complained that the Poet had appeared to give vent to a feeling of anger against the British people in one of his lectures.*]

London, *April 12th, 1921*

Dear Madam,

I received your letter late that morning, and was sorry to learn that you had come to this hotel while I was engaged.

It is not unlikely that some unsuspected remnant of race-consciousness in your mind made you imagine that I gave vent to my feeling of anger against the British people in my lecture. I deeply feel for all the races who are being insulted and injured by the ruthless exploitation of the powerful nations belonging to the West or the East. I feel as much for the Negroes, brutally lynched in America, often for economic reasons, and for the Koreans, who are the latest victims of Japanese imperialism, as for any wrongs done to the helpless multitude of my own country. I feel certain that Christ, were He living at the present day, would have been angry with the nations who attempt to thrive upon the life-blood of their victim races, just as He was angry with those who defiled God's temple with their unholy presence and profession. Surely He would have taken upon Himself the chastisement of these miscreants, especially when those who professed to be His disciples, whose ostensible vocation was to preach peace and brotherhood of man, either kept a discreet silence whenever man's history waited for a voice of judgement or showed signs of virulence against the weak and down-trodden greatly surpassing that of men whose profession it was blindly to kill human beings.

On the other hand, though I sometimes congratulate myself on my own freedom from race-consciousness, very likely a sufficient amount of it is lingering in my subconscious mind, making itself evident to outsiders in my writings through special emphasis of indignation at any unjust suffering or humiliation that my own country is made to undergo. I hope that I can claim forgiveness for this weakness, considering that I never try to condone any wrongs done by my own countrymen against others belonging to different countries from ours.

Autour Du Monde, Paris, *April 18th, 1921*

I have come back to the domain of dust from my short aeroplane career in mid-air, when my namesake from the high heaven, the Sun[1] shed upon me his smile of amused tenderness and some vagabond clouds of the April sky seemed to wonder in their minds if I were about to join their ranks.

Whenever I find time and sit alone before the window, I gravely nod my head and say to myself in a sad voice: "Those who have been born foolish can gladden the heart of God only when they have the freedom of solitariness and can spread their idle wings in the air and flit and hum for nothing at all. You, poet, are one such creature—you have to be alone to fulfil your nature. What is all this that you are planning? Must you guide the multitude and work with them for the building of an Institution?"

All through my life I have ever worked alone; for my life and my work have been one. I am like the tree, which builds up its timber by its own living process; and therefore it needs leisure and space, sunlight and air and not bricks and mortar, masons and the civil engineer.

All my poems have their roots in my dreams. But an International University needs a foundation, and not roots. It needs to be solidly built upon international boards and committees and funds contributed by men of prudence and foresight. Foresight is a gift which I wholly lack. I may have some insight, but no foresight at all. Foresight has the power of calculation:

1. Referring to his name Rabi, which means the Sun.

insight has the power of vision. He may have faith in insight to whom it belongs; and therefore he is not afraid of making mistakes or even of apparent failures. But foresight is impatient of all deficiencies. It constantly dwells on the possibilities of mistakes, only because it has not the vision of the whole. Therefore its plans are mostly solid and inflexible.

In the establishment of the International University the foresight of the experienced will never forsake me; it will go straight to the helm and take charge; and only then the prudent who give money and the wise who give advice will be satisfied. But where will remain the place for the foolish and the irresponsible?

The whole thing will have to be established on a permanent basis; but this so-called permanence is only bought at the cost of life and freedom. The cage is permanent, not the nest. And yet all that is truly permanent has to pass through an endless series of impermanences. The spring flowers are permanent, because they know how to die. The temple made of stone cannot make truce with death by accepting it. Proud of its bricks and mortar, it constantly opposes death, till it is defeated in the end.

Our Santiniketan depends for its permanence upon life. But an International University tries to build its permanence with the help of rules and regulations. But—

Never mind! Let me forget it for a moment. Possibly I am exaggerating. The reason is, the day is full of gloom. It has been snowing and raining; the road is muddy; and I am home-sick.

I am requested by some association to read a paper at one of their meetings. They asked me for a summary, which they will circulate among the members. I enclose a copy of it which I have given to them for circulation.

THE SUMMARY OF A LECTURE

From the beginning of their history the Western races have had to deal with Nature as their antagonist. This fact has emphasized in their minds the dualistic aspect of truth, the eternal conflict between good and evil. Thus it has kept up the spirit of fight in the heart of their civilization. They seek victory and cultivate power.

The environment in which the Aryan immigrants found themselves in India was that of the forest. The forest, unlike the desert or sea, is living; it gives shelter and nourishment to life. In such surroundings, the ancient forest-dwellers of India realized the spirit of harmony with the universe and emphasized in their minds the monistic aspect of Truth. They sought the realization of their souls through union with all.

The spirit of fight and the spirit of harmony both have their importance in the scheme of things. For making a musical instrument, the obduracy of materials has to be forced to yield to the purpose of the instrument-maker. But music itself is a revelation of beauty, it is not an outcome of fight; it springs from an inner realization of harmony. The musical instrument and the music both have their own importance for humanity.

The civilization that fights and conquers for Man, and the civilization that realizes for him the fundamental unity in the depth of existence, are complementary to each other. When they join hands, human nature finds its balance; and its pursuits, through rugged paths, attain their ultimate meaning in an ideal of perfection.

Autour Du Monde, Paris, *April 21st, 1921*

When I sent my appeal for an International Institution to the Western people, I made use of the word "University" for the sake of convenience. But that word has not only an inner meaning, but also an outer association in the minds of those who use it; and that fact tortures my idea into its own rigid shape. It is unfortunate.

I should not allow my idea to be pinned to a word for a foreign museum, like a dead butterfly. It must be known, not by a definition, but by its own life-growth.

In the past I saved our Santiniketan School from being trampled into smoothness by the steam-roller of the Education

Department. Our school is poor in resources and equipment, but it has the wealth of truth in it which no money can ever buy; and I am proud of the fact that it is not a machine-made article perfectly modelled in a workshop—it is our very own.

If we must have a University, it should spring from our own life and be maintained by our own life. Someone may say that such freedom is dangerous and that a machine will help to lessen our personal responsibility and make things easy for us. Yes! Life has its risks, and freedom has its responsibility; and yet they are preferable on account of their own immense value, and not for any other ulterior results.

So long, I have been able to retain my perfect independence and self-respect, because I had faith in my own resources and proudly worked within their sovereign limits. My bird must still retain its freedom of wings and not be tamed into a sumptuous nonentity by any controlling agency outside its own living organism. I know that the idea of an International University is complex, but I must make it simple in my own way. I shall be content if it attracts round it men who have neither name nor fame nor worldly means, but who have the mind and faith; who are to create a great future with their dreams.

Very likely I shall never be able to work with a Board of Trustees, influential and highly respectable—for I am a vagabond at heart. But the powerful people of the world, the lords of the earth, make it difficult for me to carry out my work. I know it, and I have had experience of it in connection with Santiniketan. But I am not afraid of failure. I am only afraid of being tempted away from truth, in pursuit of success. The temptation assaults me occasionally; but it comes from the outside atmosphere. My own abiding faith is in life and light and freedom. And my prayer is:

"Lead me from the unreal to Truth."

This letter of mine is to let you know that I free myself from the bondage of help and go back to join with you the great "Brotherhood of the Tramps," who seem helpless, but are recruited by God for His own army.

Strasbourg, *April 29th, 1921*

I am writing this from Strasbourg, where I am going to read my lecture at the University this evening.

I miss you very much at this moment; for I feel certain it would overwhelm you with happiness could you be with me now, realizing the great outburst of love for me in the continental countries of Europe which I have visited. I have never asked for it, or striven for it, and I never can believe that I have deserved it. However, if it be more than is due to me, I am in no way responsible for this mistake. For I could have remained perfectly happy in my obscurity to the end of my days, on the banks of the Ganges, with the wild-ducks as my only neighbours on the desolate sand islands.

"I have only sown my dreams in the air," for the greater part of my life, and I never turned back to see if they bore any harvest. But the harvest now surprises me, almost obstructs my path, and I cannot make up my mind to claim it for my own. All the same, it is a great good fortune to be accepted by one's fellow-beings from across the distance of geography, history and language; and through this fact we realize how truly One is the mind of Man, and what aberrations are the conflicts of hatred and the competitions of self-interest.

We are going to Switzerland to-morrow, and our next destination will be Germany. I am to spend my birthday this year in Zürich. I have had my second birth in the West, and there is rejoicing at the event. But by nature all men are *dwija* or twice-born—first they are born to their home, and then, for their fulfilment, they have to be born to the larger world. Do you not feel yourself that you have had your second birth among us? And with this second birth you have found your true place in the heart of humanity.

It is a beautiful town, this Strasbourg, and to-day the morning light is beautiful. The sunshine has mingled with my blood and tinged my thoughts with its gold, and I feel ready to sing:

"Brothers, let us squander this morning with futile songs."

This is a delightful room where I am sitting now, with its windows looking over the fringe of the Black Forest. Our hostess is a charming lady, with a fascinating little baby, whose plump fingers love to explore the mystery of my eye-glasses.

We have a number of Indian students in this place, among whom is Lala Harkishen Lal's son, who asks me to send you his respectful regards. He is a fine young man, frank and cheerful, loved by his teachers.

We have missed this week's letters, which are now evidently lost beyond recovery. It is difficult for me to forgive the Mediterranean for doing me this disservice! The present week's mail is due, and if Thos. Cook & Son are prompt about it we shall find our letters to-day!

Geneva, *May 6th, 1921*

To-day is my birthday. But I do not feel it; for in reality it is a day which is not for me, but for those who love me. And away from you, this day is merely a date in the calendar. I wish I had a little time to myself to-day, but this has not been possible. The day has been crowded with visitors and the talk has been incessant, some part of which has unfortunately lapsed into politics, giving rise to a temperature in my mental atmosphere of which I always repent.

Political controversies occasionally overtake me like a sudden fit of ague, without giving sufficient notice; and then they leave me as suddenly, leaving behind a feeling of *malaise*. Politics are so wholly against my nature; and yet, belonging to an unfortunate country, born to an abnormal situation, we find it so difficult to avoid their outbursts. Now when I am alone I am wishing that I could still my mind in the depth of that infinite peace where all the wrongs of the world are slowly-tuned up, out of their discordance, into the eternal rhythm of the flowers and stars.

But men are suffering all over the world, and my heart is sick. I wish I had the power to pierce this suffering with music and bring the message of abiding joy from the deeper regions of the world soul, and repeat to the people who are angry and to the people whose heads are bowed down in shame: "From joy all things are born, by joy they are maintained, and into joy they proceed and find their end."

Why should I be the one to air our grievances and give shrieking expression to the feeling of resentment? I pray for the great tranquillity of truth, from which have welled forth the immortal words that are to heal the wounds of the world and soothe the throbbing heat of hatred into forbearance.

The East and the West have met—this great fact of history has so far produced only our pitiful politics, because it has not yet been turned into truth. Such a truthless fact is a burden for both parties. For the burden of gain is no less than the burden of loss—it is the burden of the enormity of corpulence. The fact of the meeting of the East and the West still remains concentrated on the surface—it is external. The result is, all our attention is diverted to this surface where we are hurt, or where we can only think of material profits.

But deep in the heart of this meeting is surely maturing the seed of a great future of union. When we realize it, our mind regains its detachment from the painful tension of the immediate present and attains its faith in the eternal—it is relieved from the hysterical convulsions of exasperated despair. We have learnt from our ancestors that the Advaitam is the eternal significance of all passing events—which is the principle of unity in the heart of dualism. The dualism of East and West contains that unity, and therefore it is sure to be fulfilled in union.

You have expressed that great truth in your life. In your love for India you carry that message of Eternity. In you, the apparent conflict of the East and the West has unveiled the great beauty of its inner reconciliation. We, who are clamouring for vengeance, only conscious of the separateness, and therefore expecting absolute separation, have not read the great purpose of our history right.

For passion is darkness. It exaggerates isolated facts and makes our minds stumble against them at every step. Love is the light that reveals to us the perfection of unity and saves us from the constant oppression of the detached—of the immediate.

And therefore I embrace you, take my inspiration from your love and send you my birthday *namaskar*.[1]

Near Zürich, *May 10th, 1921*

I have just received a birthday greeting from Germany through a committee consisting of men like Eucken, Harnack, Hauptmann and others, and with it a most generous gift, consisting of at least four hundred copies of valuable German books. It has deeply touched my heart, and I feel certain that it will find response in the hearts of my countrymen.

To-morrow I have my invitation at Zürich, and on the 13th of this month I leave Switzerland for Germany. Haven't I said to you, in some letter of mine, that my life has followed the course of my celestial namesake, the Sun, and that the last part of my hours is claimed by the West? How genuine has been the claim I never realized before I had visited the continent of Europe. I feel deeply thankful for this privilege, not only because it is sweet to realize appreciation from one's fellow-beings, but because it has helped me to feel how near we are to the people who in all appearances are so different from ourselves.

Such an opportunity has become rare to us in India because we have been segregated from the rest of the world. This has acted upon the minds of our people in two contrary ways. It has generated that provincialism of vision in us which either leads to an immoderate boastfulness, urging us to assert that India is unique in every way—absolutely different from other countries—or to a self-depreciation which has the sombre attitude of suicide. If we can come into real touch with the West through the disinterested medium of intellectual co-operation, we shall gain a true perspective of the human world, realize our own position in it, and have faith in the possibility of widening and deepening our connection with it. We ought to know that a perfect isolation of life and culture is not a thing of which any race can be proud. The dark stars are isolated, but stars that are luminous belong to the eternal chorus of lights.

1. Greeting.

Greece was not shut up in the solitude of her culture, nor was India, when she was in the full radiance of her glory. We have a Sanskrit expression, "That which is not given is lost." India, in order to find herself, must give herself. But this power of giving can only be perfected when it is accompanied by the power of receiving. That which cannot give, but can only reject, is dead. The cry, which has been raised to-day, of rejecting Western culture only means the paralysing of our own power to give anything to the West. For, in the human world, as I have said, giving is exchanging. It is not one-sided. Our education will attain its perfection, not by refusing to accept all lessons from the West, but by realizing its own inheritance. This will give us the means to pay for such lessons. Our true wealth, intellectual as well as material, lies not in the acquisition itself, but in our own independent means of acquisition.

So long as our intellectual attainments were solely dependent on an alien giver, we have been accepting and not acquiring. Therefore these attainments have mostly been barren of production, as I have discussed in my pamphlet on Education. But it would be wrong to blame the Western culture itself for such futility. The blame lies in our not using our own receptacle for this culture. Intellectual parasitism causes degeneracy in the intellectual organs of the mind. It is not the food, but the parasitism, that has to be avoided.

At the same time, I strongly protest against Mahatma Gandhi's depreciation of such great personalities of modern India as Ram Mohun Roy in his zeal for declaiming against our modern education.[1] Every Indian ought to be proud of the fact that, in spite of immense disadvantages, India still has been able to produce greatness of personality in her children, such as we find in Ram Mohun Roy. Mahatmaji has quoted the instances of Nanak, Kabir and other saints of mediaeval India. They were great because in their life and teaching they made organic union of the Hindu and Muhammadan cultures—and such realization

1. Mahatma Gandhi had been reported as saying that Ram Mohun Roy was a pigmy as compared with Kabir and Nanak, who had never had any touch with the West.

of the spiritual unity through all differences of appearance is truly Indian.

In the modern age, Ram Mohun Roy had that comprehensiveness of mind to be able to realize the fundamental unity of spirit in the Hindu, Muhammadan and Christian cultures. Therefore he represented India in the fullness of truth; and this truth is based, not upon rejection, but on perfect comprehension. Ram Mohun Roy could be perfectly natural in his acceptance of the West, only because his education had been perfectly Eastern—he had the full inheritance of the Indian wisdom. He was never a schoolboy of the West, and therefore he had the dignity to be a friend of the West. If he is not understood by modern India, this only shows that the pure light of her own truth has been obscured for the moment by the storm-clouds of passion.

Hamburg, *May 17th, 1921*

It has been a perpetual sunshine of kindness for me all through my travels in this country. While it delights me, it makes me feel embarrassed. What have I to give to these people? What have they received from me? But the fact is, they are waiting for the daybreak after the orgies of the night, and they have their expectation of light from the East.

Do we feel in the soul of India that stir of the morning which is for all the world? Is the one string of her *ektara*[1] being tuned, which is to give the key-note to the music of a great future of Man—the note which will send a thrill of response from shore to shore? Love of God in the hearts of the mediaeval saints of India—like Kabir and Nanak—came down in showers of human love, drowning the border-lines of separation between Hindus and Mussulmans.

They were giants, not dwarfs, because they had spiritual vision, whose full range was in the Eternal—crossing all the barriers of the moment. The human world in our day is much larger than in theirs; conflicts of national self-interest and race-traditions are stronger and more complex; the political

1. A one-stringed instrument.

dust-storms are blinding; the whirlwinds of race antipathy are fiercely persistent; the sufferings caused by them are world-wide and deep. The present age is waiting for a divine word, great and simple, which creates and heals. What has moved me profoundly is the fact that suffering Man in this continent has turned his face to the East.

It is not the man of politics, or the man of letters, but the simple man whose faith is living. Let us believe in his instinct; let his expectation guide us to our wealth. In spite of the immense distractions of our latter-day degeneracy, India still cherishes in her heart the immortal mantram of Peace, of Goodness, of Unity—

"Santam, Sivam, Advaitam."

The message of the "One in the All," which had been proclaimed in the shade of India's forest solitude, is waiting to bring reconciliation to the men who are fighting in the dark and have lost the recognition of their brotherhood.

Of all men in modern India, Ram Mohun Roy was the first man and the greatest who realized this truth. He held up high the pure light of the Upanishads that shows the path whereby the conquerors of the self "enter into the heart of the all"—the light which is not for rejection, but for comprehension.

The Mussulmans came to India with a culture which was aggressively antagonistic to her own. But in her saints the spirit of the Upanishads worked in order to attain the fundamental harmony between things that were apparently irreconcilable. In the time of Ram Mohun Roy the West had come to the East with a shock that caused panic in the heart of India. The natural cry was for exclusion. But this was the cry of fear, the cry of weakness, the cry of the dwarf. Through the great mind of Ram Mohun Roy the true spirit of India asserted itself and accepted the West, not by the rejection of the soul of India, but by the comprehension of the soul of the West.

The mantram which gives our spiritual vision its right of entrance into the soul of all things is the mantram of India, the mantram of Peace, of Goodness, of Unity—Santam, Sivam, Advaitam. The distracted mind of the West is knocking at the gate of India for this. And is it to be met there with a hoarse shout of exclusion?

Hamburg, *May 20th, 1921*

I trust that my long voyage has now come nearly to its end. Every moment I hear the call of the beach and see the vision of the evening lamp watching behind the window for the return of the weary traveller. But there is one thought that never ceases to buzz in my mind. It is that the weather-beaten boat, after its voyage across the sea, may be utilized as the ferry for the miscellaneous errands of daily traffic.

Today, life is nowhere normal in the world. The atmosphere is swarming with problems. Singers are not allowed to sing; they have to shout messages. But, my dear friend, is my life to be one perpetual polar summer, an endless monotony of a day of lidless light, of ceaseless duties, with never a night of stars to open before my vision the gateway of the Infinite? Is the fact of death a mere fact of stoppage? Does it not speak to us of our right of entrance into a region beyond the bounds of patriotism? When am I going to make my final adjustment of life and be ready for the invitation to the world of Spirit?

We are taught by our Western schoolmaster that there is nothing of importance that is not shown in the national school map; that only *my* country is my earth and heaven; that only in *my* country are united my life and my immortality. And when we try to reject the West, in our pride of country, we, like a ragged scamp, pick the pocket of the same West and pilfer that same spirit of rejection.

But our fathers had a clearer consciousness of a truth of freedom, which was never clipped of its wings and shut up in a geographical cage. I feel that my time has come for the realization of that truth; and I pray that I may never die a patriot, or a politician, but as a free spirit; not as a journalist, but as a poet.

Stockholm, *May 27th, 1921*

I have been following the track of spring from Switzerland to Denmark, and from Denmark to Sweden, watching everywhere flowers breaking out in a frenzy of colours. And it seems to me like the earth's shouting of victory, and flinging up its coloured cap to the sky. My path in the West also has had the same exuberant outburst of welcome.

At first I felt the impulse to describe it to you in detail; for I was sure it would give you great delight. But now I shrink from doing it. For somehow it does not cause exultation in my own mind, but makes me sad. It would be absurd for me to claim what has been offered to me as fully mine. The fact is, there is a rising tide of heart in the West rushing towards the shores of the East, following some mysterious law of attraction. The unbounded pride of the European peoples has suddenly found a check, and their mind appears to be receding from the channel it had cut for itself.

The giant, being weary, is seeking peace; and as the fountain of peace has ever flowed from the East, the face of troubled Europe is instinctively turned to-day towards the East. Europe is like a child who has been hurt in the midst of her game. She is shunning the crowd and looking out for her mother. And has not the East been the mother of spiritual humanity, giving it life from its own life?

How pitiful it is that we, in India, are unaware of this claim for succour from Europe which has come to our door; that we fail to realize the great honour of the call to serve humanity in her hour of need!

Bewildered at heart by the great demonstrations made in my honour in these countries, I have often tried to find out the real cause. I have been told that it was because I loved humanity. I hope that this is true; and all through my writings, my love of man has found its utterance and touched human hearts across all barriers. If it *be* true, then let that truest note in my writings guide my own life henceforth!

The other day, when I was resting alone in my room in the hotel at Hamburg, timidly there entered two shy and sweet German girls, with a bunch of roses for their offering to me. One of them, who spoke broken English, said to me: "I love

India." I asked her: "Why do you love India?" She answered: "Because you love God."

The praise was too great for me to accept with any degree of complaisance. But I hope its meaning was in the expectation from me which it carried, and therefore was a blessing. Or possibly she meant that my country loved God, and therefore she loved India. That also was an expectation whose meaning we should try to appreciate and understand.

The nations love their own countries; and that national love has only given rise to hatred and suspicion of one another. The world is waiting for a country that loves God and not herself. Only that country will have the claim to be loved by men of all countries.

When we hear "Bande Mataram" from the housetops, we shout to our neighbours: "You are not our brothers." But that is not true. Therefore, because it is untrue, it pollutes the air, and darkens the sky. Whatever may be its use for the present, it is like the house being set on fire simply for roasting the pig! Love of self, whether national or individual, can have no other destination except suicide. Love of God is our only fulfilment; it has in it the ultimate solution of all problems and difficulties.

On the day after to-morrow we shall be leaving Sweden for Berlin. The Czecho-Slovakian Government has promised us an air trip from Berlin to Prague, and from Prague to Munich. From Munich we are expected to visit Darmstadt, where a gathering of some notable persons of Germany will be held to meet us. It will be over on or about the 15th of June, and then through France and Spain we shall be able to take our ship at the beginning of July—if not earlier.

Berlin, *May 28th, 1921*

I am leaving Germany to-night for Vienna. From there I go to Czechoslovakia, and then to Paris—and then, to the Mediterranean Sea! Our steamer sails on the 2nd of July, and so this letter is likely to be my last.

You can have no idea what an outbreak of love has followed me and enveloped me everywhere I have been in

Scandinavia and Germany. All the same, my longing is to go back to my own people. I have lived my life there, done my work there, given my love there, and I must not mind if the harvest of my life has not had its full payment there. The ripening of the harvest itself brings its ample reward for me. And therefore the call comes to me from the field where the sunlight is waiting for me; where the seasons, each in turn, are making their inquiries about my home-coming. They know me, who all my life have sowed there the seeds of my dreams. But the shadows of evening are deepening on my path, and I am tired. I do not want praise or blame from my countrymen. I want to take my rest under the stars.

Berlin, *June 4th, 1921*

To-day my visit to Berlin has come to an end. To-night we are starting for Munich. It has been a wonderful experience in this country for me! Such fame as I have got I cannot take at all seriously. It is too readily given, and too immediately. It has not had the perspective of time. And this is why I feel frightened and tired at it—and even sad.

I am like a house-lamp, whose place is in a corner, and whose association is that of intimacy of love. But when my life is made to take part in a firework display, I apologize to the stars and feel humble.

I saw *Post Office* acted in a Berlin theatre. The girl who took the part of Amal was delightful in her acting, and altogether the whole thing was a success. But it was a different interpretation from that of ours in our own acting in Vichitra. I had been trying to define the difference in my mind, when Dr. Otto of Marburg University, who was among the audience, hit upon it. He said that the German interpretation was suggestive of a fairy-story, full of elusive beauty, whereas the inner significance of this play is spiritual.

I remember, at the time when I wrote it, my own feeling which inspired me to write it. Amal represents the man whose soul has received the call of the open road—he seeks freedom from the comfortable enclosure of habits sanctioned by the prudent and from walls of rigid opinion built for him by the respectable. But Madhab, the worldly-wise, considers his restlessness to be the sign of a fatal malady; and his adviser, the physician, the custodian of conventional platitudes—with his quotations from prescribed textbooks full of maxims—gravely nods his head and says that freedom is unsafe and every care should be taken to keep the sick man within walls. And so the precaution is taken.

But there is the post office in front of his window, and Amal waits for the king's letter to come to him direct from the king, bringing to him the message of emancipation. At last the closed gate is opened by the king's own physician, and that which is "death" to the world of hoarded wealth and certified creeds brings him awakening in the world of spiritual freedom.

The only thing that accompanies him in his awakenment is the flower of love given to him by Sudha.

I know the value of this love, and therefore my petition to the Queen was:

"Let me be the gardener of thy flower garden"—the gardener, whose only reward is daily to offer his garlands to the Queen.

Do you think that *Post Office* has some meaning at this time for my country in this respect, that her freedom must come direct from the King's Messenger, and not from the British Parliament; and that when her soul awakes nothing will be able to keep her within walls? Has she received her letter yet from the King?

Ask Dinu what is the original of the following translation:

My *Vina* breaks out in strange disquiet measure,
My heart to-day is tremulous with the heart-throbs of the world.
Who is the restless youth that comes, his mantle fluttering in the breeze?
The woodland resounds with the murmur of joy at the dance lyric of the light,
The anklet-bells of the dancer quiver in the sky with an unheard tinkle,

To whose cadence the forest leaves clap their hands.
The hope for the touch of a nearing footstep spreads a whisper in the grass.
And the wind breaks its fetters, distraught with the perfume of the Unknown.

To-day is the 5th of June. Our steamer sails on the 3rd of July.

Darmstadt, *June 10th, 1921*

In Darmstadt they have a gathering of people from all parts of Germany to meet me. We have our meeting in the Grand Duke of Hesse's garden, where my audience will bring before me their questions. I give them monologues in answer, and Count Keyserling translates them into German for those who cannot follow my English.

Yesterday I reached this place, and in the afternoon we had our first meeting.

The first question put to me by a Canadian German was: "What is the future of this scientific civilization?"

After I had answered him, he again asked me: "How is the problem of over-population to be solved?"

After my answer, I was asked to give them some idea about the true character of Buddhism.

These three subjects took up fully three hours. It is delightful to feel the earnestness of these people. They have the habit of mind to think out the deeper problems of life; they deal seriously with ideas. In India, in our modern schools, we merely receive our ideas from textbooks, for the purpose of passing examinations. Besides that, our modern schoolmasters are Englishmen; and they, of all the Western nations, are the least susceptible to ideas. They are good, honest and reliable, but they have a vigorous excess of animal spirits which seek for exercise in racing, fox-hunting, boxing-matches, etc., and they offer stubborn resistance to all contagion of ideas.

Therefore our English educationalists do not inspire our minds. We do not realize that ideas are necessary in order to enable us to live a true life. We do not possess a genuine enthusiasm, which is the gift of the soul. Our principal object and occupation are going to be the dissipations of politics, whose goal is success, whose path is the zigzag of compromise—that politics which in every country has lowered the standard of morality, has given rise to a perpetual contest of lies and deception, cruelties and hypocrisies, and has increased inordinately national habits of vulgar vainglory.

S.S. "Morea," *July 5th, 1921*

Land has its claims upon one, in return for its hospitality, but sea has none; it repudiates humanity with a magnificent indifference; its water is solely occupied in an eternal dialogue with the sky—the two inseparable companions who retain their irresponsible infancy as on the first day of their creation.

Land imposes on us our mission of usefulness, and we have to be occupied with lectures and textbooks; and our guardians have the right to rebuke us when we waste good paper in making literary paper-boats. But the sea has no inspiration of moral obligation for us; it offers no foundation for a settled life; its waves raise their signals and have only one word of command: "Pass on."

I have observed, on board a steamer, how men and women easily give way to their instinct of flirtation, because water has the power of washing away our sense of responsibility, and those who on land resemble the oak in their firmness behave like floating seaweed when on the sea. The sea makes us forget that men are creatures who have their innumerable roots and are answerable to their soil.

For the same reason, when I used to have my dwelling on the bosom of the great river Padma, I was nothing more than a lyrical poet. But since I have taken my shelter at Santiniketan I have developed all the symptoms of growing into a schoolmaster, and there is grave danger of my ending my career as a veritable prophet! Already everybody has begun asking me for "Messages"; and the day may come when I shall be afraid to disappoint them. For when prophets do appear unexpectedly to fulfil their mission, they are stoned to death; and when those whom men warmly expect to be prophets fail to act their part to the end, they are laughed to extinction. The former have their compensation; for they fulfil their purpose, even through their martyrdom. But for the latter, their tragic end is utter wastefulness; it satisfies neither man nor Gods.

Who is there to save a poet from disaster? Can anybody give me back my good-for-nothingness? Can anyone restore to me the provision with which I began life's journey to the realm of inutility? One day I shall have to fight my way out of my own reputation; for the call of my Padma river still comes to me through this huge and growing barrier. It says to me: "Poet, where are you?" And all my heart and soul try to seek out that poet. It has become difficult to find him. For the great multitude of men have heaped honours on him, and he cannot be extricated from under them. I must stop here—for the ship's engine is throbbing in a measure which is not that of my pen.

S.S. "Morea," *July 6th, 1921*

I suppose you have read in the newspapers that in Europe I met with an enthusiastic welcome. No doubt I was thankful to the people for their kind feelings towards me; but somehow, deep in my heart I was bewildered and almost pained.

Any expression of feeling by a great multitude of men must have in it a large measure of unreality. It cannot help exaggerating itself simply because of the cumulative effect of emotion upon the crowd-mind. It is like a sound in a hall, which is echoed back from innumerable corners. An immense amount of it is only contagion—it is irrational, and every member of the crowd has the freedom to draw upon his own imagination for building up his opinion. Their idea of me cannot be the real me. I am sorry for it and for myself. It makes me feel a longing to take shelter in my former obscurity. It is hateful to have to live in a world made up of other people's illusions. I have seen people press round me to touch the hem of my robe, to kiss it in reverence—it saddens my heart. How am I to convince these people that I am of them and not above them, and that there are many among them who are worthy of reverence from me?

And yet I know for certain that there is not a single individual in their midst who is a poet as I am. But reverence of this kind is not for a poet. The poet is for conducting ceremonial in the festival of life; and for his reward he is to have his open invitation to all feasts wherever he is appreciated. If he is successful, he is appointed to the perpetual comradeship of Man—not as a guide, but as a companion. But if, by some mad freak of fate, I am set upon an altar, I shall be deprived of my own true seat—which by right is mine and not another's.

It is far better for a poet to miss his reward in this life rather than to have a false reward, or to have his reward in an excessive measure. The man who constantly receives honour from admiring crowds has the grave danger of developing a habit of mental parasitism upon such honour. He consciously, or unconsciously, grows to have a kind of craving for it, and feels injured when his allowance is curtailed or withdrawn.

I become frightened of such a possibility in me, for it is vulgar. Unfortunately, when a person has some mission of doing some kind of public good, his popularity becomes the best asset for him. His own people most readily follow him, when other people have the same readiness—and this makes it a matter of temptation for such an individual. A large number of his followers will consider themselves as deceived by him when the fickle flow of popularity changes its course.

S.S. "Morea," *July 7th, 1921*

In this modern age of the philosophy of relativity I suppose I cannot claim for myself the quality of absolute poetdom. It is evident that the poet in me changes its features and spontaneously assumes the character of the preacher with the change of its position. I have evolved in me a certain philosophy of life which has in it a strong emotional element, and therefore it can sing as well as speak. It is like a cloud that can break out in a shower of rain, or merely tinge itself in colours and offer decorations to the festival of the sky. For this reason I give rise to expectations which are almost of a contrary character—I am asked to give gladness, and I am asked to give help.

To give gladness requires inspiration; to give help requires organization—the one depends principally upon myself, and the other upon means and materials that are outside me. Here come in difficulties which make me pause. Poesy creates its own solitude for the poet. The consequent detachment of mind which is necessary for creative life is lost or broken when the poet has to choose a constructive programme. The work of construction requires continuous employment of attention and energy—it cannot afford to grant leave to the poet to retire and come to himself.

This creates conflict within my nature and very often makes me think that the guidance of the Good is not always for the Best. And yet, its call being natural to me, I cannot ignore it altogether. But what constantly hurts me is the fact that, in a work of organization, I have to deal with and make use of men who have more faith in the material part than in the creative ideal.

My work is not for the success of the work itself, but for the realization of the ideal. But those in whose minds the reality of the ideal is not clear, and love for the ideal is not strong, try to find their compensation in the success of the work; and they are therefore ready for all kinds of compromise.

I know that the idea which I have in mind requires the elimination of all passions that have their place in the narrow range of life; but most people believe that these passions are the steam-power which gives velocity to our motives. They quote precedents; they say that pure idea has never achieved any result. But when you say that the result is not greater than the idea itself, then they laugh at you!

During the last fourteen months of my campaign for an International University, I have said to myself over and over again: "Never let your pride be hurt at any prospect of failure; for failure can never affect truth." My weakness creeps in where I love. When those whom I love feel exultant at the expectation of success, it urges me to procure this toy for them.

S.S. "Morea," *July 8th, 1921*

I must not exaggerate. Let me admit that the realization of ideals has its external part, which depends for its development upon materials. And materials—both human and non-human—offer resistance to success, and therefore must not be lightly spoken of.

But what I had in my mind was this, that the mastery of grammar and the creation of literature may not coincide. Emphasis upon grammar may hinder perfectness of expression. Success in materials may go contrary to the fulfilment of ideals. For material success has its temptation. Often our idealism is exploited for the sake of obtaining success—we have seen that in the late war. In consequence, the battle has been won, but the ideal has not been reached.

Ever since the scheme of the International University has been made public, the conflict in my mind has been unceasing—the conflict between the vision of the ideal and the vision of success. The plan itself is big and has a scope for the ambition of men who love to show their power and gain it. It is not merely ambition which lures our minds; it is the wrong value which we set upon certain results. To be certain of the inner truth requires imagination and faith, and therefore it is always in danger of being missed, even when it is near at hand; whereas external success is obvious.

You remember how Chitra, in my play of that name, became jealous of the physical beauty lent to her by the Gods—because it was a mere success, not truth itself. Truth can afford to be ignored, but not to be allied to unreality for the sake of success.

Unfortunately facts are cited to show that all over the world the prudent and the wise are in the habit of making a pact with Mephistopheles to build roads to reach their God. Only they do not know that God has *not* been reached—and that success and God are not the same thing. When I think of all this, I feel a longing for the simplicity of poverty, which, like the covering of certain fruits, conceals and protects the richness and freshness of the deeper ideal. All the same, as I have said, the pursuit of success must not be abandoned for mere want of energy and spirit. Let it represent our sacrifice for the truth, and not for itself.

S.S. "Morea," *July 9th, 1921*

All true ideals claim our best, and it cannot be said with regard to them that we can be content with the half, when the whole is threatened. Ideals are not like money. They are a living reality. Their wholeness is indivisible. A beggar woman may be satisfied with an eight-anna bit when sixteen annas are denied her; but a half-portion of her child she will never consent to accept!

I know that there is a call for me to work towards the true union of East and West. I have unconsciously been getting ready for this mission. When I wrote my *Sadhana* lectures, I was not aware that I had been fulfilling my destiny. All through my tour I was told that my *Sadhana* had been of real help to my Western readers. The accident which made me translate *Gitanjali* and the sudden and unaccountable longing which took me over to Europe at the beginning of my fiftieth year—all combined to push me forward to a path whose destination I did not clearly know when I first took it. This, my last tour in Europe, has made it definitely known to me.

But, as I have said before, the claims of all great ideals have to be fully paid. Not merely the negative moral injunction of non-violence will suffice. It is a truism to say that the creative force needed for true union in human society is love. Justice is only an accompaniment to it, like the beating of a tom-tom to the song. We in the East have long been suffering humiliation at the hands of the West. It is enormously difficult for us either to cultivate, or express, any love for Western races—especially as it may have the appearance of snobbishness or prudence. The talk and behaviour of the Moderate Party in India fail to inspire us because of this—because their moderation springs from the colourless principle of expediency. The bond of expediency between the powerful and the weak must have some element in it which is degrading. It brings to us gifts for which we can claim no credit whatever, except, perhaps, persistency of expectation and unbaffled employment of importunity.

Self-sacrifice on the part of the gainer, and not solely on the part of the giver, imparts true value to the gift. When our claims are feeble, and our method of realizing them is altogether unheroic, then the very boons granted to us make us poorer. That is why the Moderates in India look so pitifully obscure by the side of the Extremists.

However, my point is that, as an idealist, it is immensely difficult for me to nourish any feeling of love for those people who themselves are neither eager to offer it to us nor care to claim it from us. But never let me look at that condition as an absolute one. There are screens between us which have to be removed—possibly they are due to the too great inequality of circumstances and opportunities between the two parties. Let us, by every means in our power, struggle against our antipathies—all the while taking care to keep wide open channels of communication through which individuals, from both sides, may have facilities to meet in the spirit of good-fellowship. I cannot tell you how thankful I feel to you, who have made it easier for me to love your people. For your own relationship with India has not been based upon a sense of duty, but upon genuine love. It makes me feel sad when I see this lesson of your love being lost—when it fails to inspire our people with the realization that love of humanity is with you far truer than patriotism.

I deeply regret that you could not accompany me in my last tour in Europe, though I understand the reasons that prevented you. If you had been with me, you would have been able fully to realize the great truth of the mission we have undertaken. To the majority of my countrymen the course of experience through which I passed will ever remain vague; and my appeal to them to view the history of our own country in the large background of humanity is not likely to carry any force. For my work I shall ever depend upon your comradeship, and therefore I feel sad that the reality of the ideal which has possessed me has missed its one signal chance of coming close to your heart. The perspective against which you have been recently setting up your scheme of life has been vastly different from mine. You have taken up responsibilities that may have to follow their own channels away from those that I shall have to choose; and the loneliness of my task, which has been my fatality in my past life, will follow me to the end of my days. But I must not complain. I shall follow the call of my providence, and I know that to respond to it in my own manner is fulfilment in itself, whatever may be its results.

S.S. "Morea," *July 12th, 1921*

For the last fourteen months my one thought was to bring India into touch with the living activities of the larger world of humanity. It was not because I thought that India would be the sole gainer by this contact, but because I was certain that when the dormant mind of India was roused from its torpor she would be able to offer something for the needs of the human race which would be valuable.

Through different modes of political co-operation and non-co-operation India has assumed up to the present an attitude of asking boons from others. I have been dreaming of some form of co-operation through which she would be in a position to offer her own gifts to the world. In the West the mind of man is in full activity. It is vigorously thinking and working towards the solution of all the problems of life. This fullness of intellectual vigour itself gives its inspiration to mental vitality. But in our Indian Universities we simply have the results of this energy, not the living velocity itself. So our mind is burdened and not quickened by our education. This has made me realize that we do not want schoolmasters from the West, but fellow-workers in the pursuit of truth.

My own aspiration for my country is that the mind of India should join its forces to the great movement of mind which is in the present-day world. Every success that we may attain in this effort will at once lead us directly to feel the unity of Man. Whether the League of Nations acknowledges this unity or not, it is the same to us. We have to realize it through our own creative mind.

The moment that we take part in the building up of civilization we are instantly released from our own self-seclusion—from our mental solitary cell. We have not yet gained full confidence that we have the power to join hands with the great builders—the great workers of the world. Either our boastfulness breaks its voice in unnatural shrieking or our self-denunciation makes an abnormal display of itself in an aggressive flutter of humility.

But I am certain that we have every claim to this confidence, and that we must do everything to realize it. We do not want bragging; we need for ourselves the dignity of the man who knows that he has some purpose to fulfil for all people and for all time. This has made me bold to invite students and scholars from different parts of the world to an Indian University to meet there our students and scholars in a spirit of collaboration. I wonder if this idea of mine will find any response in the hearts of my countrymen of the present day.

S.S. "Morea," *July 13th, 1921*

In our music, each *ragini*[1] has its special scale in which some notes are absent and some are added, and the sequence of them is different in different *raginis*. The idea of India in my mind has its different *raginis,* presenting different aspects.

During my absence in the West my idea of India had its own special grouping of notes, and consequently the vision had its own special emotional value. When, in my travels, I was communicating with you, I had not the least notion that your India and mine were vastly different at that moment. I came to be aware of this fact when, at Aden, a number of Indian newspapers of different dates came into my hands, I felt, for the first time in these fourteen months, that I should have to make another attempt between my aspiration and my country.

But misgivings come to my mind as to whether any proper adjustment will be possible. I hate constant conflicts and bickerings—always to be shouting at the top of my voice in order to make myself heard above the shouts of other parties.

1. Mode or tune.

The India about which I had been dreaming belongs to the world. The India that I shall reach shortly belongs tremendously to itself. But which of these must I serve?

Months ago, while sitting each day at my window in a New York hotel, my heart had been aching morning after morning for the time of my return—the day that should bring me back to the arms of Mother India. But to-day my heart is sad—like this dark heaving sea, under the rainy sky. I have been wondering in my own mind, during the last few days, whether it was not my mission to remain in Europe at least another year, where I was asked to stay. But it is too late now. From this time forward I must make the effort to train my attitude of mind to a condition for which I am not ready.

S.S. "Morea," *July 14th, 1921*

There is an idealism which is a form of egotism egregiously self-assertive. The confidence which one has in one's own ideas may not arise from an unmixed love of truth. It may be a subtle form of bigotry of self. There is an idealism ready to kill freedom in others in order to find freedom for its own plan.

I feel, at times, afraid lest such a tyranny of idealism should ever take possession of my own mind. For it would mean that my faith in truth had grown weaker than my faith in myself. Pride of self insidiously creeps into our schemes for ameliorating the conditions of our fellow human beings; and when failure occurs, we are hurt because the schemes are *our* schemes.

Egotism of this kind is blindly oblivious of other people's missions in life. It tries to impose one vast monotony of taste upon individuals who have temperament and capacities fit for other kinds of work. It is like the tyranny of conscription which compels teachers to dig and poets to kill their fellow-men. This, being against God's own purpose, is terribly wasteful. In fact, all tyrants in idealism try to usurp the rights of Providence for their own purpose.

The gloom of sadness which has been brooding over my mind for the last few days must be the shadow of my own egotism, whose flame of hope is dimmed by a fear. For some months I had been feeling sure that everybody would think my thoughts and carry on my work. But this confidence in me and in my plan has suddenly found a check and I am apprehensive.

No, this is wrong for me, and it is also a source of wrong for others. Let me be glad because a great idea, with all its beauty and truth, has alighted upon my mind. I alone am responsible for carrying out its commands. It has its own wings of freedom to bear it to its own goal; and its call is music, and not an injunction. There is no failure for truth—failure is only for me—and what does that matter?

Henceforth I shall have the chance of talking with you face to face. Yet distance has its own significance, and letters have their power of speech which tongues do not possess. And therefore, when we meet, some part of our thoughts will remain unuttered for the want of a great space and silence between us.

S.S. "Morea," *July 15th, 1921*

Before I finish this last letter to you, my friend, let me thank you with all my heart for your unfailing generosity in sending me letters all through my absence from India. They have been to me like a constant supply of food and water to a caravan travelling through a desert. I was sorely in need of them during the dreary months I spent in the United States. I promised to myself that I should try to pay you back in kind. I think I have kept my promise, and I hope you have got my letters in a regular weekly series, unless there have been gaps owing to the suspicions of professional eavesdroppers who watch over the destinies of the British Empire.

I suppose that the first few weeks I was lazy and depended upon Pearson to supply you with news, and therefore I am busy now in making up for the deficits. But about one thing I can never hope to compete with you. As a letter-writer you are incomparable! Mine are no more letters than lobsters are fish. They are like fragments of a book; like meteors that are shot off a planet. They are shot at you, and with a flash most of them vanish into ashes; whereas yours come down like showers of rain upon the thirsty land. Yet you must consider one thing in my favour—it is that I am heavily handicapped in my race with you, because I write in a language that is not my own, and this greatly adds to the original inertia I always have to overcome in writing any letter in any language whatsoever. On the other hand, writing letters is as easy to you as it is easy for our *Sal* avenue to put forth its leaves in the beginning of the spring months. However, I wonder if even *you* will be able to cope with my correspondence on my return! It has grown amazingly exuberant. Good-bye.

APPENDIX I

[*The following letter was sent to the Editor of the* Manchester Guardian, *Mr C.P. Scott, by Rabindranath Tagore, with reference to his friend* W.W. *Pearson, and was published on November 27, 1923.*]

The news has reached us of W.W. Pearson's death through an accident which happened while he was travelling in Italy on the eve of his departure for India. He is not known to the wide public, but we feel sure that his loss is not merely a loss to the individuals who came into intimate touch with him. We seldom met with anyone whose love of humanity was so concretely real, whose ideal of service so assimilated to his personality, as it had been with him. The gift of friendliness, which he was ever ready to bestow upon the obscure, upon those who had nothing to attract the attention of their neighbours, was spontaneous in its generosity, completely free from all tinge of conscious or unconscious egotism, enjoying the luxury of the satisfied pride of goodness. The constant help which he rendered to those who were in need of it could have no reward in public recognition; it was as simple and silent as the daily fulfilling of his own personal requirements. His patriotism was for the world of man; he intimately suffered for all injustice or cruelty inflicted upon any people in any part of the earth, and in his chivalrous attempt to befriend them he bravely courted punishment from his own countrymen. He had accepted Santiniketan Asram for his home, where he felt he could realize his desire to serve the cause of humanity and express his love for India, which was deeply genuine in his nature, all his aspirations of life centering in her.

I know he has numerous friends in this country and outside India who admire the noble unselfishness of heart which he possessed, and who mourn his loss. I feel sure they will appreciate our idea of setting up some permanent memorial in his name in our Asram, which was so dear to him. He had a great desire to see the hospital in connection with our institution rebuilt and equipped in an adequate manner, for which he was working and contributing money whenever possible. I believe if we can carry out this wish of his and construct a hospital building, and a special ward for children attached to it, this will be the best form of perpetuating his memory, reminding us of his sympathy for those who suffer.

APPENDIX II

[*The following letter from the Poet to his friend W.W. Pearson was found among his papers and was too late for insertion in the last chapter of this volume. I have therefore included it as an appendix.*]

Santiniketan, *July 4th, 1923*

I have just got your letter in which you ask me to give you my opinion concerning the importance of Institutional Religion.

As an abstract idea, I have nothing to say against it; for it is like the Caste System, perfect when ideally represented. Men can be classified according to their inherent differences in temperament. If all the natural Brahmins came together in order to carry on the special work which was only for them to perform, then through their mutual encouragement and co-operation an immensely potent force could be generated for the good of mankind. But directly a group is formed, its own group-personality almost invariably gives rise to an egoism which judges its own value by its external success and its physical duration. The Sect struggles for bigness and self-preservation even at the cost of truth. The growing consciousness of its own distinction and importance develops into a pride which—like the pride of wealth and office—becomes a temptation.

It is extremely difficult to become truly a Christian in conduct and life; but by following the easy path of belonging to a Christian Sect one seems to acquire the merit of being a Christian and also to have the right to despise even one's betters who by chance or by choice do not profess Christianity.

This has proved to be true of all religions which crystallize themselves into sectarianism. Religious communities are more often formed and established upon custom and the herd instinct than upon Truth. The children born to a Christian family are included in the religious community, not because they have shown in any way their fitness to belong to it, but because of the accident of birth. They do not have the time or the opportunity to discover their own individual inclination towards the religion they profess. They are persistently hypnotized into the belief that they are 'Christians.' For this reason we often witness the scene of men preaching Christianity as missionaries—or even as bishops—to their un-Christian fellow-beings, whom they might have killed as soldiers, or held down for ever under their heels as diplomats, had they followed their own true vocations.

An Institution which brings together individuals who are profoundly true and sincere in their common aspirations is a great help to all its members. But if, by its very constitution, it offers accommodation to those who merely have uniformity of habits and not unity of true faith, it necessarily becomes a breeding-place of hypocrisy and untruth. And because all organizations, by the very virtue of their power of combination, mechanically acquire a certain amount of force, such untruths and hypocrisies find ready opportunity to create widespread mischief.

Christ, like all other spiritual personalities, was solitary in moral greatness. He had a pure relationship of love and truth with all humanity. His Spirit works in solitude in the depth of men's souls. Therefore we find great-hearted individuals on the side of those people who are oppressed and insulted. On the other hand, we often find the Christian Church on the side of those vested interests which are engaged in exploiting the weak. This happens because the Church, as an organization, is a power which has its own natural alliance with other powers that are not only non-religious but very often irreligious. In fact, it is ready to make its bargain with those very powers that crucified Christ.

It is a truism to say that the character of the majority of the members constituting a religious community determines the level of its ideals. For this cause an Institution which is indiscriminate in the choice of its materials, and possesses an inordinate greed for the augmentation of its own numbers, very often becomes merely the most efficient organ for expressing the collective passion of its members. Have you not noticed this in the time of the late European War? And does not the profession of a sectarian Christianity fashion in the time of peace a cloak of respectability which covers a multitude of sins?

I know that a community of God-seekers is a great shelter for man. But directly this grows into an Institution it is apt to give ready access to the Devil by its back-door.

Mahatmaji and the Depressed Humanity

RABINDRANATH'S TELEGRAM TO MAHATMAJI

Santiniketan, 19–9–32

Mahatma Gandhi, Yeravda Jail, Poona.

It is worth sacrificing precious life for the sake of India's unity and her social integrity. Though we cannot anticipate what effect it may have upon our rulers who may not understand its immense importance for our people we feel certain that the supreme appeal of such self offering to the conscience of our own countrymen will not be in vain. I fervently hope that we will not callously allow such national tragedy to reach its extreme length. Our sorrowing hearts will follow your sublime penance with reverence and love.

RABINDRANATH TAGORE

MAHATMAJI'S WIRE TO RABINDRANATH

Poona, 20-9-32

Gurudev, Santiniketan.

Have always experienced God's mercy. Very early this morning I wrote seeking your blessing if you could approve action, and behold I have it in abundance in your message just received. Thank you.

GANDHI

MAHATMAJI'S LETTER TO RABINDRANATH

Censored, *Sd./-Illegible, Major, I.M.S. Superintendent, Yeravda Central Prison*

Dear Gurudev,

This is early morning 3 o'clock of Tuesday. I enter the fiery gate at noon—If you can bless the effort, I want it. You have been to me a true friend because you have been a candid friend often speaking your thoughts aloud. I had looked forward to a firm opinion from you one way or the other. But you have refused to criticize. Though it can now only be during my fast, I will yet prize your criticism, if your heart condemns my action. I am not too proud to make an open confession of my blunder, whatever the cost of the confession, if I find myself in error. If your heart approves of the action I want your blessing. It will sustain me. I hope I have made myself clear. My love.

Y.C.P.
20 $^{9}/_{32}$ (Sd.) M.K. Gandhi
10-30 a.m.

Just as I was handing this to the Superintendent, I got your loving and magnificent wire. It will sustain me in the midst of the storm I am about to enter. I am sending you a wire. Thank you.

M.K.G.

20TH SEPTEMBER*

A shadow is darkening to-day over India like a shadow cast by an eclipsed sun. The people of a whole country is suffering from a poignant pain of anxiety the universality of which carries in it a great dignity of consolation. Mahatmaji who through his life of dedication has made India his own in truth has commenced his vow of extreme self-sacrifice.

Each country has its own inner geography where her spirit dwells and where physical force can never conquer even an inch of ground. Those rulers who come from outside remain outside the gate and directly they are called away from the cloud-topping tower of their foreign possessions the stupendous fabric of unreality vanishes into the void. But the great soul who achieves victory through the power of truth continues his dominion even when he is physically no longer present. And we all know such achievement belongs to Mahatmaji. And the fact that he has staked his life for a further and final realization of his hope fills us with awe and makes us think.

At this solemn moment we have a cause for fear. It is our unfortunate habit to reduce the truth that belongs to the inner spirit into signs and observances that are external and after a

* Address to the staff and students of Santiniketan and Sriniketan.

cheap welcome to bid it adieu. Our leaders have requested us to observe fasting for this day, and there is no harm in it. But there is the risk of some unthinking people putting it in the same category with the fasting that Mahatmaji has begun to observe. Nothing can be more disastrous for us than the utter lessening of the value of a heroic expression of truth by paying it the homage of a mere ceremonial expression of feeling by a people emotionally inclined.

The penance which Mahatmaji has taken upon himself is not a ritual, but a message to all India and to the world. If we must make that message our own we should accept it in right manner through proper process of realization. The gift of sacrifice has to be received in a spirit of sacrifice.

Let us try to understand the meaning of his message. From the beginning of human history there has continued the cleavage between classes, those favoured by circumstances exploiting the weakness of others and building the stronghold of their own pride of superiority upon the humiliation of a large section of the community. Though this practice has been prevalent for long yet we must assert that it is against the true spirit of man. No civilized society can thrive upon victims whose humanity has been permanently mutilated, whose minds have been compelled to dwell in the dark. Those whom we keep down inevitably drag us down and obstruct our movement in the path of progress. The indignity with which we burden them grows into an intolerable burden to the whole country; we insult our own humanity by insulting Man where he is helpless or where he is not of our own kin.

To-day there are thousands in India, confined in prisons indefinitely and without trial, inhumanly treated, and there can be no doubt that not only are they a heavy burden upon the Government but they permanently lower its dignity. The contemptuous vindictiveness ruthlessly pursued against prisoners whether political or belonging to other classes reveals the primitive barbarism lurking in the dark recesses of civilization, perpetually burdening it with hard problems and tainting its soul. We on our part in India have banished a considerable number of our own people into a narrow enclosure of insult branding them with the sign of permanent degradation. A dungeon does not solely consist of brick and mortar confinement, but setting narrow limits to man's self-respect is a moral prison more cruel for victims than the physical one and more demoralising for those who encourage it passively or with pious fervour.

The concrete fact of inequalities between individuals and races cannot be ignored, but to accept it as absolute and utilize it to deprive men of their human rights and comradeship is a social crime that multiplies fast in its heinousness. We who imagine ourselves superior to those whom we have tied down to their abasement are punished by enfeebling them and losing them from us. The weakness engendered by such alienation has been one of the principal causes of defeat in all our historical conflicts. Where numerous divisions have been made among the people by dark gaps of dishonour balance is upset and social structure is ever in danger of toppling over. The signs of such trials are not lacking in the Western Continents where the chasm between wealth and want is widening and is darkly nourishing earthquakes in its depth. The moral channels of communication should never be obstructed if man must be saved from degeneracy or destruction.

Mahatmaji has repeatedly pointed out the danger of those divisions in our country that are permanent insults to humanity, but our attention has not been drawn to the importance of its rectification with the same force as it has been to the importance of the Khaddar. The social inequities upon which all our enemies find their principal support have our time-honoured loyalty making it difficult for us to uproot them. Against that deep-seated moral weakness in our society Mahatmaji has pronounced his ultimatum and though it may be our misfortune to lose him in the battlefield the fight will be passed on to every one of us to be carried on to the final end. It is the gift of the fight which he is going to offer to us and if we do not know how to accept it humbly and yet with proud determination, if we cheaply dismiss it with some ceremonials to which we are accustomed and allow the noble life to be wasted with its great meaning missed then our people will passively roll down the slope of degradation to the blankness of utter futility.

It is not possible for us to realize what effect Mahatmaji's action will have upon the people who govern us, and it is not for us today to discuss its political aspects.

Only one thing we must make clear to those who seem to have our destiny in their hands. We have observed that the English people are puzzled at the step that Mahatmaji has been compelled to take. They confess that they fail to understand it. I believe that the reason of their failure is mainly owing to the fact that the language of Mahatmaji is fundamentally different from their own. His method of protest is not in accord with the method which they usually follow in cases of grave political crisis. I ask them to remember the terrible days of atrocities that reddened in blood at their door when a dismemberment was being forced between Ireland and the rest of Great Britain. Those Englishmen who imagined it to be disastrous to the integrity of their Empire did not scruple to kill and be killed, even to tear into shreds the decency of civilized codes of honour. The West is accustomed to such violent outbursts in times of desperation and therefore such a procedure did not seem strange to them though to some of them it must have appeared wrong. The dismemberment of a large portion of Hindu society is certainly fatal to its wholeness and when all our appeals are stubbornly dismissed the reason should not be incomprehensible to other people as to why Mahatmaji is voicing the extreme form of protest on behalf of India I ask them to imagine what would have happened when the Roman Catholic community of England suffered from a forcible deprivation of its common rights, if some foreign power would come and with efficient benevolence alienate them from the rest of the nation. Very likely the people would resort to the method of protest which they consider as honourable in its red fury of violence. In our case the feeling may be similar though Mahatmaji has made use of its expression which is his own. The message of non-violence so often expressed by him in words and in deeds finds to-day its final exposition in a great language which should be easiest to understand.

RABINDRANATH TAGORE

RABINDRANATH'S APPEAL TO COUNTRYMEN*

I appeal to my countrymen that they must not delay a moment effectively to prove that they are in earnest to eradicate from their neighbourhood untouchability in all its ramifications. The movement should be universal and immediate, its expressions clear and indubitable. All manner of humiliation and disabilities from which any class in India suffers should be removed by heroic efforts and self-sacrifice. Whoever of us fails in this time of grave crisis to try his utmost to avert the calamity facing India would be held responsible for one of the saddest tragedies that could happen to us and to the world.

22-9-32.

RABINDRANATH TAGORE

TELEGRAM TO SRIJUT MAHADEV DESAI

Santiniketan, 23-9-32

Mahadev Desai, Yeravda Jail, Poona.

Gurudeva eager start Poona if Mahatmaji has no objection. Wire health and if compromise reached.

AMIYA CHAKRAVARTY

TELEGRAM TO SRIJUT MAHADEV DESAI

Santiniketan, 23-9-32

Mahadev Desai, Yeravda Jail, Poona.

I try my hardest to keep my faith firm in ultimate victory of truth as expressed in a great life to be sacrificed for its cause, but my heart bleeds to think what it would cost our country and I struggle with all my power to convince myself that India can afford it in her present time of crisis. It is needless to tell you how anxious I am to know the details of Mahatmaji's condition.

RABINDRANATH TAGORE

---

* Issued through Free Press and The Associated Press of India.

MAHATMAJI'S TELEGRAM TO RABINDRANATH

Poona, 23-9-32

Gurudev, Santiniketan.

Have read your loving message to Mahadev also Amiya's. You have put fresh heart in me. Do indeed come if your health permits. Mahadev will send you daily wires. Talks about settlement still proceeding. Love. Will wire again if necessary.

GANDHI

WIRE FROM SJ. SATISH CH. DAS GUPTA

Poona, 23-9-32

Gurudev, Santiniketan.

Mahadev wishes me express gratefulness your kind telegram and says in this battle between light and forces of darkness combined your presence near Gandhiji would be sure inspiration and healing balm.

SATIS DAS GUPTA

CABLEGRAM FROM SIR PRABHASHANKAR PATTANI

Rabindranath Tagore, Calcutta.

Shall be grateful for cabling real India situation address care India Office.

PATTANI

REPLY TO THE ABOVE

Sir Prabhashankar Pattani, India Office, London.

Whole country profoundly stirred by Mahatmaji's penance. Sweeping reforms proceeding apace. Every chance of the palpably unjust Communal Award being rectified by our own people.

RABINDRANATH TAGORE

WITH MAHATMAJI IN POONA*

We left for Poona with hope in our hearts even though the atmosphere was tense with foreboding. The journey is long, giving time for anxious thoughts to dwell on what may await us at the end. My companions buy newspapers at every big railway stall—the news is not encouraging. Mahatmaji, according to the physicians, seems to have definitely entered the danger zone, his muscles yielding now that his naturally meagre surplus of fat has almost been exhausted. Apoplexy may result any time. Discussions with different groups, prolonged and intricate, continue all these days mercilessly to exact his best energies. And yet Mahatmaji has indeed triumphed, curbing intense physical agony and mental strain with an unbending will. Compromise seems to have been achieved, retaining the depressed communities within the Hindu fold, and frustrating attempts to create divisions by the separate electorate award. The final resolution is now with the British Cabinet though there is no reasonable ground for their withholding sanction as the Prime Minister has already committed himself to accept what our own communities may jointly recognize as just.

Wavering between hope and fear, we reached Kalyan on the 26th September morning. We met Srimati Basanti and Urmila on the platform—they had arrived some hours before by the B.N. Ry. Mail. Without delay we started for Poona by the car which our hostess there had sent for us.

The hilly road through the Western Ghats is picturesque. Entering the city of Poona we found armoured cars and machine guns being manoeuvred on the military grounds; soldiers paraded along the city roads. Lady Thackersay herself graciously received us at her doorstep; as we went up the stairs to our rooms the girls of her school standing on either side welcomed us with songs and ceremonial garland, and sandal-paste.

---

* Talk to staff and students of Visva-bharati on returning from Poona. Rabindranath left for Poona on the 24th September by the E.I. Ry Bombay Mail with Sj. Surendranath Kar and Amiya Chakravarty.

Entering the house I had sensed anxiety in the air; there was a shadow of suspense in every face. On questioning I found that Mahatmaji's condition was precarious. No answer had come from London. I sent an urgent cable to the Premier.

There was no need for sending it. Soon the rumour reached us that the expected news had arrived. But we had no means of verifying that rumour till many hours later.

Today is Mahatmaji's day of silence. He has expressed his desire to break it with me at one o'clock. On our way to the Yeravda prison, at some distance from the gate, our car was stopped—a sentry on duty had been asked not to let any car pass till further orders. I had thought that in India now-a-days the road towards the jail entrance is generous. Round our car gathered a medley crowd.

As a gentleman from our side proceeded to obtain sanction from the prison authorities Sriman Devadas came along in a car, the jail-permit in his hand. Later on I heard that Mahatmaji had felt that our car had been obstructed in the way—though he had no information on that point—and sent his son to fetch us.

Big iron doors swung wide open one after the other and closed behind us. To our front is the arrogance of high walls, a fettered sky, straight cut metalled roads projecting ahead, a few trees.

Two major experiences of my life have come rather late. Recently I have crossed the threshold of the University; and in spite of a slight obstruction here am I today inside a regular prison house.

Climbing a few steps to the left and passing through a door I enter a walled-in enclosure with two blocks of cells, some distance apart. In the middle courtyard under the thick shade of a young mango tree lies Mahatmaji on his bed.

Mahatmaji drew me near to himself, and kept me there for some time. He expressed deep joy in seeing me.

I praised my luck for having come on the crest of good news. It was nearly half past one. The message from London had by now spread all over India, and it had even been discussed at the Assembly—so I heard later. The newspaper men had also known of it. There seems only to have been no hurry in saving him whose life-stream hour by hour was rapidly dwindling into a vanishing point. One felt surprised at the cruelly tortuous length of Red Tape. Upto four in the afternoon our anxiety mounted higher. One hears that the information had arrived in official Poona at 10 a.m.

On all sides are friends. I recognized among them Mahadev, Vallabhbhai, Rajagopalachari, Rajendraprasad, Srimati Kasturibai and Sarojini as well as Jawaharlal's wife Kamala were there.

Mahatmaji's slender body was emaciated to a degree, his voice was barely audible. He was being given water with soda to counteract the growing acidity in his stomach. The responsibility of his physicians was grave.

Yet his inner vigour was undiminished, intellectual flow active, his radiant personality as ever tireless. From before his fast difficult problems had weighed on his mind; he had carried on intricate discussions; his correspondence with politicians across the seas must have been a harsh experience. During his fast, as every one knows, claims and clamour of different parties have not spared him. Not a sign, however, of mental fatigue, not the slightest shadow was there to obscure the lucid language of his thoughts. Transcending the extreme rigours of his body this great manifestation of his invincible soul was before us moving us to profound admiration. I could hardly have fully realized how great is the strength of this frail man had I not come near to him like this.

To-day to millions of hearts in India have reached the message of this immortal spirit resting under the shadow of death's altar. No barriers could stand in its way, those of distance, of brick and mortar, of hostile politics. The obstruction of century-old inertia has crumbled before it into dust.

Mahadev said that Mahatmaji had been keenly awaiting my arrival. I cannot offer any help in the solution of political problems, for I lack necessary experience and inclination; but I am happy to have given him some satisfaction by my personal presence.

We move on to a distance as it would tire him to be surrounded. We patiently await for the message to arrive. The afternoon light arches over the bare high walls. In groups, white Khaddar clothed men and women quietly hold discussions. Noticeable is the disciplined calm of this gathering inside the jail. No hint is there of unguarded behaviour taking advantage of relaxed regulations. This strength of character naturally evokes trust, the prison authorities therefore have respectfully allowed them unhampered to mix with each other. They have not accepted any privileges transgressing Mahatmaji's implied assurance to the authorities. The dignity of natural self-respect is theirs; one can easily understand that they fully deserve the responsibility which rests on them to establish India's Swaraj on unflinching service of Truth.

At last with the Government's red sealed envelope in hand appears the Inspector General of Prisons. There seems to be a hint of happiness in his face. Slowly Mahatmaji reads the document. I asked Sarojini to request others to move away from him now. After he has finished reading, Mahatmaji calls his friends to discuss the communication amongst themselves and expresses his wish that it should be shown to Dr Ambedkar.

This letter is pondered over; I too read it. A production of diplomatic minds, it needs careful perusal. One understands that it does not go against Mahatmaji's wishes. Pandit Hridaynath Kunzru is deputed to explain the document in detail to Mahatmaji. His clear analysis leaves no room for doubt in Mahatmaji's mind. The great penance of the fast is now over.

Mahatmaji's cot is removed near to the shade of the prison wall. Spreading the jail blankets the gathering is seated. The lemon juice is prepared by Srimati Kamala Nehru; according to the request of the Inspector General of Prisons, it is to be given to Mahatmaji by Srimati Kasturibai. Mahadev tells me that my Gitanjali song "When the heart is dried and parched up..." is a favourite of Mahatmaji's. I had forgotten the tune which once I gave it; I sing it to an improvised tune. Pandit Shyam Shastri reads out from the Vedas. Srimati Kasturibai hands over to Mahatmaji the glass of fruit juice which he takes and slowly sips. Then the members of Sabarmati Ashram and others sing in chorus the hymn "Vaishnava Jana To". Fruits and sweets are distributed, we all partake of it.

Within gaol barricades this great festival takes place. Never has happened such an event in human history. The *Jajna* (the sacrificial rite) was begun inside the prison and here too is reached its great fulfilment.

At night Pandit Kunzru and other notable leaders now assembled in Poona came to me with the request that I should preside at the mammoth meeting to be held tomorrow to celebrate Mahatmaji's birthday anniversary. Pundit Malaviya, they said, would arrive tomorrow from Bombay. Punditji, I proposed, should preside, I would read out a short address in which I would try adequately to express my own sentiments. It was impossible not to consent to join even a big gathering on an occasion so auspicious, overruling considerations of my age and health.

Next evening in the open grounds of Sivaji Mandir a vast gathering had met to do honour to their master. With difficulty, I entered wondering what would happen about subsequent exit. Malaviyaji in his chaste Hindi explained beautifully that our scriptures never support class or racial discrimination in the name of religion; quoting chapter and verse he proved his thesis. I knew it was impossible for my voice any more to make itself audible to a meeting of this size. So I spoke a few words; Sriman Govind Malaviya, son of Punditji undertook to read out the text of my address. It was surprising to find that he could do it so perfectly considering that the evening light was dim and that he saw the paper now for the first time.

My written speech has already appeared fully in the papers. Just before coming to the meeting I had gone to Yeravda prison and presented it to Mahatmaji.

Mrs Motilal Nehru addressing her brothers and sisters said that they should never pause in their fight against untouchability which was a blot on the fair name of our civilization. Srijukta Rajagopalachari, Rajendraprasad, and other leaders exhorted their audience with great feeling to remove this evil which was disrupting our society and thwarting at every step our larger aspirations. Srijut Rajagopalachari wanted to take with him a birthday present for Mahatmaji in his jail. Let it be their promise never again to tolerate untouchability in their lives. At the end of the meeting the entire audience raising their hands accepted the vow of purifying our social life of grave wrongs that humiliate our humanity. It was evident that the message of today had reached the hearts of our audience—it would have been impossible even a few days before for thousands of men and women to accept unanimously such a difficult resolve.

My work is done. Next morning I spent many hours with Mahatmaji. Pundit Malaviya and myself had long discussions with him on a wide range of subjects. In a day Mahatmaji had regained unexpected physical strength, his voice was firmer, his blood pressure nearly normal. Visitors pour in with greetings of devoted love, to take the dust of his feet. He talks smilingly with each person. Children come with gifts of flowers, how happy he is with them. Discussions continue with his friends on social problems. His great concern now is to achieve a harmony between our two great communities, the Hindus and Mahomedans.

His great life which today luminously reveals itself on a large background has brought to us the message of discovering man the Great in all humanity. May this message be fulfilled. The true path to emancipation lies in man's unity; our political dependence is nourished by the innumerable sects and divisions that keep our peoples apart. The day has come when human civilization must move forward breaking through the fetters of the Ages—towards broader understanding based on mutual faith and love.

RABINDRANATH TAGORE

CABLE FROM C.F. ANDREWS

London, 24-9-32

Rabindranath Tagore, Poona.

Marvellous result appearing.
Dearest Love
Tell Bapu.

CHARLIE

MAHATMAJI BREAKS FAST

WIRE FROM POONA

Poona, 26-9-32

Rabindranath Tagore, Santiniketan.

Mahatmaji broke fast five p.m. Gurudeva spent four hours Yeravda Jail, sang just before breaking fast. Will visit Mahatmaji again tomorrow. Great rejoicing.

AMIYA; SUREN

CABLE FROM C.F. ANDREWS

London, 26-9-32

Rabindranath Tagore, Santiniketan.

Thank God Mahatma's life is spared.

CHARLIE

MESSAGE ON MAHATMAJI'S BIRTHDAY

Poona, 27-9-32.

On this day of our rejoicing over our reconciliation with the depressed classes of India we still suffer from a bitter sense of disappointment for not being able to realize the confidence of our Mahomedan brethren which is so absolutely necessary for the fulfilment of our national life. We assure them that the great fight which has recently been taken up by our country against the inequitous custom of untouchability has not made us forget the greater ordeal of purification through which India must pass in order to bring together the two great neighbours Hindus and Mahomedans in a perfect spirit of trust and cooperation. Both communities must be united in a bond of comradeship and stand side by side in the arduous adventure of India's freedom which to be real must come from within the heart of our common humanity and build on the basis of uncompromising honesty and love.

I heartily endorse the statement which Mahatmaji has sent to the Press and I appeal to our countrymen that they must never pause till the evils of disparity and discord are completely rooted out from the soil of India. Let us today take upon ourselves, all men and women of India, this great task which lies before us and dare meet the challenge which it has sent from one end of our country to the other.

RABINDRANATH TAGORE

ON MAHATMAJI'S BIRTHDAY*

Mahatmaji's birthday appears today before us in awful majesty of death which has just left him victorious.

Ordinarily men are born to a limited neighbourhood where related to their kinsmen they carry on the course of their common-place life till they die. Every year they also enjoy their special day which assures them of their birth right of a seat in the hearts of their few friends and relations. But great souls are born into a large sphere of life, they are acknowledged by peoples and nations; in celebrating their birthday we not only realize them to be our own for all time, but through them feel our spiritual intimacy with the world of Man. They extend the range of our personal self, giving it a universal background, the significance of eternal humanity.

---

* Speech delivered at Sivaji Mandir, Poona on 27th September 1932.

It is our great good fortune today that such a man has indeed come to us and what is still rarer that we have not repudiated him as we have so often done with the messengers of freedom and truth. His inspiration is actively in work all through India and even beyond its boundaries; it has awakened our consciousness to a truth which goes far beyond the limits of our self-interest. His life itself is a constant call to us to emancipation in service and self-dedication.

Today is the day of our national acknowledgement of Mahatmaji as the great brother who in the present age is the central bond of our brotherhood in our Motherland. I hope we shall be earnestly solemn in our expression of it and never cheapen the meaning of this occasion by merely indulging in emotional pride. Let us be worthy of the call of this Age and accept from Mahatmaji's hand the responsibility which he has accepted for himself.

We know in the Upanishads, God who ever dwells in the hearts of all men; has been mentioned as Mahatma. The epithet is rightly given to the man of God whom we are honouring today, for his dwelling is not within the narrow enclosure of individual consciousness, his dwelling is in the heart of untold multitudes who are born today in India and who are yet to come. And this greatness of his soul which has the power to comprehend other souls has made possible what never has yet happened in our history when even the masses have been roused to the great fact that India is not merely a geographical entity but is a living truth, in which they live and move and have their being.

Today in our determined effort to join Mahatmaji in his noble task of removing the burden of Ages, the burden of disrespect upon the bent back of those who have been stigmatized for the accident of their birth, the sin of wilful denial to a large body of our countrymen of sympathy which is the birthright of all human beings—we are not only casting off the chain of India's moral enslavement but indicating a path for all humanity. We are challenging victimisation wherever and in whatever form it may exist, to stand the test of relentless questioning of conscience which Mahatmaji has brought to bear upon our day.

When Mahatmaji began his penance there were cynics in our own country and abroad who mocked and jeered at him. And yet before our very eyes the wonder has happened. Hard rocks of tradition have been blasted, irrational prohibitions cramping our national life are already showing signs of tottering. Great has been the achievement due to his penance but it will be a greater glory to him and to us if we can fulfil his vow by fighting to the finish the evils of untouchability, of intolerance, of all that hinders the comradeship of man and man and obstructs our path to freedom and righteousness.

My friends, I appeal to you, do not betray your great man and your own humanity by any deviation of your initiative from the pursuit of justice and love towards your fellowmen who have suffered humiliation for ages and remained dumb in a pathetic apathy of resignation never even blaming providence and their own cruel destiny. But the angry voice has at last come from the divine guide of our history with its warning message that they cut at the root of freedom who in their unreasoning pride obstruct the freedom of social communication among their own kindreds.

RABINDRANATH TAGORE

CABLE FROM SIR PRABHASHANKAR PATTANI

Geneva, 29-9-32

Dr Rabindranath Tagore, Santiniketan.

Thanks for cabling. Thank God India has risen to its culture and communal peace is restored through Gandhiji's penance. He wired to us here that Gurudev was tower of strength at this juncture.

PATTANI

LETTER TO MIRA BEN, ARTHUR ROAD PRISON, BOMBAY

Santiniketan, 1-10-32

Dear Mira,

Mahatmaji showed me your letter which gave us both great joy. We missed you very much indeed but knew that you were with us in spirit in those anxious moments of suffering and the happiness that followed.

I found Mahatmaji much better when I left and hope that he is now gradually coming back to normal health. My pilgrimage to Poona has been auspicious throughout.

Yours affectionately,
RABINDRANATH TAGORE

LETTER FROM MIRA BEN

Arthur Road Prison, Bombay, 17-10-32

Revered Gurudev,

How happy I was to receive your loving letter.

From the day I read in the paper that you had started for Yeravda from Santiniketan I kept thinking of the joy your coming would give to Bapu. I counted the days and hours, and felt how you were going to get there just at the moment when the Fast would be broken. I pictured it all in my mind just as, I heard afterwards, it had all happened.

It helped me to bear the terrible strain of those hours.

And now I get such cheering letters from Bapu—full of thankfulness and hope. His health too, seems to have recovered in a wonderful way.

As I watch the developments which are following the Fast, my heart overflows with thanksgiving to God.

Ever affectionately,
Yours MIRA

MAHATMAJI'S STATEMENT ON BREAKING FAST*

The fast taken in the name of God was broken in His name in the presence of Gurudev and the leper prisoner Parachure Shastri, a learned Pandit, seated opposite each other, and a company of loving and loved ones who had gathered round me. The breaking was preceded by the Poet singing one of his Bengali hymns, then mantras from the Upanishads by Parachure Shastri, and my favourite hymn 'Vaishnavajana Te.' The hand of God has been visible in the glorious manifestation throughout the length and breadth of India during the past seven days. Cables received from many parts of the world, blessing the fast, have sustained me through the agony of the body, mind and soul that I passed through during the seven days.

But the cause was worth going through that agony, and the sacrificial fire once lit shall not be put out till there is the slightest trace of untouchability still left in Hinduism; and if it is God's will that it does not end with my life, I have confidence that there are several thousands of earnest reformers who will lay down their lives in order to purify Hinduism of this awful curse.

The settlement arrived at, so far as I can see, is a generous gesture on all sides. It is a meeting of hearts, and my Hindu gratitude is due to Dr Ambedkar, Rao Bahadur Srinivasan and their party on the one hand and Rao Bahadur M.C. Rajah on the other. They could have taken up an uncompromising and defiant attitude by way of punishment to the so-called Caste Hindus for the sins of generations. If they had done so, I at least could not have resented their attitude and my death would have been but a trifling price exacted for the tortures that the outcasts of Hinduism have been going through for unknown generations. But they chose a nobler path and have thus shown that they have followed the precept of forgiveness enjoined by all religions. Let me hope that the Caste Hindus will prove themselves worthy of this forgiveness and carry out to the letter and spirit every clause of the settlement with all its implications.

* Issued on 26 September evening.

The settlement is but the beginning of the end. The political part of it, very important though it no doubt is, occupies but a small space in the vast field of reform that has to be tackled by Caste Hindus during the coming days, namely the complete removal of social and religious disabilities under which a large part of the Hindu population has been groaning.

I should be guilty of a breach of trust, if I do not warn fellow reformers and Caste Hindus in general that the breaking of the fast carried with it a sure promise of its resumption, if this is not relentlessly pursued and achieved within a measurable period. I had thought of laying down a period, but I feel that I may not do so without a definite call from within. The message of freedom shall penetrate every 'untouchable' home, and that can only happen if reformers will cover every village. And yet in the wave of enthusiasm and in an inordinate desire to spare me the repetition of the agony there should be no coercion. We must, by patient toil and self-suffering, convert the ignorant and superstitious but never seek to compel them by force.

I wish too that the almost ideal solution that has been arrived at may be followed by the other communities and that we might see a dawn of a new era of mutual trust, mutual give and take, and a recognition of the fundamental unity of all communities.

I would here single out the Hindu-Moslem-Sikh question. I am the same to the Musalman today that I was in 1920-1922. I should be just as prepared to lay down my life as I was in Delhi to achieve an organic unity and permanent peace between them, and I hope and pray that there will be, as a result of this upheaval, a spontaneous move in this direction, and then surely the other communities can no longer stand out.

In conclusion I would like to thank the Government and the jail staff and the medical men appointed by the Government to look after me. Extreme care and attention was bestowed upon me. Nothing was left undone. The jail staff worked under terrible pressure and I observed that they did not grudge this labour. I thank them all from high to low.

I thank the British Cabinet for hastening the decision on the settlement. The terms of the decision sent to me, I have not approached without misgivings. It accepts, I suppose, very naturally only that part of the Agreement that refers to the British Cabinet's communal decision. I expect that they had constitutional difficulty in now announcing their acceptance of the whole agreement.

But I would like to assure my Harijan friends, as I would like henceforth to name them, that so far as I am concerned, I am wedded to the whole of that agreement and that they may hold my life as hostage for its due fulfilment unless we ourselves arrive at any other and better settlement of our own free will.

M.K. GANDHI

East and West

GILBERT MURRAY—RABINDRANATH TAGORE

Yatscombe, Boar's Hill, Oxford,
August 17th, 1934

My dear Tagore

I venture to trouble you with this letter for several reasons. First, you are a great poet, probably the most famous poet now living in the world, and poetry is to me almost the chief pleasure and interest in life. Your life and work are inspired by a spirit of harmony, and it is in the interest of harmony between man and man that I make my appeal. You are a Thinker, and in this distracted world, where nation stands armed against nation and the old liberal statesmanship of the nineteenth century seems to have given way to a blind temper of competition, I cannot but look to the Thinkers of the world to stand together, not in one nation but in all nations, reminding all who care to listen of the reality of human brotherhood and the impossibility of basing a durable civilized society on any foundation save peace and the will to act justly.

All generalizations about whole nations or groups of nations are superficial and inaccurate, even when made by scientific students without personal bias. And most of these actually current are made by prejudiced and utterly unscientific partisans. People talk loosely of the difference in character between "Nordic" and "Latin" nations, or, in still looser phrase, between "East" and "West", violently denouncing the one and praising the other. Even when there is no actual prejudice at work, the comparisons, though sometimes suggestive, are never exact. For one thing, neither side of the comparison is uniform: every German is different from every other German, every Italian from every other Italian: nor can you make any single statement that will be true of all Indians or of all Englishmen. And besides, the differences of habits and ways of thought between, say, one fairly typical Bengali and one typical Yorkshireman, are so infinite in number that they cannot be added together in a definite catalogue, and for the most part so utterly unimportant that they would not be worth cataloguing. I am always puzzled by the people who ask me "Do I like Indians", or it may be Americans, or Frenchmen: and can only answer, as I would about my own countrymen, that I like some and do not like others.

Yet the differences are there, and are felt though they cannot be analysed. Indeed the mischief is that they are felt far too much; infinitesimal peculiarities are noted and interpreted as having some great moral significance. We are accustomed to our own people and do not seek for profound psychological explanations of their chance looks and ways. But when we meet a foreigner we feel a surge of curiosity and criticism rising within us. We want eagerly to know what this strange being is really like, and we have so little evidence to go upon that we exaggerate the importance of all we have. A slightly louder voice, a less ceremonious address, a ruddier face, will suggest insolence and brutality: the opposite will seem to be symptoms of timidity and insincerity. Similarly, an act of courtesy to which we are not accustomed will be gratefully remembered for years; a breach of the sort of courtesy which we expect will be furiously resented. And, inevitably when this course of ingenious misinterpretation is once begun, it is easy to get abundant confirmation of all one's prejudices. It is said to be, in point of law, impossible to draw an indictment against a nation: as a matter of literature, it is only too easy. One could write a "Mother India" about every nation—an appalling indictment, and false as a whole, while every statement in it might be true. I remember an English newspaper in the 90's which, finding nothing more mischievous to do at the moment, used to collect and publish a list of all the crimes committed by members of the French army. And since the French army was very large the crimes were proportionately numerous, and the effect as horrifying as the editor desired. Many of us read a famous German scholar's book, "England", published during the war. It dwelt upon the disgusting faults of the English and the merits of the writer's own countrymen, and perhaps, in the long run, it was as useful to us as it was harmful to them. But of course the whole method of such books is wrong. The first step towards international understanding must be a recognition that our own national habits are not the unfailing canon by which those of other peoples must be judged, and that the beginning of all improvement must be a certain reasonable humility.

It is not hard, in theory at least, to make this first step. Indeed it is a duty generally recognised by English Liberals. The historical works of my friend, Edward Thompson, on Indian subjects are an example. But it is hard indeed to carry out consistently, and even to begin needs some imaginative effort.

An Indian friend of mine once told me that as a small child he had been taught to regard the Englishman as something scarcely human, a kind of Demon, which had every day both to shed blood and be drugged with alcohol, or else its rage became terrible. This, I suppose, was strictly true, at any rate of some average British officers on a hunting expedition. They did expect every day to shed blood and to cheer themselves with alcohol—two acts which to my Indian friend were equally abominable; and I can quite believe that their tempers wore rather thin when they were disappointed of either. Yet no doubt, apart from this little weakness for blood and alcohol, they were excellent people.

I remember many years ago a visit of yours to England, when a number of people met to give you a public welcome in some hall in London, and, among other features in the entertainment, an English singer sang one of your poems. It was a gentle philosophical poem, dependent for its whole effect upon a spirit of quiet and calm. I should have liked to hear it spoken to the accompaniment of some antique stringed instrument like a harp or a cithara. But on this occasion it had been set to modern European music of a *bravura* style, and when the singer began, her piercing soprano made me wince. I looked to see how you were bearing it. No doubt you suffered, but you were the centre of all eyes and your statuesque courtesy was undisturbed.

Yes, the differences are there: they are real and perhaps to a certain extent they are national or racial, though not so much as people imagine. I was once on a Committee where a certain Indian member was making himself very tiresome (there are tiresome Indians as well as tiresome Europeans) by his touchiness and vanity. And a wise old Japanese friend of mine told me afterwards how he had wondered within himself: "Is that sort of behaviour Asiatic, and ought I to feel ashamed? Or is it Indo-European, so that I am left untouched?" Of course it was neither. It was only human. There are touchy and vain people in all parts of the world, just as there are criminals in all parts; just as there are thinkers, artists, poets, men of learning; just as there are saints and sages. And it is valuable to remember that, as Plato pointed out long ago, while criminals tend to cheat and fight one another, and stupid people to misunderstand one another, there is a certain germ of mutual sympathy between people of good will or good intelligence. An artist cannot help liking good art, a poet good poetry, a man of science good scientific work, from whatever country it may spring. And that common love of beauty or truth, a spirit indifferent to races and frontiers, ought, among all the political discords and antagonisms of the world, to be a steady well-spring of good understanding, a permanent agency of union and brotherhood.

There is no need for sentimentality, no need for pretence. If I enjoy the beauty of your poetry, if I sympathize with your rejection of honours from a government which you had ceased to respect, that makes already a sufficient bond between us: there is no need for me to share, or pretend to share, or make a great effort to share, your views on every subject, or because I admire certain things that are Indian to turn round and denounce Western Civilization. Men of imagination appreciate what is different from themselves: that is the great power which imagination gives. For example, I have just been reading your play called in French "La Machine", and see in it, if I am not mistaken, your hatred of machines as such, and of all the mechanization of modern life. Now I happen to admire machines and the engineers who make them. I respect their educational influence. I feel that if a boy's horse or dog will not do what he wants he will probably try to make it do so by losing his temper and beating it; but if his bicycle or his wireless will not work, he knows it is no good losing his temper. He has to think and work, to find out what is wrong and to put it right: which is a priceless lesson for any boy. Then the use of machinery teaches conscientiousness to the mechanic. I often think of the thousands and thousands of aeroplanes that are plying their daily tasks throughout Europe and America; each one of them consisting of thousands and thousands of parts, every single one of which must be properly adjusted and made fast by the workmen before the machine starts. A mistake, almost any mistake, is quite likely to be fatal. But the engineers, quite ordinary men for the most part, are so trained that they do not make a mistake, and the rest of us have such confidence in their accuracy and conscientiousness that we travel in their aeroplanes freely and without a qualm. This seems to me a quite wonderful fact, that masses of men should have been made so trustworthy and reliable. It is the Age of Machines that, for the first time in history, has made them so. I write this not to argue but merely to illustrate; to show that difference of opinion, habit or training need not cause alienation. You can remain profoundly Indian and I a regular westerner, without disturbance to our mutual sympathy.

I even believe in the healthiness and high moral quality of our poor distressed civilization. It made the most ghastly war in history, but it hated itself for doing so. As a result of the war it is now full of oppressions, cruelties, stupidities and public delusions of a kind which were thought to be obsolete and for ever discarded a century ago. But I doubt if ever before there was what theologians would call such a general sense of sin, such widespread consciousness of the folly and wickedness in which most nations and governments are involved, or such a determined effort, in spite of failure after failure, to get rid at last of war and the fear of war and all the baseness and savagery which that fear engenders. I still have hope for the future of this tortured and criminal generation: perhaps you have lost hope and perhaps you will prove right. But the divergence of view need make no rift between us.

My beloved and admired colleague, Mme Curie, when she threw herself into the work of Intellectual Co-operation, gave one special reason for doing so. She had seen, during the World War, how often the intellectual leaders in the various nations had been not better but, if anything, worse than the common people in the bitterness and injustice of their feelings. She had seen that this was a great evil and one that could be remedied. The artists and thinkers, the people whose work or whose words move multitudes, ought to know one another, to understand one another, to work together at the formation of some great League of Mind or Thought independent of miserable frontiers and tariffs and governmental follies, a League or Society of those who live the life of the intellect and through the diverse channels of art or science aim at the attainment of beauty, truth and human brotherhood.

I need not appeal to you, Tagore, to join in this quest; you already belong to it, you are inevitably one of its great leaders. I only ask you to recognize the greatness of your own work for the intellectual union of East and West, of thinker with thinker and poet with poet, and to appreciate the work that may be done by the intellectuals of India not merely for their own national aims, however just and reasonable they may be; there is a higher task to be attempted in healing the discords of the political and material world by the magic of that inward community of spiritual life which even amid our worst failures reveals to us Children of Men our brotherhood and our high destiny.

Believe me, with deep respect,

Yours sincerely,
GILBERT MURRAY

"Uttarayan" Santiniketan, Bengal
September 16th, 1934

My dear Professor Murray

In the midst of my busy seclusion in a corner of this Educational Colony in India comes your letter bearing its call for close understanding of the problems that face our common humanity. I have no difficulty in responding to your friendly voice, for it is not only the voice of a friend whom I have the privilege to know and love; but it also carries the highest authority of European culture and scholarship, and is therefore eminently fitted to represent the great humanity of Europe.

I must confess at once that I do not see any solution of the intricate evils of disharmonious relationship between nations, nor can I point out any path which may lead us immediately to the levels of sanity. Like yourself, I find much that is deeply distressing in modern conditions, and I am in complete agreement with you again in believing that at no other period of history has mankind as a whole been more alive to the need of human co-operation, more conscious of the inevitable and inescapable moral links which hold together the fabric of human civilization. I cannot afford to lose my faith in this inner spirit of Man, nor in the sureness of human progress which following the upward path of struggle and travail is constantly achieving, through cyclic darkness and doubt, its ever-widening ranges of fulfilment. Willingly therefore I harness myself, in my advanced age, to the arduous responsibility of creating in our Educational Colony in Santiniketan a spirit of genuine international collaboration based on a definite pursuit of knowledge, a pursuit carried on in an atmosphere of friendly community life, harmonized with Nature, and offering freedom of individual self-expression. This work which I have to continue in the face of desperately adverse circumstance, has yet struck root in the soil of India, and sent out its branches to a wider arena of humanity, and it carries, I believe, a very deep affinity with the activities of the League of Intellectual Co-operation with which I am already associated.

My occasional misgivings about the modern pursuit of Science is directed not against Science, for Science itself can be neither good or evil, but its wrong use. If I may just touch here on your reference to machines, I would say that machines should not be allowed to mechanize human life but contribute to its well-being, which as you rightly point out, it is constantly doing when it is man's sanity which controls the use of machinery.

I would like here to quote a passage from one of my writings published in April 1929 which I think may interest you. You will find that it is impossible for me not to accept the true spirit of Science as a pure expression of the creative soul of man.

"Personally I do not believe that Europe is occupied only with material things. She may have lost her faith in religion, but not in humanity. Man, in his essential nature, is spiritual and can never remain solely material. If, however, we in the East merely realize Europe in this external aspect, we shall be seriously at fault. For in Europe the ideals of human activity are truly of the soul. They are not paralyzed by shackles of scriptural injunctions. Their sanction lies in the heart of man and not in something external to him.

"It is this attitude of mind in Europe which is essentially spiritual....

"When the aeroplane goes up in the sky, we may wonder at it as the perfection of material power; but behind this lies the human spirit, strong and alive. It is this spirit of man which has refused to recognize the boundaries of nature as final. Nature has put the fear of death in man's mind to moderate his power within the limits of safety; but man in Europe has snapped his fingers at Death and torn asunder the bonds. Only then did he earn the right to fly—a right of the gods.

"But even here the adverse forces—the Titans—are alive, who are ready to rain down death from the air. But the Titans are not in sole possession. In Europe, there is a constant war between the gods and the Titans. Often the Titans are victorious; but the victory is sometimes with the gods...."

What really must concern us in our generalization or in our detailed study of truth is, as you indicate, a sincere recognition of reality and an unflinching loyalty to it.

May I therefore, in trying to pursue the middle path of harmony, deal with some details of our present problems of India, and also put them in relation to the larger aspect of international relationship as I view it. In offering you gleanings from my thoughts covering a number of my mature years of experience, I may perhaps help in clearing up, to a certain extent, the nature of some of our vital problems. On the clear recognition of these internal as well as international problems must depend the possibility of genuine understanding and co-operation both between the different communities of India and between India as a whole and Europe. This, I believe, is also the guiding principle of the League of Nations which has asserted itself time and again in spite of the pressure of political vicissitudes.

II

Now that mutual intercourse has become easy, and the different peoples and nations of the world have come to know one another in various relations, one might have thought that the time had arrived to merge their differences in a common unity. But the significant thing is, that the more the doors are opening and the walls breaking down outwardly, the greater is the force which the consciousness of individual distinction is gaining within. There was a time when we believed that men were remaining separate, because of the obstacles between them; but the removal of these, to the largest possible extent, is not seen to have the effect of doing away with the differences between diverse sections of mankind.

Individuality is precious, because only through it we can realize the universal. Unfortunately there are people who take enormous pride in magnifying their speciality and proclaiming to the world that they are fixed for ever on their pedestal of uniqueness. They forget that only discords are unique and therefore can claim their own separate place outside the universal world of music.

It should be the function of religion to provide us with this universal ideal of truth and maintain it in its purity. But men have often made perverse use of their religion, building with it permanent walls to ensure their own separateness. Christianity, when it minimises its spiritual truth, which is universal, and emphasises its dogmatic side, which is a mere accretion of time, has the same effect of creating a mental obstruction which leads to the misunderstanding of people who are outside its pale. A great deal of the unmerited contempt and cruelty, which the non-western peoples have suffered in their political, commercial or other relations at the hands of the West, is owing to sectarian calumnies with which even the western children's textbooks are contaminated. Nevertheless this sectarian religion does not occupy the greater part of the western life and therefore in its heart still remains the possibility of a better human relationship than what prevails now between the races.

We have seen Europe cruelly unscrupulous in its politics and commerce, widely spreading slavery over the face of the earth in various names and forms. And yet, in this very same Europe, protest is always alive against its own iniquities. Martyrs are never absent whose lives of sacrifice are the penance for the wrongs done by their own kindred. The individuality which is western is not to be designated by any sect-name of a particular religion, but is distinguished by its eager attitude towards truth, in two of its aspects, scientific and humanistic. This openness of mind to truth has also its moral value and so in the West it has often been noticed that, while those who are professedly pious have sided with tyrannical power, encouraging repression of freedom, the men of intellect, the sceptics, have bravely stood for justice and the rights of man.

I do not mean to say that those who seek truth always find truth, and we know that men in the West are apt to borrow the sanction of science under false pretences to give expression to their passions and prejudices. To many thinkers there has appeared a clear connection between Darwin's theories and the "imperialism", Teutonic and other, which was so marked a feature during the sixties. We have also read western authors who, admirably mimicking scientific mannerism, assert, as you point out, that only the so-called Nordic race has the proper quality and therefore the right to rule the world, extolling its characteristic ruthlessness as giving it the claim to universal dominance. But we must not forget that such aberrations of science, padded with wrong or imperfect data, will be knocked down by science itself. The stream of water in a river does carry sand, but so long as the stream can still flow it will push away the sand from its own path. If the mental attitude is right we need not be afraid of mistakes. That is why the individual in the West has no unsurpassable barrier between himself and the rest of humanity. He may have his prejudices, but no irrational injunctions to keep him in internment away from the wide world of men.

Unfortunately for us, however, the one outstanding visible relationship of Europe with Asia today is that of exploitation; in other words, its origins are commercial and material. It is physical strength that is most apparent to us in Europe's enormous dominion and commerce, illimitable in its extent and immeasurable in its appetite. Our spirit sickens at it. Everywhere we come against barriers in the way of direct human kinship. The harshness of these external contacts is galling, and therefore the feeling of unrest ever grows more oppressive. There is no people in the whole of Asia today which does not look upon Europe with fear and suspicion.

There was a time when we were fascinated by Europe. She had inspired us with a new hope. We believed that her chief mission was to preach the gospel of liberty to the world. We had come then to know only her ideal side through her literature and art. But slowly, Asia and Africa have become the main spheres of Europe's secular activities, where her chief preoccupations have been the earning of dividends, the administration of empires, and the extension of commerce.

Europe's warehouses and business offices, her police outposts and soldiers' barracks, have been multiplied, while her human relationships have declined.

Towards those who are being exploited, there always is wont to grow up a feeling of contempt. For exploitation itself becomes easier, if we can succeed in creating a callousness towards those who are its victims. Just as whenever we go out fishing we are inclined to regard fishes as the least sensitive of all living creatures, so it becomes quite pleasant to loot the Orient, if only we can make our own moral justification easy by relegating coloured races to the lowest groupings of mankind.

Thus modern Europe, scientific and puissant, has portioned out this wide earth into two divisions. Through her filter, whatever is finest in Europe cannot pass through to reach us in the East. In our traffic with her, we have learnt, as the biggest fact of all, that she is efficient, terribly efficient. We may feel astounded by this efficiency; but if, through fear, we bring to it our homage of respect, then we ourselves need to realize that we are fast going down to the very depths of misfortune; for to do such homage is like the crude barbarity of bringing sacrificial offerings to some god which thirsts for blood. It is on account of this fact, and in order to retain her self-respect, that the whole of Asia today denies the moral superiority of Europe. At the same time, to withstand her ravages, Asia is preparing to imitate the ruthless aspect which slays, which eats raw flesh, which tries to make the swallowing process easier by putting the blame on the victim.

But this, as we realize is only one side, however real and painful, of the Western civilization as it appears to us in the East.

Western humanity, when not affected by its unnatural relationship with the East, preserves a singular strength of moral conduct in the domain of its social life, which has its great inspiration for all of us. It is easy enough for us, when someone reviles us for our social evils, to point at worse evils in Europe; but this is negative. The bigger thing to remember is, that in Europe these evils are not stagnant. There, the spiritual force in man is ever trying to come to grips. While, for instance, we find in Europe the evil Giant's fortress of Nationalism, we also find Jack the Giant-Killer. For, there is growing up the international mind. This Giant-Killer, the international mind—though small in size—is real. In India, even when we are loudest in our denunciation of Europe, it is often her Giant's fortress that we long to build with awe and worship. We insult Jack with ridicule and suspicion. The chief reason for this is, that in India we have ourselves become material-minded. We are wanting in faith and courage. Since in our country the gods are sleeping, therefore, when the Titans come, they devour all our sacrificial offerings—there is never a hint of strife. The germs of disease are everywhere; but man can resist disease only when his vital force is active and powerful.

So, too, even when the worship of the blood-thirsty and false gods of self-seeking are rampant on all sides, man can lift up his head to the skies if his spirit is awake. Both matter and spirit are active. They alone become entirely materialistic who are only half men, who cripple the native majesty of the spirit before the blind repetition of unintelligent activities; who are niggardly in knowledge and palsied in action; who are ever insulting themselves by setting up a meaningless ritualism in the place of true worship; who have no difficulty whatever in believing that there is special sanctity inherent in particular forms and peculiar rites, even when their significance is neither known nor knowable.

I know how reluctant it makes us feel to give any credit for humanity to the western civilization when we observe the brutalities into which this nationalism of theirs breaks out, instances of which are so numerous all the world over—in the late war, in the lynching of Negroes, in cowardly outrages allowed to be committed by European soldiers upon helpless Indians, in the rapacity and vandalism practised in Peking during the Boxer war by the very nations who are never tired of vulgarly applying barbaric epithets to each other according to the vicissitudes of political expediency and passion. But while I have never sought to gloss over or keep out of mind any of these ugly phenomena, I still aver that in the life of the West they have a large tract where their mind is free; whence the circulation of their thought-currents can surround the world. This freedom of the mind's ventilation following the constant growth of a vigorous life bears in it the promise of righting the wrong and purifying the noxious accumulation within.

To me the mere political necessity is unimportant; it is for the sake of our humanity, for the full growth of our soul, that we must turn our mind towards the ideal of the spiritual unity of man. We must use our social strength, not to guard ourselves against the touch of others, considering it as contamination, but generously to extend hospitality to the world, taking all its risks however numerous and grave. We must manfully accept the responsibility of moral freedom, which disdains to barricade itself within dead formulae of external regulation, timidly seeking its security in utter stagnation. Men who live in dread of the spirit of enquiry and lack courage to launch out in the adventure of truth, can never achieve freedom in any department of life. Freedom is not for those who are not lovers of freedom and who only allow it standing space in the porter's vestibule for the sake of some temporary purpose, while worshipping, in the inner shrine of their life, the spirit of blind obedience.

In India what is needed more than anything else, is the broad mind which, only because it is conscious of its own vigorous individuality, is not afraid of accepting truth from all sources. Fortunately for us we know what such a mind has meant in an individual who belongs to modern India. I speak of Rammohun Roy. His learning, because of its depth and comprehensiveness, did not merely furnish him with materials for scholarship, but trained his mind for the free acceptance of truth. Rammohun Roy developed the courage and capacity to discriminate between things that are essential and those that are non-essential in the culture which was his by inheritance. This helped him to realize that truth can never be foreign, that money and material may exclusively belong to the particular country which produces them, but not knowledge, or ideas, or immortal forms of art.

The very magnitude of mind of such men becomes almost a grievance for smaller personalities, and Rammohun has been misunderstood by his own countrymen because he had in him this modern spirit of freedom and comprehensive grasp of truth. We must, however, never make the mistake of thinking that great men who are belittled by their contemporary compatriots do not represent their countries; for countries are not always true to themselves.

In Rammohun Roy's life we find a concrete illustration of what India seeks, the true indication of her goal. Thoroughly steeped in the best culture of his country, he was capable of finding himself at home in the larger world. His culture was not for rejection of those cultures which came from foreign sources; on the contrary, it had an uncommon power of sympathy which could adjust itself to them with respectful receptiveness.

The ideal I have formed of the culture which should be universal in India, has become clear to me from the life of Rammohun Roy. I have come to feel that the mind which has been matured in the atmosphere of a profound knowledge of its own country, and of the perfect thoughts that have been produced in that land, is ready to accept and assimilate the cultures that come from foreign countries. He who has no wealth of his own can only beg, and those who are compelled to follow the profession of beggary at the gate of the intellectually rich may gain occasional scraps of mental food, but they are sure to lose the strength of their intellectual character and their minds are doomed to become timid in thought and in creative endeavour.

All this time we have been receiving education on purely western lines. When this first began, western culture was imbued with a supreme contempt for that of the East. And to this day, consequently, we have been brought up in this contempt. This speaks of internal dissensions within the temple of Mother Saraswati. Her eastern sons kept closed the door leading to the western side for fear of adulteration, and her western sons barred their eastern windows through want of respect. Meanwhile the system of education in India remained, and still remains, absurdly un-Indian, making no adequate provision for our own culture. We have, here, not even anything like the facility which the German student enjoys in Germany for the study of the lore of Hindu and Moslem. And if we have become conscious of this vital deficiency in our education, that is because of the spirit of the times.

A certain number of us do not admit that our culture has any special features of value. These good people I leave out of account. But the number of those others is not few, who while admitting this value in theory, ignore it more or less in practice. Very often, the flourishing of the banner of this culture is not for the sake of the love of truth but for that of national vain-gloriousness—like brandishing a musical instrument in athletic display before one's own admiring family, instead of using it to make music.

This section of our people while never neglecting to make proud boast of their country's glory, have an absurdly narrow conception of the ideal in which that glory consists. Their indiscriminate reverence is for the actual, not for the eternal. The habits and customs of our decadence which have set up barriers between us and the world, splitting us into mutually exclusive sections, making us weak and bowing our heads in shame at every turn of our later history—these are the idols of their special worship, which they endow with endless virtues of their own imagining. They consider it to be their sacred mission to retain in perpetuity the waste matter sloughed off by age, as the true insignia of our Hindu civilization; to extol the gleam of the will-o-the-wisp, born of the noxious miasma of decay, as more time-hallowed than the light of sun, moon and stars.

In our greed for immediate political result, we are apt to ascribe the fact of our tendency towards separateness to accidental circumstances, refusing to see that a code of behaviour, which has not the sanction of reason, and yet has the support of religion, must result in the creation of irreconciliable divisions between men. In reason alone can we have our common meeting ground; for that which is against reason needs must be peculiar and exclusive, offering constant friction until worn away by the ever-active, rational mind of man. So when, for a body of men, popular custom is artificially protected by a religion which is allowed to usurp the entire range of human knowledge and conduct, it becomes a potent factor in maintaining an immense gap of aloofness and antagonism between closest neighbours.

The evolving Hindu social ideal has never been present to us as a whole, so that we have only a vague conception of what the Hindu has achieved in the past, or can attempt in the future. The partial view, before us at any moment, appears at the time to be the most important, so we can hardly bring ourselves to the true ideal, but tend to destroy it. And there we stand fasting and telling beads, emaciated with doing penance, shrinking into a corner away from the rest of the world.

We forget that Hindu civilization was once very much alive, crossing the seas, planting colonies, giving to and taking from all the world. It had its arts, its commerce, its vast and strenuous field of work. In its history, new ideas had their opportunity. Its women also, had their learning, their bravery, their place in the civic life. In every page of the Mahabharata we shall find proofs that it was no rigid, cast-iron type of civilization. The men of those days did not, like marionettes, play the same set piece over and over again. They progressed through mistakes, made discoveries through experiment, and gained truth through striving. They belonged to a free and varied *Samaj*, quick with life, driven into ever new enterprise by its active vigour.

This, however, was society which orthodoxy today would hardly recognize as Hindu, because it was living and had a growth which was revealing its inner unity through outer changes. So the *dharma* (principle) of life which thinks and doubts, accepts and rejects, progresses, changes and evolves, cannot, according to orthodoxy, be a part of the Hindu Dharma. Man shows his mental feebleness when he loses his faith in life because it is difficult to govern, and is only willing to take the responsibility of the dead because they are content to lie still under an elaborately decorated tomb-stone of his own make. We must know that life carries its own weight, while the burden of the dead is heavy to bear—an intolerable burden which has been pressing upon our country for ages.

The fact stands out clearly today that the Divinity dwelling within the heart of man cannot be kept immured any longer in the darkness of particular temples. The day of the *Ratha-yatra*, the Car Festival, has arrived when He shall come out on the high way of the world, into the thick of the joys and sorrows, the mutual commerce, of the throng of men. Each of us must set to work to build such car as we can, to take its place in the grand procession. The material of some may be of value, of others cheap. Some may break down on the way, others last till the end. But the day has come at last when all the cars must set out.

III

Your letter has been a confirmation to me of the deep faith in the ultimate truths of humanity which we both try to serve and which sustains our being. I have tried to express how religion today as it exists in its prevalent institutionalised forms both in the West and the East has failed in its function to control and guide the forces of humanity; how the growth of nationalism and wide commerce of ideas through speeded-up communication have often augmented external differences instead of bringing humanity together. Development of organizing power, mastery over Nature's resources have subserved secret passions or the openly flaunted greed of unashamed national glorification. And yet I do not feel despondent about the future. For the great fact remains that man has never stopped in his urge for self-expression, in his brave quest of knowledge; not only so, there is today all over the world in spite of selfishness and unreason a greater *awareness* of truth. The fury of despotic tyranny, the denial of civic sanity and the violence with which the citadels of international federation are constantly assaulted, combine to betray an uncomfortable and increased consciousness in the mind of man of the inescapable responsibilities of humanity. It is this stirring of the human conscience to which we must look for a reassertion of man in religion, in political and economic affairs, in the spheres of education and social intercourse. It is apparent that innumerable individuals in every land are rising up vitalized by this faith, men and women who have suffered and sought the meaning of life and who are ready to stake their all for raising a new structure of human civilization on the foundation of international understanding and fellowship. In this fact lies the great hope of humanity—this emergence in every nation, in spite of repression and the suicidal fever of national warmindedness, of the clean and radiant fires of individual consciousness. When I read some of the outstanding modern books published after the War I realize how the brighter spirits of young Europe are now alive to the challenge of our times. Nothing can be of greater joy to us in India than to find how unimpeachably great some of your scholars, historians, artists and literary men are in their fearless advocacy of truth, their passion for righteousness. In India, too, there is a great awakening everywhere, mainly under the inspiration of Mahatma Gandhi's singular purity of will and conduct, which is creating a new generation of clear-minded servers of our peoples. To these individuals of every land and race, these youthful spirits burning like clean flame on the altar of humanity, I offer my obeisance from the sunset-crested end of my road.

I feel proud that I have been born in this great Age. I know that it must take time before we can adjust our minds to a condition which is not only new, but almost exactly the opposite of the old. Let us announce to the world that the light of the morning has come, not for entrenching ourselves behind barriers, but for meeting in mutual understanding and trust on the common field of co-operation; never for nourishing a spirit of rejection, but for that glad acceptance which constantly carries in itself the giving out of the best that we have.

Yours sincerely,
RABINDRANATH TAGORE

LECTURES AND ADDRESSES

Race Conflict

The problem of race conflict has ever been present in the history of mankind. This conflict has been at the basis of all great civilizations. It is like the clash of elements in the material world giving rise to complex combinations and evolutions of higher growth.

It was the concussion of peoples brought up in different surroundings and with different outlook upon life that started the original energy resulting in complicated social organizations. All civilizations are mixed products. Only barbarism is simple, monadic and unalloyed.

When differences have to be taken into account perforce, when there is no possible escape from them, then men are compelled to find out some central bond which can bring into unity all the diverse elements. This is really the seeking after truth, the search for the one in the many, the universal through the individuals.

Naturally, in the commencement its appearance is simple and crude. Some common visible object of worship is held as a symbol of the oneness of the people. It is very often gross and frightful. For when man has to depend upon external standards of life these have to be made as conspicuous as possible, and nothing is so compelling to primitive imagination as fear.

But, as the community grows larger and, by conquest and other means, peoples of different traditions unite, then fetishes multiply and more gods than one have to be recognized. In that case, these symbols lose their power as common bonds, and they have to be replaced by something whose appeal is not so much to the senses and whose significance is more universal.

Thus, gradually, as the problem grows more and more wide and complex, the solution of it becomes deeper and more far-reaching, and human solidarity seeks for its foundation something which is abiding and comprehensive. This is the purpose of all history, man seeking truth through complexities of experience impelled by the impetus of the immensity of evergrowing life.

There was a time when owing to the restricted means of communication different races and nations lived in a state of comparative segregation and consequently their social laws and institutions had an intensely local character. They were narrowly racial and aggressively hostile to the aliens. People did not have frequent occasion to learn how to adjust themselves with outsiders. They had to take to violent measures when they collided with alien people. They simplified the problem to its narrowest limits and either absolutely excluded and exterminated all foreign elements or completely amalgamated them.

Men have not yet outgrown this training of racial or national self-sufficiency. They are still burdened with the age-long inheritance of a suspicion of aliens which is the primitive instinct of animals. They still have a lurking ferocity ready to come out at the slightest provocation when in contact with people outside their social boundaries. They have not yet acquired fairness of mind when judging other races and dealing with them. They have not that power of adjusting their mental vision which would enable them to understand the people who are not nearest to them. They strive their utmost to prove the superiority and originality of their own religion and philosophy and they are reluctant to acknowledge that, truth, because it is truth, naturally manifests itself in different countries in different garbs. They are ever prone to put more stress on differences which are external and lose sight of the inner harmony.

This is the result of being brought up in the home training of isolation, which makes one unfit for the citizenship of the world. But this cannot continue for long and with the advent of the new age of science and commerce men have been brought nearer to each other than they ever were before and they are face to face with the highest problem of human history, the problem of race conflict.

This problem has been waiting to be solved by experience, through the expansion of history. It is not a mere matter of sentiment or of intellect. We had prophets who preached equality of man, and philosophy and literature which gave us a broader view of reality than is contained in the limits of racial traditions and habits. But this race problem with its vast complexity was never before us—we were not in living contact with it. Humanity, till now, has played with this sentiment of brotherhood of man as a girl does with her doll. It reveals the truth of the feeling which is innate in the heart of man, still it lacks the reality of life. But the playtime is passed and what was only in the sentiment has grown into our life fraught with immense responsibilities.

Of all the ancient civilizations, I think, that of India was compelled to recognize this race problem in all seriousness and for ages she has been engaged unravelling the most bafflingly complicated tangle of race-differences. Europe was fortunate in having neighbouring races more or less homogeneous, for, most of them were of the same origin. So, though in Europe there were bitter feuds between different peoples, there was not that physical antipathy between them which the difference in colour of skin and in feature tends to produce. In England it did not take long for the Norman and Saxon elements to coalesce and lose their distinctions. Not only in colour and features but in their ideals of life the western peoples are so near each other that practically they are acting as one in building up their civilization.

But it has been otherwise with India. At the beginning of Indian history the white-skinned Aryans had encounters with the aboriginal people who were dark and who were intellectually inferior to them. Then there were the Dravidians who had their own civilization and whose gods and modes of worship and social system were totally different from those of the newcomers, which must have proved a more active barrier between them than full-fledged barbarism.

In tropical countries life is not so strenuous as it is where the climate is cold. There the necessities of life are comparatively small and nature more prodigal in her bounties; therefore in those countries strifes between contending parties die away for want of incentives. So, in India, after a period of fierce struggles, men of different colours and creeds, different physical features and mental attitudes settled together side by side. As men are not inert matter but living beings, this juxtaposition of different elements became an ever-present problem for India. But with all its disadvantages this it was that stimulated men's minds to find out the essential unity in diversity of forms, to know that, however different be the symbols and rituals, God, whom they try to represent, is one without a second, and to realize him truly is to realize him in the soul of all beings.

When differences are too jarring, man cannot accept them as final; so, either he wipes them out with blood, or coerces them in some kind of superficial homogeneity, or he finds out a deeper unity which he knows is the highest truth.

India chose the last alternative; and all through the political vicissitudes that tossed her about for centuries, when her sister civilizations of Greece and Rome exhausted their life force, her spiritual vitality still continued and she still retains her dignity of soul. I do not say for a moment that the difficulties about the race differences have been altogether removed in India. On the contrary, new elements have been added, new complications introduced, and all the great religions of the world have taken their roots in the soil of India. In her attempts at bringing into order this immense mass of heterogeneity India has passed through successive periods of expansion and contraction of her ideals. And her latest has been that of setting up rigid lines of regulations to keep different sections at arm's length to prevent confusion and clash.

But such a negative attitude cannot last long, and mere mechanical contrivances can never work satisfactorily in human society. If, by any chance, men are brought together who are not products of the same history and not moulded in the same traditions, they never can rest till they can find out some broad basis of union which is positive in its nature and which makes for love. And I am sure, in India we have that spiritual ideal, if dormant but still living, which can tolerate all differences in the exterior while recognizing the inner unity. I feel sure, in India, we have that golden key forged by ancient wisdom and love which will one day open the barred gates to bring together to the feast of good fellowship men who have lived separated for generations.

From a very remote period of her history till now all the great personalities of India have been working in the same direction. The Gospel of universal love that Buddha preached was the outcome of a movement long preceding him, which endeavoured to get at the kernel of spiritual unity, breaking through all divergence of symbols and ceremonies and individual preferences.

With the advent of the Mohamedan power not only a new political situations was created in India but new ideas in religion and social customs were brought before the people with a violent force. Nevertheless, it had not the effect of generating an antagonistic fanatical movement among Hindus. On the contrary, all the great religious geniuses that were born during this period in India sought a reconciliation of the old with the new ideals in a deeper synthesis, which was possible because of the inherited spirit of toleration and accumulated wisdom of ages. In all these movements there was the repeated call to the people to forget all distinctions of castes and creeds and accept the highest privilege of brotherhood of man by uniting in love of God.

The same thing has occurred again when India has been closely brought in contact with the Christian civilization with the coming of the English. The Brahmo Samaj movement in India is the movement for the spiritual reconciliation of the East and West, the reconciliation resting upon the broad basis of spiritual wisdom laid in the Upanishads. There is again the same call to the people to rise above all artificial barriers of caste and recognise the common bond of brotherhood in the name of God.

In no other country in the world is the conflux of races different in every respect so great as in India. Therefore it never could have been possible for her to come to such a simple solution of the difficulty as national unity. The fetish of nationalism is powerless to bring her warring elements into a harmony; she must appeal to the highest power in man, the spiritual power, she must come to her God. There has been going on in India a long continued contention between rigid forms of exclusiveness which is mechanical and a recognition of the unity of mankind which is spiritual. Here, as in every land, the social convention is on the side of the pride of caste, and the higher nature and the deeper wisdom of the people assert in the lives of its greatest personalities the validity of the claims of all men to justice and love. On the one hand there is the regulation which forbids eating and drinking at the same board for men of different castes and on the other hand there comes the voice from the ancient past which preaches that he who realizes his own self in the self of all individuals realizes truly. And I have not the least doubt in my mind that it is the urging of this spiritual impulse in man which will win in the end, and will mould all the social forms in such a way that they may not hinder its purpose but become its instrument.

I bring before you this instance of Indian history to show that a problem must be a living one to rouse man's mind for its solution. It has become so in the present age. Races widely separated in their geographical position and historical growth, in their modes of thought and manners of expression have been brought near each other in closer relations. To each man the human world has been enlarged to an extent never dreamt of in former days. That we are not ready for these changed circumstances is becoming painfully evident every day. The caste feeling is running fearfully high. The western people are cultivating an arrogant exclusiveness against all other races. While keeping for themselves their prerogatives of exploiting weaker nations by threat of force they securely bar their own gates against them in a manner cruelly barbarous and inhospitable. Sentiments of humanity are openly discredited and poets of world-wide reputation are exulting in the triumph of brute force, Nations wakened from a lethargy of centuries and bravely struggling for a larger life are held back by others more fortunate, waiting to turn to their own advantage the situation created by the breaking up of old order. Want of consideration for people held to be inferior to themselves, rising into inhuman atrocities where privacy is secured, is not uncommon with the people proud of their colour and the impunity of their position.

Yet, in spite of these untoward aspects of the case I assert strongly that the solution is most assured when difficulties are greatest. It is a matter for congratulation that today the civilized man is seriously confronted with this problem of race conflict.

And the greatest thing that this age can be proud of is the birth of Man in the consciousness of men. Its bed has not been provided for, it is born in poverty, its infancy is lying neglected in a wayside stall, spurned by wealth and power. But its day of triumph is approaching. It is waiting for its poets and prophets and host of humble workers and they will not tarry for long. When the call of humanity is poignantly insistent then the higher nature of man cannot but respond. In the darkest periods of his drunken orgies of power and national pride man may flout and jeer at it, daub it as an expression of weakness and sentimentalism, but in that very paroxysm of arrogance, when his attitude is most hostile and his attacks most reckless against it, he is suddenly reminded that it is the direst form of suicide to kill the highest truth that is in him. When organized national selfishness, racial antipathy and commercial self-seeking begin to display their ugly deformities in all their nakedness, then comes the time for man to know that his salvation is not in political organizations and extended trade relations, not in any mechanical rearrangement of social system, but in a deeper transformation of life, in the liberation of consciousness in love, in the realization of God in man.

1912

The Spirit of Japan

One morning the whole world looked up in surprise, when Japan broke through her walls of old habits in a night and came out triumphant. It was done in such an incredibly short time, that it seemed like a change of dress and not like the slow building up of a new structure. She showed the confident strength of maturity and the freshness and infinite potentiality of new life at the same moment. The fear was entertained that it was a mere freak of history, a child's game of Time, the blowing up of a soap bubble, perfect in its rondure and colouring, hollow in its heart and without substance. But Japan has proved conclusively that this sudden revealment of her power is not a short-lived wonder, a chance product of time and tide, thrown up from the depth of obscurity to be swept away the next moment into the sea of oblivion.

The truth is that Japan is old and new at the same time. She has her legacy of ancient culture from the East,—the culture that enjoins man to look for his true wealth and power in his inner soul, the culture that gives self-possession in the face of loss and danger, self-sacrifice without counting the cost or hoping for gain, defiance of death, acceptance of countless social obligations that we owe to man as a social being,—the culture that has given us the vision of the infinite in all finite things, through which we have come to realize that the universe is living with a life and permeated with a soul, that it is not a huge machine which had been turned out by a demon of accidence or fashioned by a teleological God who lives in a far away heaven. In a word modern Japan has come out of the immemorial East like a lotus blossoming in an easy grace, all the while keeping its firm hold upon the profound depth from which it has sprung.

And Japan, the child of the Ancient East, has also fearlessly claimed all the gifts of the modern age for herself. She has shown her bold spirit in breaking through the confinements of habits, useless accumulations of the lazy mind, seeking safety in its thrift and its lock and keys. Thus she has come in contact with the living time and has accepted with an amazing eagerness and aptitude the responsibilities of modern civilization.

This it is which has given heart to the rest of Asia. We have seen that the life and the strength are there in us, only the dead crust has to be removed; that we must nakedly take our plunge into the youth-giving stream of the time-flood. We have seen that taking shelter in the dead is death itself, and only taking all the risk of life to the fullest extent is living.

Japan has taught us that we must learn the watchword of the age, in which we live, and answer has to be given to the sentinel of time, if we must escape annihilation. Japan has sent forth her word over Asia, that the old seed has the life germ in it, only it has to be planted in the soil of the new age.

I, for myself, cannot believe that Japan has become what she is by imitating the West. We cannot imitate life, we cannot simulate strength for long, nay, what is more, a mere imitation is a source of weakness. For it hampers our true nature, it is always in our way. It is like dressing our skeleton with another man's skin, giving rise to eternal feuds between the skin and the bones at every movement.

I have not had the opportunity of coming into intimate touch with Japan and forming my own opinion of what she truly is, where is her strength and where lie her dangers. For a person like myself belonging to the East, her present problems and her methods of solution of those problems are matters of utmost interest. The whole world waits to see what this great Eastern nation is going to do with the opportunities and responsibilities she has accepted from the hands of the modern time. If it be a mere reproduction of the West, then the great expectation she has raised will remain unfulfilled. For there are grave questions that the Western civilization has presented before the world but not completely answered. The conflict between the individual and the state, labour and capital, the man and the woman; the conflict between the greed of material gain and the spiritual life of man, the organized selfishness of nations and the higher ideals of humanity; the conflict between all the ugly complexities inseparable from giant organizations of commerce and state and the natural instincts of man crying for simplicity and beauty and fullness of leisure,—all these have to be brought to a harmony in a manner not yet dreamt of.

We have seen this great stream of civilization choking itself from debris carried by its innumerable channels. We have seen that with all its vaunted love of humanity it has proved itself the greatest menace to Man, far worse than the sudden outbursts of nomadic barbarism from which men suffered in the early ages of history. We have seen that, in spite of its boasted love of freedom, it has produced worse forms of slavery than ever were current in earlier societies,—slavery whose chains are unbreakable, either because they are unseen, or because they assume the names and appearance of freedom. We have seen, under the spell of its gigantic sordidness, man losing faith in all the heroic ideals of life which have made him great.

Therefore you cannot with a light heart accept the modern civilization with all its tendencies, methods and structures, and dream that they are inevitable. You must apply your Eastern mind, your spiritual strength, your love of simplicity, your recognition of social obligation, in order to cut out a new path for this great unwieldy car of progress, shrieking out its loud discords as it runs. You must minimize the immense sacrifice of man's life and freedom that it claims in its every movement. For generations you have felt and thought and worked, have enjoyed and worshipped in your own special manner; and this cannot be cast off like old clothes. It is in your blood, in the marrow of your bones, in the texture of your flesh, in the tissue of your brains; and it must modify everything you lay your hands upon, without your knowing, even against your wishes. Once you did solve the problems of man to your own satisfaction, you had your philosophy of life and evolved your own art of living. All this you must apply to the present situation and out of it will arise a new creation and not a mere repetition, a creation which the soul of your people will own for itself and proudly offer to the world as its tribute to the welfare of man. Of all countries in Asia, here in Japan you have the freedom to use the materials you have gathered from the West according to your genius and your need. You are fortunately not hampered from the outside, therefore your responsibility is all the greater, for in your voice Asia shall answer the questions that Europe has submitted to the conference of Man. In your land the experiments will be carried on by which the East will change the aspects of the modern civilization, infusing life in it where it is a machine, substituting human heart for cold expediency, not caring so much for power and success as for harmonious and living growth, for truth and beauty.

I cannot but bring to your mind those days when the whole of Eastern Asia from Burma to Japan was united with India in the closest tie of friendship, the only natural tie which can exist between nations. There was a living communication of hearts, a nervous system evolved through which messages ran between us about the deepest needs of humanity. We did not stand in fear of each other, we had not to arm ourselves to keep each other in check; our relation was not that of self-interest, of exploration and spoliation of each other's pockets; ideas and ideals were exchanged, gifts of the highest love were offered and taken; no difference of languages and customs hindered us in approaching each other heart to heart; no pride of race or insolent consciousness of superiority, physical or mental, marred our relation; our arts and literatures put forth new leaves and flowers under the influence of this sunlight of united hearts; and races belonging to different lands and languages and histories acknowledged the highest unity of man and the deepest bond of love. May we not also remember that in those days of peace and goodwill, of men uniting for those supreme ends of life, your nature laid by for itself the balm of immortality which has helped your people to be born again in a new age, to be able to survive its old outworn structures and take on a new young body, to come out unscathed from the shock of the most wonderful revolution that the world has ever seen? I cannot help thinking that it is only the divine in man that can perform this miracle of transmuting the old into the new, the weak into the strong, the insult into a glorious victory. And that divine in you was born, not in these sordid days of screeching machinery and gigantic selfishness, not amidst the blatant lies of statecraft and the smug self-satisfaction of prosperous hypocrisy, but in the dawn-light of that heroic manhood when heaven came nearer the earth, and man had faith in his own soul and the soul whose revelation is the world.

What has impressed me most in this country is the conviction that you have realized nature's secrets, not by methods of analytical knowledge, but by sympathy. You have known her language of lines and music of colours, the symmetry in her irregularities, and the cadence in her freedom of movements; you have seen how she leads her immense crowds of things yet avoids all frictions; how the very conflicts in her creations break out in dance and music; how her exuberance has the aspect of the fullness of self-abandonment, and not a mere dissipation of display. You have discovered that nature reserves her power in forms of beauty; and it is this beauty which, like a mother, nourishes all the giant forces at her breast, keeping them in active vigour, yet in repose. You have known that energies of nature save themselves from wearing out by the rhythm of a perfect grace, and that she with the tenderness of her curved lines takes away fatigue from the world's muscles. I have felt that you have been able to assimilate these secrets into your life, and the truth which lies in the beauty of all things has passed into your souls. A mere knowledge of things can be had in a short enough time, but their spirit can only be acquired by centuries of training and self-control. Dominating nature from outside is a much simpler thing than making her your own in love's delight, which is a work of true genius. Your race has shown that genius, not by acquirements, but by creation; not by display of things, but by manifestation of its own inner being. This creative power there is in all nations, and it is ever active in getting hold of men's natures and giving them a form according to its ideals. But here, in Japan, it seems to have achieved its success, and deeply sunk into the minds of all men, and permeated their muscles and nerves. Your instincts have become true, your senses keen, and your hands have acquired natural skill. The genius of Europe has given her people the power of organization, which has specially made itself manifest in politics and commerce and in coordinating scientific knowledge. The genius of Japan has given you the vision of beauty in nature and the power of realizing it in your life. And, because of this fact, the power of organization has come so easily to your help when you needed it. For the rhythm of beauty is the inner spirit, whose outer body is organization.

All particular civilization is the interpretation of particular human experience. Europe seems to have felt emphatically the conflict of things in the universe, which can only be brought under control by conquest. Therefore she is ever ready for fight, and the best portion of her attention is occupied in organizing forces. But Japan has felt, in her world, the touch of some presence, which has evoked in her soul a feeling of reverent adoration. She does not boast of her mastery of nature, but to her she brings, with infinite care and joy, her offerings of love. Her relationship with the world is the deeper relationship of heart. This spiritual bond of love she has established with the hills of her country, with the sea and the streams, with the forests in all their flowery moods and varied physiognomy of branches; she has taken into her heart and the rustling whispers and sighing of the woodlands and sobbing of the waves; the sun and the moon she has studied in all the modulations of their lights and shades, and she is glad to close her shops to greet the seasons in her orchards and gardens and cornfields. This opening of the heart to the soul of the world is not confined to a section of your privileged classes, it is not the forced product of exotic culture, but it belongs to all your men and women of all conditions. This experience of your soul, in meeting a personality in the heart of the world, has been embodied in your civilization. It is civilization of human relationship. Your duty towards your state has naturally assumed the character of filial duty, your nation becoming one family with your Emperor as its head. Your national unity has not been evolved from the comradeship of arms for defensive and offensive purposes, or from partnership in raiding adventures, dividing among each member the danger and spoils of robbery. It is not an outcome of the necessity of organization for some ulterior purpose, but it is an extension of the family and the obligations of the heart in a wide field of space and time.

And this has made me all the more apprehensive of the change, which threatens Japanese civilization, as something like a menace to one's own person. For the huge heterogeneity of the modern age, whose only common bond is usefulness, is nowhere so pitifully exposed against the dignity and hidden power of reticent beauty, as in Japan.

But the danger lies in this, that organized ugliness storm the mind and carries the day by its mass, by its aggressive persistence, by its power of mockery directed against the deeper sentiments of heart. Its harsh obtrusiveness makes it forcibly visible to us, overcoming our senses,—and we bring to its altar sacrifices as does a savage to the fetish which appears powerful because of its hideousness. Therefore its rivalry to things that are modest and profound and have the subtle delicacy of life is to be dreaded.

I am quite sure that there are men in your nation, who are not in sympathy with your national ideals; whose object is to gain, and not to grow. They are loud in their boast, that they have modernized Japan. While I agree with them so far as to say, that the spirit of the race should harmonize with the spirit of the time, I must warn them that modernizing is a mere affectation of modernism, just as affectation of poesy is poetising. It is nothing but mimicry,—only affectation is louder than the original, and it is too literal. One must bear in mind, that those who have the true modern spirit need not modernise, just as those who are truly brave are not braggarts. "Modernism is not in the dress of the Europeans; or in the hideous structures, where their children are interned when they take their lessons; or in the square houses with flat straight wall-surfaces, pierced with parallel lines of windows, where these people are caged in their lifetime; certainly modernism is not in their ladies' bonnets, carrying on them loads of incongruities." These are not modern, but merely European. True modernism is freedom of mind, not slavery of taste. It is independence of thought and action, not tutelage under European schoolmasters. It is science, but not its wrong application in life,—a mere imitation of our science teachers who reduce it into a superstition absurdly invoking its aid for all impossible purposes.

I do not for a moment suggest, that Japan should be unmindful of acquiring modern weapons of self-protection. But this should never be allowed to go beyond her instinct of self-preservation. She must know that the real power is not in the weapons themselves, but in the man who wields those weapons; and when he, in his eagerness for power, multiplies his weapons at the cost of his own soul, then it is he who is in even greater danger than his enemies.

Things that are living are so easily hurt; therefore they require protection. In nature, life protects itself within coverings, which are built with life's own material. Therefore they are in harmony with life's growth, or else when the time comes they easily give way and are forgotten. The living man has his true protection in his spiritual ideals, which have their vital connection with his life and grow with his growth. But, unfortunately, all his armour is not living,—some of it is made of steel, inert and mechanical. Therefore, while making use of it, man has to be careful to protect himself from its tyranny. If he is weak enough to grow smaller to fit himself to his covering, then it becomes a process of gradual suicide by shrinkage of the soul. And Japan must have a firm faith in the moral law of existence to be able to assert to herself, that the Western nations are following that path of suicide, where they are smothering their humanity under the immense weight of organizations in order to keep themselves in power and hold others in subjection.

Therefore I cannot think that the imitation of the outward aspects of the West, which is becoming more and more evident in modern Japan, is essential to her strength or stability. It is burdening her true nature and causing weakness, which will be felt more deeply as time goes on. The habits, which are being formed by the modern Japanese from their boyhood,—the habits of the Western life, the habits of the alien culture,—will prove, one day, a serious obstacle to the understanding of their own true nature. And then, if the children of Japan forget their past, if they stand as barriers, choking the stream that flows from the mountain peak of their ancient history, their future will be deprived of the water of life that has made her culture so fertile with richness of beauty and strength.

What is still more dangerous for Japan is not this imitation of the outer features of the West, but the acceptance of the motive force of the Western civilization as her own. Her social ideals are already showing signs of defeat at the hands of politics, and her modern tendency seems to incline towards political gambling in which the players stake their souls to win their game. I can see her motto, taken from science, "Survival of the Fittest," writ large at the entrance of her present-day history —the motto whose meaning is, "Help yourself, and never heed what it costs to others"; the motto of the blind man, who only believes in what he can touch, because he cannot see. But those who can see, know that men are so closely knit, that when you strike others the blow comes back to yourself. The moral law, which is the greatest discovery of man, is the discovery of this wonderful truth, that man becomes all the truer, the more he realizes himself in others. This truth has not only a subjective value, but is manifested in every department of our life. And nations, who sedulously cultivate moral blindness as the cult of patriotism, will end their existence in a sudden and violent manner. In past ages we had foreign invasions, there had been cruelty and bloodshed, intrigues of jealousy and avarice, but they never touched the soul of the people deeply; for the people, as a body, never participated in these games. They were merely the outcome of individual ambitions. The people themselves, being free from the responsibilities of the baser and more heinous side of those adventures, had all the advantage of the heroic and the human disciplines derived from them. This developed their unflinching loyalty, their single-minded devotion to the obligations of honour, their power of complete self-surrender and fearless acceptance of death and danger. Therefore the ideals, whose seats were in the hearts of the people, would not undergo any serious change owing to the policies adopted by the kings or generals. But now, where the spirit of the Western civilization prevails, the whole people is being taught from boyhood, to foster hatreds and ambitions by all kinds of means,—by the manufacture of half-truths and untruths in history, by persistent misrepresentation of other races and the culture of unfavourable sentiments towards them, by setting up memorials of events, very often false, which for the sake of humanity should be speedily forgotten, thus continually brewing evil menace towards neighbours and nations other than their own. This is poisoning the very fountain-head of humanity. It is discrediting the ideals, which were born of the lives of men, who were our greatest and best. It is holding up gigantic selfishness as the one universal religion for all nations of the world. We can take anything else from the hands of science, but not this elixir of moral death. Never think for a moment, that the hurts you inflict upon other races will not infect you, and the enmities you sow around your homes will be a wall of protection to you for all time to come. To imbue the minds of a whole people with an abnormal vanity of its own superiority, to teach it to take pride in its moral callousness and ill-begotten wealth, to perpetuate humiliation of defeated nations by exhibiting trophies won from war, and using these in schools in order to breed in children's minds contempt for others, is imitating the West where she has a festering sore, whose swelling is a swelling of disease eating into its vitality.

Our food crops, which are necessary for our sustenance, are products of centuries of selection and care. But the vegetation, which we have not to transform into our lives, does not require the patient thoughts of generations. It is not easy to get rid of weeds; but it is easy, by process of neglect, to ruin your food crops and let them revert to their primitive state of wildness. Likewise the culture, which has so kindly adapted itself to your soil,—so intimate with life, so human,—not only needed tilling and weeding in past ages, but still needs anxious work and watching. What is merely modern,—as science and methods of organization,—can be transplanted; but what is vitally human has fibres so delicate, and roots so numerous and far-reaching, that it dies when moved from its soil. Therefore I am afraid of the rude pressure of the political ideals of the West upon your own. In political civilization, the state is an abstraction and relationship of men utilitarian. Because it has no roots in sentiments, it is so dangerously easy to handle. Half a century has been enough for you to master this machine; and there are men among you, whose fondness for it exceeds their love for the living ideals which were born with the birth of your nation and nursed in your centuries. It is like a child, who, in the excitement of his play, imagines he likes his playthings better than his mother.

Where man is at his greatest, he is unconscious. Your civilization, whose mainspring is the bond of human relationship, has been nourished in the depth of a healthy life beyond reach of prying self-analysis. But a mere political relationship is all conscious; it is an eruptive inflammation of aggressiveness. It has forcibly burst upon your notice. And the time has come, when you have to be roused into full consciousness of the truth by which you live, so that you may not be taken unawares. The past has been God's gift to you; about the present, you must make your own choice.

So the questions you have to put to yourselves are these,—"Have we read the world wrong, and based our relation to it upon an ignorance of human nature? Is the instinct of the West right, where she builds her national welfare behind the barricade of a universal distrust of humanity?"

You must have detected a strong accent of fear, whenever the West has discussed the possibility of the rise of an Eastern race. The reason of it is this, that the power, by whose help she thrives, is an evil power; so long as it is held on her own side she can be safe, while the rest of the world trembles. The vital ambition of the present civilization of Europe is to have the exclusive possession of the devil. All her armaments and diplomacy are directed upon this one object. But these costly rituals for invocation of the evil spirit lead through a path of prosperity to the brink of cataclysm. The furies of terror, which the West has let loose upon God's world, come back to threaten herself and goad her into preparations of more and more frightfulness; this gives her no rest and makes her forget all else but the perils that she causes to others and incurs herself. To the worship of this devil of politics she sacrifices other countries as victims. She feeds upon their dead flesh and grows fat upon it, so long as the carcasses remain fresh,—but they are sure to rot at last, and the dead will take their revenge, by spreading pollution far and wide and poisoning the vitality of the feeder. Japan had all her wealth of humanity, her harmony of heroism and beauty, her depth of self-control and richness of self-expression; yet the Western nations felt no respect for her, till she proved that the bloodhounds of Satan are not only bred in the kennels of Europe, but can also be domesticated in Japan and fed with man's miseries. They admit Japan's equality with themselves, only when they know that Japan also possesses the key to open the floodgate of hell-fire upon the fair earth, whenever she chooses, and can dance, in their own measure, the devil dance of pillage, murder, and ravishment of innocent women, while the world goes to ruin. We know that, in the early stage of man's moral immaturity, he only feels reverence for the god whose malevolence he dreads. But is this the ideal of man which we can look up to with pride? After centuries of civilization nations fearing each other like the prowling wild beasts of the night time; shutting their doors of hospitality; combining only for purpose of aggression or defence; hiding in their holes their trade secrets, state secrets, secrets of their armaments; making peace offerings to the barking dogs of each other with the meat which does not belong to them; holding down fallen races struggling to stand upon their feet; counting their safety only upon the feebleness of the rest of humanity; with their right hands dispensing religion to weaker peoples, while robbing them with their left,—is there anything in this to make us envious? Are we to bend our knees to the spirit of this civilization, which is sowing broadcast over all the world seeds of fear, greed, suspicion, unashamed lies of its diplomacy, and unctuous lies of its profession of peace and goodwill and universal brotherhood of Man? Can we have no doubt in our minds, when we rush to the Western market to buy this foreign product in exchange for our own inheritance? I am aware how difficult it is to know one's self; and the man, who is intoxicated, furiously denies his drunkenness; yet the West herself is anxiously thinking of her problems and trying experiments. But she is like a glutton, who has not the heart to give up his intemperance in eating, and fondly clings to the hope that he can cure his nightmares of indigestion by medicine. Europe is not ready to give up her political inhumanity, with all the baser passions of man attendant upon it; she believes only in modification of systems, and not in change of heart.

We are willing to buy their machine-made systems, not with our heart, but with our brains. We shall try them and build sheds for them, but not enshrine them in our homes, or temples. There are races, who worship the animals they kill; we can buy meat from them, when we are hungry, but not the worship which goes with the killing. We must not vitiate our children's minds with the superstition, that business is business, war is war, politics is politics. We must know that man's business has to be more than mere business, and so have to be his war and politics. You had your own industry in Japan; how scrupulously honest and true it was, you can see by its products,—by their grace and strength, their conscientiousness in details, where they can hardly be observed. But the tidal wave of falsehood has swept over your land from that part of the world, where business is business, and honesty is followed in it merely as the best policy. Have you never felt shame, when you see the trade advertisements, not only plastering the whole town with lies and exaggerations, but invading the green fields, where the peasants do their honest labour, and the hill-tops, which greet the first pure light of the morning? It is so easy to dull our sense of honour and delicacy of mind with constant abrasion, while falsehoods stalk abroad with proud steps in the name of trade, politics and patriotism, that any protest against their perpetual intrusion into our lives is considered to be sentimentalism, unworthy of true manliness.

And it has come to pass, that the children of those heroes, who would keep their word at the point of death, who would disdain to cheat men for vulgar profit, who even in their fight would much rather court defeat than be dishonourable, have become energetic in dealing with falsehoods and do not feel humiliated by gaining advantage from them. And this has been effected by the charm of the word 'modern'. But if undiluted utility be modern, beauty is of all ages; if mean selfishness be modern, the human ideals are no new inventions. And we must know for certain, that however modern may be the proficiency, which clips and cripples man for the sake of methods and machines, it will never live to be old.

But while trying to free our minds from the arrogant claims of Europe and to help ourselves out of the quicksands of our infatuation, we may go to the other extreme and blind ourselves with a wholesale suspicion of the West. The reaction of disillusionment is just as unreal as the first shock of illusion. We must try to come to that normal state of mind, by which we can clearly discern our own danger and avoid it, without being unjust towards the source of that danger. There is always the natural temptation in us of wishing to pay back Europe in her own coin, and return contempt for contempt and evil for evil. But that again would be to imitate Europe in one of her worst features which comes out in her behaviour to people whom she describes as yellow or red, brown or black. And this is a point on which we in the East have to acknowledge our guilt and own that our sin has been as great, if not greater, when we insulted humanity by treating with utter disdain and cruelty men who belonged to a particular creed, colour or caste. It is really because we are afraid of our own weakness, which allows itself to be overcome by the sight of power, that we try to substitute for it another weakness which makes itself blind to the glories of the West. When we truly know the Europe which is great and good, we can effectively save ourselves from the Europe which is mean and grasping. It is easy to be unfair in one's judgment when one is faced with human miseries,—and pessimism is the result of building theories while the mind is suffering. To despair of humanity is only possible, if we lose faith in the power which brings to it strength, when its defeat is greatest, and calls out new life from the depth of its destruction. We must admit that there is a living soul in the West which is struggling unobserved against the hugeness of the organizations under which men, women and children are being crushed, and whose mechanical necessities are ignoring laws that are spiritual and human,—the soul whose sensibilities refuse to be dulled completely by dangerous habits of heedlessness in dealings with races for whom it lacks natural sympathy. The West could never have risen to the eminence she has reached, if her strength were merely the strength of the brute, or of the machine. The divine in her heart is suffering from the injuries inflicted by her hands upon the world,—and from this pain of her higher nature flows the secret balm which will bring healing to those injuries. Time after time she has fought against herself and has undone the chains, which with her own hands she had fastened round helpless limbs; and though she forced poison down the throat of a great nation at the point of the sword for gain of money, she herself woke up to withdraw from it, to wash her hands clean again. This shows hidden springs of humanity in spots which look dead and barren. It proves that the deeper truth in her nature, which can survive such career of cruel cowardliness, is not greed, but reverence for unselfish ideals. It would be altogether unjust, both to us and to Europe, to say that she has fascinated the modern Eastern mind by the mere exhibition of her power. Through the smoke of cannons and dust of markets the light of her moral nature has shone bright, and she has brought to us the ideal of ethical freedom, whose foundation lies deeper than social conventions and whose province of activity is world-wide.

The East has instinctively felt, even through her aversion, that she has a great deal to learn from Europe, not merely about the materials of power, but about its inner source, which is of mind and of the moral nature of man. Europe has been teaching us the higher obligations of public good above those of the family and the clan, and the sacredness of law, which makes society independent of individual caprice, secures for it continuity of progress, and guarantees justice to all men of all positions in life. Above all things Europe has held high before our minds the banner of liberty, through centuries of martyrdom and achievement,—liberty of conscience, liberty of thought and action, liberty in the ideals of art and literature. And because Europe has won our deep respect, she has become so dangerous for us where she is turbulently weak and false,—dangerous like poison when it is served along with our best food. There is one safety for us upon which we hope we may count, and that is, that we can claim Europe herself, as our ally, in our resistance to her temptations and to her violent encroachments; for she has ever carried her own standard of perfection, by which we can measure her falls and gauge her degrees of failure, by which we can call her before her own tribunal and put her to shame,—the shame which is the sign of the true pride of nobleness.

But our fear is, that the poison may be more powerful than the food, and what is strength in her to-day may not be the sign of health, but the contrary; for it may be temporarily caused by the upsetting of the balance of life. Our fear is that evil has a fateful fascination, when it assumes dimensions which are colossal,—and though at last it is sure to lose its centre of gravity, by its abnormal disproportion, the mischief which it creates before its fall may be beyond reparation.

Therefore I ask you to have the strength of faith and clarity of mind to know for certain, that the lumbering structure of modern progress, riveted by the iron bolts of efficiency, which runs upon the wheels of ambition, cannot hold together for long. Collisions are certain to occur; for it has to travel upon organized lines, it is too heavy to choose its own course freely; and once it is off the rails, its endless train of vehicles is dislocated. A day will come, when it will fall in a heap of ruin and cause serious obstruction to the traffic of the world. Do we not see signs of this even now? Does not the voice come to us, through the din of war, the shrieks of hatred, the wailings of despair, through the churning up of the unspeakable filth which has been accumulating for ages in the bottom of this civilization,—the voice which cries to our soul, that the tower of national selfishness, which goes by the name of patriotism, which has raised its banner of treason against heaven, must totter and fall with a crash, weighed down by its own bulk, its flag kissing the dust, its light extinguished? My brothers, when the red light of conflagration sends up its crackle of laughter to the stars, keep your faith upon those stars and not upon the fire of destruction. For when this conflagration consumes itself and dies down, leaving its memorial in ashes, the eternal light will again shine in the East,—the East which has been the birth-place of the morning sun of man's history. And who knows if that day has not already dawned, and the sun not risen, in the

Easternmost horizon of Asia? And I offer, as did my ancestor rishis, my salutation to that sunrise of the East, which is destined once again to illumine the whole world.

I know my voice is too feeble to raise itself above the uproar of this bustling time, and it is easy for any street urchin to fling against me the epithet of 'unpractical'. It will stick to my coat-tail, never to be washed away, effectively excluding me from the consideration of all respectable persons. I know what a risk one runs from the vigorously athletic crowds to be styled an idealist in these days, when thrones have lost their dignity and prophets have become an anachronism, when the sound that drowns all voices is the noise of the marketplace. Yet when, one day, standing on the outskirts of Yokohama town, bristling with its display of modern miscellanies, I watched the sunset in your southern sea, and saw its peace and majesty among your pine-clad hills,—with the great Fujiyama growing faint against the golden horizon, like a god overcome with his own radiance,—the music of eternity welled up through the evening silence, and I felt that the sky and the earth and the lyrics of the dawn and the dayfall are with the poets and idealists, and not with the marketsmen robustly contemptuous of all sentiments,—that, after the forgetfulness of his own divinity, man will remember again that heaven is always in touch with his world, which can never be abandoned for good to the hounding wolves of the modern era, scenting human blood and howling to the skies.

1915

The Meeting of the East and the West

For over a century and a half India has borne a foreign rule which is western. Whether she has been benefited by it, whether her arts and industries have made progress, her wealth increased and her opportunities of self-government multiplied, are a matter of controversy which is of very little material interest to the present generation of our countrymen, as it cannot change facts. Even from the point of view of historical curiosity it has a very imperfect value, for we are not allowed to remember all facts except in strict privacy. So I am not going to enter into any discussion which is sure to lead to an unsatisfactory conclusion or consequences.

But one thing about which there has been no attempt at concealment or difference of opinion is that the East and the West have remained far apart even after these years of relationship. When two different peoples have to deal with each other and yet without forming any true bond of union, it is sure to become a burden, whatever benefit may accrue from it. And when we say that we suffer from the dead weight of mutual alienation we do not mean any adverse criticism of the motive or the system of government, for the problem is vast and it affects all mankind. It inspires in our minds awe verging upon despair when we come to think that all the world has been bared open to a civilization which has not the spiritual power in it to unite, but which can only exploit and destroy and domineer and can make even its benefits an imposition from outside while claiming its price in loyalty of heart.

Therefore it must be admitted that this civilization, while it abounds in the riches of mind, lacks in a great measure to one truth which is of the highest importance to all humanity; the truth which man even in the dimmest dawn of his history felt, however vaguely it might be. This is why, when things go against them, the peoples brought up in the spirit of modern culture furiously seek for some change in organization and system, as if the human world were a mere intellectual game of chess where winning and losing depended upon the placing of pawns. They forget that for a man winning a game may be the greatest of his losses.

Men began their career of history with a faith in a Personal Being in relation to whom they had their unity among themselves. This was no mere belief in ghost but in the deeper reality of their oneness which is the basis of their moral ideals. This was the one great comprehension of truth which gave life and light to all the best creative energies of man, making us feel the touch of the infinite in our personality.

Naturally the consciousness of unity had its beginning in the limited area of race—the race which was the seed-plot of all human ideals. And therefore, and first, men had their conception of God as a tribal God which restricted their moral obligation within the bounds of their own people.

The first Aryan immigrants came to India with their tribal gods and special ceremonials and their conflict with the original inhabitants of India seemed to have no prospect of termination. In the midst of this struggle the conception of a universal soul, the spiritual bond of unity in all creatures, took its birth in the better minds of the time. This heralded a change of heart and along with it a true basis of reconciliation.

During the Mahomedan conquest of India, behind the political turmoil our inner struggle was spiritual. Like Asoka of the Buddhist age Akbar also had his vision of spiritual unity. A succession of great men of those centuries, both Hindu saints and Mahomedan sufis, was engaged in building a kingdom of souls over which ruled the one God who was the god of Mahomedans, as well as Hindus.

In India this striving after spiritual realization still shows activity. And I feel sure that the most important event of modern India has been the birth and life-work of Rammohun Roy, for it is a matter of the greatest urgency that the East and the West should meet and unite in hearts. Through Rammohun Roy was given the first true response of India when the West knocked at her door. He found the basis of our union in our own spiritual inheritance, in faith in the reality of the oneness of man in Brahma.

Other men of intellectual eminence we have seen in our days who have borrowed their lessons from the West. This schooling makes us intensely conscious of the separateness of our people giving rise to a patriotism fiercely exclusive and contemptuous. This has been the effect of the teaching of the west everywhere in the world. It has roused up a universal spirit of suspicious antipathy. It incites each people to strain all resources for taking advantages of others by force or by cunning. This cult of organized pride and self-seeking, this deliberate falsification of moral perspective in our view of humanity, has also invaded with a new force men's minds in India. If it does contain any truth along with its falsehood we must borrow it from others to mend our defect in mental balance. But, at the same time, I feel sure India is bid to give expression to the truth belonging to her own inner life.

Today the western people have come in contact with all races of the world when their moral adjustment has not yet been made true for this tremendous experience. The reality of which they are most fervidly conscious is the reality of the Nation. It has served them up to a certain point, just as some amount of boisterous selfishness, pugnacious and inconsiderate, may serve us in our boyhood, but makes mischief when carried into our adult life of larger social responsibilities. But the time has come at last when the western people are beginning to feel nearer home what the cult of the nation has been to humanity, they who have reaped all its benefits, with a great deal of its cost thrown upon the shoulders of others.

It is natural that they should realize humanity when it is nearest themselves. It increases their sensibility to a very high pitch, within a narrow range, keeping their conscience inactive where it is apt to be uncomfortable.

But when we forget truth for our own convenience, truth does not forget us. Up to a certain limit, she tolerates neglect, but she is sure to put in her appearance, to exact her dues with full arrears, on an occasion which we grumble at as inappropriate and at a provocation which seems trivial. This makes us feel the keen sense of the injustice of providence, as does the rich man of questionable history, whose time-honoured wealth has attained the decency of respectability, if he is suddenly threatened with an exposure.

We have observed that when the West is visited by a sudden calamity, she cannot understand why it should happen at all in God's world. The question has never occurred to her, with any degree of intensity, why people in other parts of the world should suffer. But she has to know that humanity is a truth which nobody can mutilate and yet escape its hurt himself. Modern civilization has to be judged not by its balance-sheet of imports and exports, luxuries of rich men, lengths of dreadnoughts, breadth of dependencies and tightness of grasping diplomacy. In this judgment of history, we from the East are the principal witnesses, who must speak the truth without flinching, however difficult it may be for us and unpleasant for others. Our voice is not the voice of authority, with the power of arms behind it, but the voice of suffering which can only count upon the power of truth to make itself heard.

There was a time when Europe had started on her search for the soul. In spite of all digressions she was certain that man must find his true wealth by becoming true. She knew that the value of his wealth was not merely subjective, but its eternal truth was in a love ever active in man's world. Then came a time when science revealed the greatness of the material universe and violently diverted Europe's attention to gaining things in place of inner perfection. Science has its own great meaning for man. It proves to him that he can bring his reason to co-operate with nature's laws, making them serve the higher ends of humanity; that he can transcend the biological world of natural selection and create his own world of moral purposes by the help of nature's own laws. It is Europe's mission to discover that Nature does not stand in the way of our self-realization, but we must deal with her with truth in order to invest our idealism with reality and make it permanent.

This higher end of science is attained where its help has been requisitioned for the general alleviation of our wants and sufferings, where its gifts are for all men. But it fearfully fails where it supplies means for personal gains and attainment of selfish power. For its temptations are so stupendously great that our moral strength is not only overcome but fights against its own forces under the cover of such high-sounding names as patriotism and nationality. This has made the relationship of human races inhuman, burdening it with repression and restriction where it faces the weak and brandishing it with vengefulness and competition of ferocity where it meets the strong. It has made war and preparation for war the normal condition of all nations, and has polluted diplomacy, the carrier of the political pestilence, with cruelty and dishonourable deception.

Yet those who have trust in human nature cannot but feel certain that the West will come out triumphant and the fruit of the centuries of her endeavour will not be trampled under foot in the mad scrimmage for things which are not of the spirit of man. Feeling the perplexity of the present-day entanglements she is groping for a better system and a wiser diplomatic arrangement. But she will have to recognize, perhaps at the end of her series of death-lessons, that it is an intellectual Pharisaism to have faith only in building pyramids of systems, that she must realize truth in order to be saved, that continually gathering fuel to feed her desire will only lead to world-wide incendiarism. One day she will wake up to set a limit to her greed and turbulent pride and find in compensation that she has an everlasting life.

Europe is great. She has been dowered by her destiny with a location and climate and race combination producing a history rich with strength, beauty and tradition of freedom. Nature in her soil challenged man to put forth all his forces never overwhelming his mind into a passivity of fatalism. It imparted in the character of her children the energy and daring which never acknowledge limits to their claims and also at the same time an intellectual sanity, a restraint in imagination, a sense of proportion in their creative works, and sense of reality in all their aspirations. They explored the secrets of existence, measured and mastered them; they discovered the principle of unity in nature not through the help of meditation or abstract logic, but by boldly crossing barriers of diversity and peeping behind the screen. They surprised themselves into nature's great storehouse of powers and there they had their fill of temptation.

Europe is fully conscious of her greatness and that itself is the reason why she does not know where her greatness may fail her. There have been periods of history when great races of men forgot their own souls in the pride and enjoyment of their power and possessions. They were not even aware of this lapse because things and institutions assumed such magnificence that all their attention was drawn outside their true selves. Just as nature in her aspect of bewildering vastness may have the effect of humiliating man, so also his own accumulation may produce the self-abasement which is spiritual apathy by stimulating all his energy towards his wealth and not his welfare. Through this present war has come the warning to Europe that her things have been getting better of her truth and in order to be served she must find her soul and her God and fulfil her purpose by carrying her ideals into all continents of the earth and not sacrifice them to her greed of money and dominion.

1918

At the Cross Roads

At the present moment the World Drama is at the change or its acts, and we do not know towards what denouement it is moving. This uncertainty has given rise to a universal perturbation of mind, from which India is not free. But having remained for long outside the arena of living and creative history, we are now, in this crisis, at a loss to know what to do, or how to think. Our mind is enveloped in the dust-storm of exaggerated hopes and fears, and this blinds us to the limitation of facts. When the promise of self-government suddenly showed signs of fulfilment, we failed to see clearly what it meant to us and how to claim it with justice. The hope of it was spread before us like a feast before the famine-stricken, and we did not know whether there was more danger in gorging ourselves or in desisting from it. The cruelty of the situation lies in the abnormal condition to which we have come through long years of deprivation.

I am fully aware that we have not had the training of taking up the tremendous responsibility of governing our country. The present upheaval in the West clearly shows what terrible power has gradually been concentrated in certain parts of the world, and what a menace it is to those who never had the opportunity or foresight to prepare to meet it. I have not the slightest doubt in any mind as to what would follow if India were completely left to herself. If the birth-throes of the new Japan were to happen at the present time, we know it would be throttled at its birth even as New Persia was.

But our problem is, how are we to receive our lessons in political wisdom discreetly gradual? When an Englishman in England discusses this, he bases his discussion on his full faith in his own countrymen. Personally, I myself have a great admiration for the English people. But it is not the best ideals of a people that govern a foreign country. The unnaturalness of the situation stands in the way, and everything tending to encourage the baser passions of man,—the contemptuous pride of power, the greed of acquisition,—comes upper-most. The responsibility of the weak is tremendous. They keep themselves too obscure to be able to claim human consideration, and the conscience of the strong grows inactive for want of proper stimulus. It is sure to cause moral degeneracy in men to exercise habitually authority upon an alien people and therefore not to encounter the checks that arise from the relationship of natural sympathy. This is evident to us, not only in the callous arrogance of the bureaucracy, but also in the policy of most of the Anglo-Indian newspapers, whose consistent chorus of clamour against the least expression of Indian aspiration, or the possibility of our gaining the slightest privilege now held by the rulers, becomes virulently cruel. It creates a vicious circle,—the helplessness of the governed sapping the moral manhood of the governors, and that again reacting upon the governed, prolonging and deepening their helplessness.

This is the reason why most of our countrymen find small consolation when they are told that the rights and the power of the government of their country will come to them gradually, as they are being made fit, from the hands which hold that power now. The gift is to be cautiously doled out to us by somebody who is critic, judge and donor combined,—and, naturally, not an over-enthusiastic donor. If we could be certain of a genuinely sympathetic guidance we would be content with very little at the commencement. But not having that full confidence in the bureaucratic agency of our donors, our people at the very outset claim those powers which, consciously or unconsciously, may be set against them in making it impossible for them to prove their fitness. No one can pretend to say that the British Government in India has been or ever can be disinterested. It is a dependency upon which depends the prosperity of England, though time may some day prove that such prosperity has not been for the good of the ruling country. But so long as the present cult of the self-worship of the Nation prevails, the subject races can only expect the fragmentary crumbs of benefit, and not the bread of life, from the hands of the powerful. It will ever be easy for the latter to find plausible arguments to keep the real power in their own hands and to prolong that state in which such arguments cannot effectively be refuted. For the ideal of the Nation is not a moral one,—all its obligations being based upon selfishness with a capital S. It principally recognizes expediency in its own conduct and power in that of its neighbours. And as expediency, in God's world, cannot wholly be dissociated from a moral foundation, it finds its place in the Nation's government of the alien people; but it is there on sufferance, it is only secondary, and therefore the Nation's relationship with the non-Europeans easily breaks out into rampage, which is, to speak mildly, not Christian.*

The question remains, what are we to do? Charity, on the one side, self-congratulatory and superior: humble acceptance of small favours on the other side, laudatory and grateful,—this is not the proper solution. We must have power in order to claim justice which is real. It is a blessing that we have the opposition of the powerful to overcome, that a boon cannot easily be given to us, even when there is some amount of willingness on the part of the giver. We must gain it through victory and never otherwise.

But whenever we speak of power and victory, the words at once conjure up pictures in our minds of Dreadnoughts, long-range guns and massacre of men by millions; because these belong to the great festival days of the religion of Nation-worship, when human sacrifices must be without limit. For, political and commercial ambition is the ambition of cannibalism, and through its years of accumulation it must get ready for its carnival of suicide.

I cannot imagine that we shall ever be able to enter into competition about their own methods and objects with these nation-worshippers, and the boon of their power which they get from their gods is not for us. We must confess that, in spite of considerable exceptions, the Hindu population of India does not consist of martial races. We do not have any natural pleasure or

---

* See passages quoted from M. Anatole France in "Gleanings" in this number.

pride in indulging in orgies of massacre for the sake of its glory. Some of our modern disciples of the West may blush to own it, but it is true that the religious training which we have got for ages has made us unfit for killing men with anything like a zest. No doubt, war was held to be a necessity, but only a particular body of men was specially trained for this work, and, for the rest of the members of society, even the killing of animals was held to be a sin. There is something very harshly unnatural and mock-heroic in the shrill pitch to which we have tuned our voice while vociferating that we are fighters and we must be fighters. I do not mean to say that by training and proper incentives a large number of us cannot be made into soldiers, but at the same time it will serve no good purpose if we delude ourselves into thinking that this is a vocation of life in which we can excel. And if, for the want of natural ferocity in our blood, we cannot excel in this the Europeans, who at present hold the world in their grasp, our soldiers' training will merely entitle us to fight in a subordinate position, which, from a material point of view, will bring us meagre benefits and from a higher one will be productive of evil.

I have been accused of going to the absurdity of the extreme for insisting upon an idealism which cannot be practical. But I assert that the absurdity is not in the idealism itself, but in our own moral shortsightedness. What they mean by saying that we must be practical is that we must live, and in this one cannot but agree, for suicide can never be an ultimate object for any creature. But fortunately for man his existence is not merely physical or even political. Man has attained all that is best in him by strongly believing that there are things for which he can afford to die. To ask him to lay down his life for some political good, and at the same time to be miserly where the moral good of humanity is in view, is to ask him to pay the highest price yet refuse to accept the thing of the highest value.

There are things in which men *do* go to extremity in the teeth of practical common sense. We have heard of instances where men, set adrift on the sea without provisions, have looked upon each other as possible food in case of emergency. But those exceptions among them who could not think of such an enormity in any conceivable circumstance, have done more permanent service to man by refusing to eat human flesh and dying, than those who survived by following the contrary course. And for nations also, it is wise not to indulge in cannibalism even at the risk of non-survival. For true survival is to live beyond life.

We must bear in mind that European civilization, which is based on militant Nationalism, is on its trial in this war. We do not know what is going to be the end of it; for this may not be the last of such wars in Europe. But one thing has been made quite evident, that the attainment of political power has not the moral ideal behind it which can give it the true permanence of finality. Greece still lives where she was truly great, not in her possessions, but in her mind, and Rome survived the wreck of Empires where she attained the immortal. For centuries the Jews have had no political existence, but they live in the best ideals of Europe leavening its intellectual and spiritual life. The political ambitions of fighting races leave no other legacy to humanity but the legacy of ruins; and the power which grows tremendous, following its narrow channel of self-seeking, is sure to burst its bonds and end in a deluge of destruction.

And therefore, let us not seek the power which is in killing men and plundering them, but the moral power to stand against it, the moral power to suffer,—not merely in passive apathy, but in the enthusiasm of active purpose. This is an age of transition. The Dawn of a great To-morrow is breaking through its bank of clouds and the call of New Life comes with its message that man's strength is of the spirit, and not of the machine of organization. It will be the greatest sign of weakness in us,—the most abject defeat,—if we still cling to the atheistic faith that those nations who thrive upon their victims are great because they are powerful, and that sacrifices have to be brought to the altar of their false gods.

I know that an instinctive faith in the adequacy of moral ideals and the inner strength of the spirit for building up the world anew from its wreckage will be held as the sign of ignorance of world politics; for it does not wholly tally with the experience of the past. But all the fearful danger of the present day has come from that experience hardening into a crust obstructing the growth of spiritual humanity,—the humanity which aspires after an infinite inner perfection. The present-day Civilized Man, disillusioned and doubting, suffers from the moral senility of prudent worldliness, that knows too much but does not believe. Faith is of the future; it may lead us into danger or apparent futility; but Truth waits there for us to be courted at the risk of death or failure.

The immense power of faith which man possesses has lately been concentrated on his material possibilities. He ignored all checks from his past experiences when he believed that he could fly in the air; and even repeated failures and deaths have not deterred him from attaining this seeming impossibility. But he has grown cynically sceptic concerning the infinite reality of the moral laws.

The time for this prudent man has come near its end. The world is waiting for the birth of the Child, who believes more than he knows, who is to be the crowned King of the future, who will come amply supplied with provisions for his daring adventures in the moral world, for his explorations in the region of man's inner being.

We have heard that Modern Russia is floundering in its bottomless abyss of idealism because she has missed the sure foothold of the stern logic of Real Politik. We know very little of the history of the present revolution in Russia, and with the scanty materials in our hands we cannot be certain if she, in her tribulations, is giving expression to man's indomitable soul against prosperity built upon moral nihilism. All that we can say is that the time to judge has not yet come,—especially as Real Politik is in such a sorry plight itself. No doubt if Modern Russia *did* try to adjust herself to the orthodox tradition of Nation-worship, she would be in a more comfortable situation to-day, but this tremendousness of her struggle and hopelessness of her tangles do not, in themselves, prove that she has gone astray. It is not unlikely that, as a nation, she will fail; but if she fails with the flag of true ideals in her hands, then her failure will fade, like the morning star, only to usher in the sunrise of the New Age. If India must have her ambition, let it not be to scramble for the unholy feast of the barbarism of the past night, but to take her place in the procession of the morning going on the pilgrimage of truth,—the truth of man's soul.

1918

The Message of The Forest

The past not only contains, in its depths, the unrealized future, but in part the realized future itself. Everybody admits the truth, that, in the grandfather, lies dormant the potential grandson, who is to carry the growth of his ancestry to a further stage, or in a new direction. But it is also true that the grandson is practically born in the grandfather. New additions are made and modifications effected, but some keynote, that is to dominate the racial life, has already been achieved in the life of the grandfather.

This is the reason, why every race of people has its tradition of the Golden Age in the past, because we never can trust our future, if it does not carry some great promise bequeathed to it. It is not enough for us to know, that our future is growing out clearer from the nebulous adumbration of a primitive age, we must also be assured that it has already shown itself distinct in its achievements in the past. Every great people hold its history so valuable because of this, because, it contains not mere memories, but hope, and therefore the image of the future. Man has his instinctive faith in heredity. He feels, that, in heredity, that which is to come has been proved in that which has been,—in great heredity, the great conclusion is perpetually present in the process. And all history is man's credential of his future, signed and sealed by his past.

The physical organization of the race has certain vital memories, which are persistent, which fashion its nose and eyes in a particular shape, regulate its stature and deal with the pigment of its skin. In the ideal of a race, there also run memories that remain constant, or, in case of alien mixture, come back repeatedly, even after the lapse of long intervals. These are the compelling forces, that secretly and inevitably fashion the future of a people and give characteristic shape to its civilization. In our Shastras, it is held that our desires are the creative factors which originate and guide our future births.

Likewise every race has its innate desires, of its former days, leading it through the repeated new births of its history. Any people which lacks, in its racial mind, these inherited aspirations, merely drifts, till it sinks in the current of time; it never creates its own history. In a word, it does not renew its birth, but is merged in the amorphous vagueness of a ghostly existence.

Therefore, it is of great importance for us to know, whether, as a people, we carry in our subconscious mind some primal aspiration, which alone can guarantee us a definite future of our own. If we still have that, strong and living, it will save us from extinction, or from the perpetual shame,—worse than death,—of the life of imitation, or parasitism. When we are threatened with loss of self-respect; when our mind is overwhelmed with the idea, that there can be only one type of civilization worth the name, and that a foreign one; when our one conscious desire is to strive with all our might, by begging, borrowing or stealing, towards some ideal of perfection which can only be related to us, as a mask to a face, or a wig to a head,—then our only hope lies in discovering some profound creative desire persistent in the heart of our race, in the subconscious mind of our people. For, in the long run, it is our subconscious nature which wins, and it is the deeper unseen current of the mind which secretly cuts its own path and reaches its own goal,—not the conscious waves on the surface, which clamorously make themselves obvious and vigorously storm at the present time.

I have said elsewhere, that the environment, in which we see the past of India, is the forest, the memory of which permeates our classical literature and still haunts our minds. The legends related in our great epics cluster under the sublime shade of those ancient forests; and, in the forest, the most intense pathos of human life found its background in the greatest of our romantic dramas. The memory of these sacred forests is the one great inheritance which India ever cherishes through all her political vicissitudes and economic disturbances.

But we must know, that these forests were not merely topographical in their significance. We have seen that the history of the Northmen of Europe is resonant with the association of the sea. That sea, also, is not a mere physical fact, but represents certain ideals of life which still guide their history and inspire all their creations. In the sea, Nature presented herself to these men in her aspect of a danger, of a barrier, which seemed to be at constant war with the land and its children. The sea was the challenge of untamed Nature to the indomitable human soul. And man did not flinch; he fought and won; and the spirit of fight continued in him. He looked upon his place in the world as extorted from a hostile scheme of things, retained in the teeth of opposition. His cry is the cry of triumph of defiant Man against the rest of the universe.

This is about the people who lived by the sea, and rode on it as on a wild champing horse, clutching it by its mane and making it render service from shore to shore. But in the level tracts of *Aryavarta* men found no barrier between their lives and the Grand Life that permeates the Universe. The forest gave them shelter and shade, fruit and flower, fodder and fuel; it entered into a close living relation with their work and leisure and necessity, and in this way made it easy for them to know their own lives as associated with the larger life. They could not think of their surroundings as lifeless, separate, or inimical. So the view of the Truth, which these men found, was distinctly different from that of those of whom we have spoken above; and their relationship with this world also took a different turn, as they came to realize that the gifts of light and air, of food and drink, did not come from either sky or tree or soil, but had their fount in the all-pervading consciousness and joy of universal life. They uttered quite simply and naturally यदिदम् किञ्च सर्व्वम् प्राण एजति निष्टतम्—"All that is, vibrates with life, having emerged from the Supreme Life."

When we know this world as alien to us then we know it as a thing mechanical, built by a divine mechanic or by a chance combination of blind forces. Then our relation to it becomes the relation of utility, and we set up our own machines or mechanical methods to deal with it and make as much profit as our knowledge of its mechanism allows us to do. Then we are apt to say that Knowledge is power. This view of things does not altogether play us false, for the machine has its place in this world. And therefore, not only this material universe, but also human beings can be used as machines and made to yield results. But the view of the world which India has taken is summed up in one compound word—सच्चिदानन्द. Its meaning is that Reality, which is essentially one, has three aspects. The first is *sat,* the principle of Being, whose first information comes to us through our senses; it relates us to all things through the relationship of common existence. The second is *chit,* the principle of Knowing; it relates us to all things through the relationship of mind. The third is *ananda*—the principle of Enjoying—which unites us with all things through the relationship of love. Our consciousness of the world as that of the sum total of things that exist or that are governed by universal laws is imperfect according to the true Indian view,—but it is perfect when our consciousness realizes all things as spiritually one with it and therefore capable of giving us joy. Our text of daily meditation contains the truth of the one and the same creative force appearing in an undivided stream of manifestation in our consciousness and in the world of which we are conscious. They are one, as the East and the West are one, which only our self divides into contradictions. For us the highest purpose of this world is not merely living in it, knowing it and making use of it, but realizing our own selves in it through expansion of sympathy and emancipation of consciousness, not alienating and dominating it but comprehending and uniting it with us in blissful union. The Man whom you only use is a machine; the Man whom you only study is a material for your knowledge. But your friend is neither a machine to you nor a psychological curiosity, (though consciously or unconsciously he does take his part as a machine of work and as an object of study for you), his ultimate value lies in his giving you opportunity to lose yourself in his love. This is his aspect of *ananda*—his truest aspect for you, which comprehends his other two aspects in harmony. And to know the highest truth of all existence as that of a friend is truly Indian. This view of the world as the world of life and love, as the manifestation of the Supreme Soul whose nature is to realize his unity in the endlessness of the varied, has come to us from the great peace of our ancient forest.

When Vikramāditya became king, Ujjain a great capital, and Kālidāsa its poet, the age of India's forest retreats had passed. Then we had taken our stand in the midst of the great concourse of humanity, and the Chinese and the Hun, the Scythian and the Persian, the Greek and the Roman, had crowded round us. But even in this age of pride and prosperity, the longing love and awe of reverence with which its poet sang about the hermitage, shows what was the dominant ideal that occupied the mind of India, what was the one current of memory that continually flowed back through her life.

In Kālidāsa's drama *Shakuntala*, also, the hermitage, which dominates the play, overshadowing even the king's palace, has the same idea running through,—the recognition of the kinship of man with conscious and unconscious creation alike.

A poet of a later age, while describing a hermitage in his *Kadambari*, tells of the posture of devoutness in the flowering lianas as they bow to the wind; of the sacrifice offered by the trees scattering their blossoms; of the grove sounding with the lessons chanted by the neophytes, and the *mantras* which the parrots, constantly hearing, had learned to pronounce; of the wild fowl enjoying *Vaishva-deva-bali-pinda*—the food offered to the divinity which is in all creatures,—and of the ducks coming up from the lake, nearby, for their portion of the grass-seed, spread in the cottage yards to dry; of the deer caressing with their tongues the young hermit boys. It is again the same story. The hermitage shines out, in all our ancient literature, as the place where the chasm between man and the rest of creation has been bridged.

In the drama of other countries, where the human characters violently drown our attention in the vortex of their passions, Nature occasionally peeps in, but she is almost always a trespasser, who has to submit urgent excuses, or bow apologetically and depart. But in all our dramas, which still retain their fame, such as *Mrichchhakatika, Shakuntala, Uttara-Rama-Charita*, Nature stands on her own right, proving that she has her great function, to impart the peace of the eternal to the human passions and to mitigate their violent agitations which often come from the instability of spiritual lameness.

The frenzied fury of passion, described in two of Shakespeare's youthful poems, stands isolated upon its own pedestal of unashamed conspicuity. It is wrenched away naked from the cover of the All; it has not the green earth or the blue sky around it; the many-coloured veil of nature has been impatiently swept away from its face, bringing to our view the fever which is in man's desires, and not the healing balm which encircles it in the universe.

Ritusamhara is clearly a work of Kalidasa's immaturity. The song of youthful love sung in it sounds from the fundamental bass notes of human passion,—it does not reach the sublime height of reticence that there is in *Shakuntala* or *Kumara Sambhava*. But the tune of these voluptuous outbreaks, being set to the varied harmony of Nature's symphony, loses its delirious shrillness in the expanse of the open sky. The moon-beams of the summer evening, resonant with the murmuring flow of fountains, add to it their own melody; in its rhythm sways the *Kadamba* grove, glistening in the first cool rain of the season; and the south breezes waft into its heart the wistfulness of the scent of the mango flowers.

In the third canto of *Kumara Sambhava,* while describing the boisterous emergence of youth at the sudden coming of *Madana* (Eros), Kalidasa has been careful to avoid giving this outburst of passion an abnormal supremacy within the narrow field of view of exclusive humanity. His genius basked in the sunshine of the human spirit, where it pervades the spring flower and the harvest of the autumn; and that genius never played at focussing it into a point of ignition upon the naked fluttering heart. Kalidasa has shown a true reverence to the divine love-making of Sati by making his narration of it as a central white lotus floating on the world-wide immensity of youth, in which the animals and trees have their rhythm of life-throbs. It is a sacred flame of longing whose lamp is the universe.

Not only its third canto, but the whole of the *Kumara Sambhava* poem is painted upon a limitless canvas. Its inner idea is deep and of all time. It answers the one question that humanity asks through all its endeavours: How is the birth of the hero to be brought about,—the brave one who can defy and vanquish the evil demon, when he sweeps upon the scene, laying waste heaven's own kingdom? This is the greatest of all problems for each individual, and it forces itself in ever-new, ever-recurring forms upon each race and nation, and this is the one problem which persists in most of our poet's works,—in his *Shakuntala, Raghuvamsha* and *Kumara Sambhava*.

It becomes evident that such a problem had become acute in Kalidasa's time, when the old simplicity of Hindu life had broken up. The Hindu kings, forgetful of their kingly duties, had become self-seeking epicureans, and India was being repeatedly devastated by the Shakas.

But what answer does the poem give to the question it raises?—Not that more armaments were needed, or that a league of powers should be formed, or that some mechanical adjustment of political balance had to be effected. Its message is that the cause of weakness lies in the inner life of the soul. It is in some break of harmony with the Good, some dissociation from the True. When gain is completed by giving up, when love is fulfilled by self-sacrifice, when passion is purified by the penance of the soul, then only is heroism born,—the heroism which can save mankind from all defeat and disaster. When the ascetic Shiva—the Good—was lost in the passive immensity of his solitude, heaven was in peril. And when beautiful Sati—the Real—was all by herself, in her unwedded self-seclusion, the demons were triumphant. Only from the union of the exuberant freedom of the Real with the tranquil restraint of the Good comes the fullest strength.

Viewed from the outside, India, in the time of Kalidasa, appeared to have reached the zenith of civilization, excelling as she did in luxury, literature and the arts. Kalidasa himself was not free from the prevailing tone, and the outer embellishment of his poetry is as daintily luxurious as must have been the decorative art of the period. This, however, is only one aspect in which his age influenced the poet.

But what sudden passion for sacrifice, for the austere discipline of the life of aspiration, troubled our Goddess of

Poesy amidst the luxury of her golden bower? It was the eternal message of the forest, that can never be silenced, and like a refrain, simple in its purity, comes up again and again, through all noisy distractions of discord,—the message to free our consciousness from the accumulations of desire, to win our immortality, by breaking through the sheath of self, the self which belongs to death. From his seat beside all the glories of Vikramaditya's throne, the poet's heart yearned for the purity of India's past age of spiritual striving. And it was this yearning which took shape and impelled him to go back to the annals of the ancient kings of Raghu's line.

'I fain would sing,' says Kalidasa, in his prologue, 'of those whose purity went back to the day of their birth, whose striving went forward till attainment, whose empire knew no bounds but the seas, whose adventurous journeys reached up to the high heaven, who offered oblations to the sacred fire in accordance with injunctions, made gifts to the needy in accordance with their wants, awarded punishments in accordance with the crime, and regulated every wakeful activity in accordance with the hour,—who accumulated treasure for the sake of redistribution, tempered their utterance for the sake of truth, desired victories for the sake of glory, entered into wedlock for the sake of progeny,—who practised learning in their childhood, attended to wealth in their youth, took to the hermitage in their old age, cast away their bodies when they had attained the supreme union. Of these would I sing, though I lack all wealth of language; for their great merits, entering my ears, have disturbed my heart.'

But it was not in a paean of praise that his poem ended. What had troubled his heart becomes clear, when we come to the end of his Raghuvamsha. What was the life story of the founder of this line of Kings? Where did it begin?

The heroic life of Raghu had its prologue in a hermitage, showing that its origin was in a life of purity and self-restraint, led there by Raghu's royal parents. The poem is not ushered in with the pomp and circumstance befitting the history of a great kingly line. King Dilip, with his consort, Queen Sudakshina, has entered upon the life of the forest. The great monarch is busy tending the cattle of the hermitage. Thus opens the Raghuvamsha amidst scenes of simplicity and self-denial. But it ends in the palace of magnificence, in the wealth and luxury which divert the current of energy from the truth of life to the heaps of things. There is brilliance in this ending, as there is in the conflagration which destroys and devastates. Peaceful as the dawn, radiant as the tawny-haired hermit boy, is the calm strength of the restrained language in which the poet tells us of the kingly glory crowned with the halo of purity,—beginning his poem, as the day begins, in the serene solemnity of its sunrise. And lavish are the colours in which he describes the end, as of the evening, eloquent for a time with its sumptuous splendour of sunset, but overtaken at last by the devouring darkness which sweeps away all its brilliance into the fathomless abyss of night.

In this beginning and this ending of his poem, lies hidden the message of the forest which found its voice in the poet's words. With a suppressed sigh he is saying: 'Look on that which was and that which is! In the days when the future glowed gloriously ahead, self-discipline was esteemed as the highest path, self-renunciation the greatest treasure, but when downfall had become imminent, the hungry fires of desire aflame at a hundred different points, dazzled the eyes of all beholders.'

When the lust of self-aggrandizement is unbridled, the harmony between enjoyment and renunciation is destroyed. By concentrating our pride or desire upon a limited field, the field of the animal life, we seek to exaggerate a portion at the expense of the whole, the wholeness which is in man's life of the spirit. From this results evil. That is why renunciation becomes necessary,—not to lead to destitution, but to restoration, to win back the All.

Kalidasa in almost all his works, has depicted this break of harmony between enjoyment and renunciation, between the life that loses itself in the sands of the self and the life that seeks its sea of eternity. And this is characteristically represented by the unbounded impetuousness of kingly splendour on one side and the serene strength of regulated desires on the other. I have already given above an illustration of this from the *Raghuvamsha*.

Even in the minor drama of *Malavikagnimitra* we find the same thing in a different manner. It must never be thought that, in this play, the poet's deliberate object was to pander to his royal patron by inviting him to a literary orgy of lasciviousness. The very *Nandi* contradicts this and shows the object towards which this play is directed. The poet begins the drama with the prayer, 'सम्मार्गालोकयन् व्यपनयतु स नस्तामसौष्ठत्तिभोगः' 'Let God, to illumine for us the path of truth, sweep away our passions, bred of darkness.' The God, to whom this prayer is uttered, says the poet, is one in whose nature Eternal Woman is ever commingled, in an ascetic purity of love,—who stands in the sacred simplicity of barenness in the midst of his infinite wealth. The unified being of Hara and Parvati is the perfect symbolism of the eternal in the wedded love of man and woman. The poet opens his drama with the invocation of this spirit of the Divine Union. It is quite evident that this invocation carries the message in it with which he greeted his kingly audience. The whole drama is to show in vivid colour the utter ugliness of the treacherous falsehoods and cruelties inherent in all passions that are unchecked. In this play the conflict of ideals is between the king and the queen,—between Agnimitra and Dharini, between the insolent offence against all that is good and true, and the unlimited peace of forgiveness that dwells deep in the self-sacrifice of love. The great significance of this contrast lies hidden in the very names of the hero and the heroine of the drama. Though the name '*Agnimitra*' is historical, yet it symbolises in the poet's mind the desolating destructiveness of uncontrolled desire,—just as did the name of *Agnivarna* in *Raghuvamsha*. *Agnimitra,*—'the friend of the fire',—the reckless person, who in his love-making is playing with fire, not knowing that, all the time, it is scorching him black, till the seed of immortality perishes at the core of his being. And what a great name is *Dharini,* signifying the fortitude and forbearance that comes of the majesty of soul! What association it carries of the infinite dignity of love purified by the sacrificial fire of self-abnegation rising far above all insult of base betrayal! Can anybody doubt what effect the performance of this drama produced upon the royal looker-on, what searching of heart, what humility, what reverence for the love that claims our best worship by the offer of its patient worship of service!

In Shakuntala, this conflict of ideals has been shown all through the drama, by the contrast of the pompous heartlessness of the king's court and the natural purity of the hermitage, the contrast of the arrogance displaying itself upon the hollow eminence of convention, and the simplicity standing upon the altitude of truth. The message of the poet is uttered by the two hermit boys, when they enter the king's palace, just before the impending catastrophe of Shakuntala's life, the naked cruelty of which is skilfully hidden by the episode of the curse, though it was unbarred a moment before through the shameless self-confession of fickleness by the king, when he listened to the lamentation of Hamsapadika, one of his numerous victims. The message is:

> अभ्यक्तमिव स्नातः शुचिरशुचिमिव प्रवुच इव सुप्तम्
> वचामिव स्वैरगतिर्जनमिह सुखसडिंगतम् अवैमि।
>
> We look upon these devotees of pleasure as he, who has bathed, looks upon the unclean, as the pure in heart upon the polluted, as the wide awake soul looks upon the slothful slumberer, and as the one, who is free to move, looks upon the shackled.

And what is the inner meaning of the curse that follows the hermit girl in this drama, till she is purified by her penance? I am sure, according to the poet, it is the same curse from which his country at that time suffered. There were two guests who knocked at the gate of Shakuntala of whom one was accepted and the other refused. The king, as an embodiment of passion and worldliness, came to her and she readily yielded to his allurements. But when after that the duty of the higher life, the spirit of the forest ideal, stood before her in the guise of an ascetic, she in her absent-mindedness did not notice him. And what was the result? She lost her world of desire for which she had forsaken her truth. And in order to regain that world as her own by right she had to follow through suffering the path of self-conquest. The poet was aware of the two guests who sought entrance into the heart of his country,—the devotee of pleasure and power who comes secretly without giving his real name and insinuates himself into trustful acceptance, and the seeker of spiritual perfection who announces himself in a master's voice, in clear notes, अयमहं भोः—'I am here!' And to his dismay he found his country baring her heart to the former to be betrayed by him. It is evident that kings of that period were deeply drawn into the eddy of self-indulgence and were fighting each other for power, the love of which leads men into the insanity of suicide. The fatal curse of falsehood is always generated when power and success are pursued for their own sake, when our baser passions shamelessly refuse all claims of justice and self-control. The poet had one lingering ray of hope in his heart. He could not but believe that his country had not lost her reverence for her *tapaswi*, the guest who brings to her door the message of everlasting life: only her mind was distracted by some temporary outbreak of temptation. He was certain that she would wake up in sanctifying sorrow, and give birth to her Bharata, the hero who would bring to her life unity and strength of truth. There was a note of assurance in the poet's voice when through his great poems Kumara-Sambhava and Shakuntala he called her to come back once again to her purity of life and realization of soul, the call which is true for other times and other countries also. For the curse still remains to be worked off by humanity for the inhospitable insult offered to the Eternal in Man.

The drama of Shakuntala opens with a hunting scene, where the king is in pursuit of an antelope. This indulgence in sport appears like a menace symbolising the spirit of the king's life clashing against the spirit of the forest-retreat, where all creatures find their protection of love. And the pleading of the forest-dwellers to the king, to spare the life of the deer, helplessly innocent and beautiful, is the pleading that rises from the heart of the whole drama.

न खलु न खलु बाणः सन्निपात्योऽयमस्मिन् ।
मृदुनि मृगशरीरे पुष्प राशाविवाग्निः ॥

Never, oh never is the arrow meet for piercing the tender body of a deer, as the fire is not for burning flowers.

The living beauty, whose representative in this drama is Shakuntala, is not aggressively strong like the callous destructiveness of lust, but, through its frailness, it is sublimely great. And it is the poet's pleading which still rings in our ears against the ugly greed of commercialism in the modern age, against its mailed fist of earth-hunger, against the lust of the strong, which is grossly intent upon killing the Beautiful and piercing the heart of the Good to the quick. Once again sounds the warning of the forest, at the conclusion of the first act, when the king is engaged in fateful dalliance with the hermit girl: 'O *Tapaswis*, hasten to rescue the living spirit of the sacred forest, for Dushyanta, the lord of earth, whose pleasure is in hunting, is come.' It is the warning of India's past, and that warning still continues against the reckless carnival of the present time, celebrated by the lords of Earth, whose pleasure is in hunting to death with their ruthless machines all that is beautiful with the delicacy of life.

In *Kumara-Sambhava,* the friend and ally of Indra, the king of the Gods, is Madana, the god of desire. And he, in his blindness, imagines that he can unite Shiva and Parvati by the delusion created by the madness of the senses. It is the same as when we try to reach our perfection through wealth and power, through the intensity of boisterous self-seeking. That is not to be. At last Parvati's love was crowned with fulfilment through her penance of self-sacrifice. The moral of the *Kumara-Sambhava* is the same as the teaching of the Upanishat: त्यक्तकेन भुञ्जी, 'enjoy through renunciation'. मा गृधः कस्यस्विज्जनम् 'Enjoyment not be through greed.'

One thing which we must remember is, that the life in ancient India was not all forest life,—nor is the heart the only organ we possess in our vital organism. But the heart lies in the centre of our body; it purifies our blood and sends our life-current through the ramifications of all the channels in our body to the extremities of our limbs. Our *tapovana* was just such a vital centre of our social body. In it throbbed the rhythm of our life's ebb and flow: it gave truth to our thoughts, right impulse to our feelings, and guiding force to our work. We distinctly see, from the works of our poet, that the teaching of the forest was not towards the inertia of passivity, but towards true heroism and victory. It was not towards suppression of action, but its purification, towards giving it freedom of life by removing obstructions.

We know of other great systems in which there is a special insistence upon sacrifice and resignation. Just as heat is an important factor in the process of creation, so is pain an essential reagent in the formation of man's life. It melts the intractable hardness of his spirit, and wears away the unyielding crust which confines his heart. But the Upanishat enjoins renunciation, not by way of acceptance of pain, but for the purpose of enjoyment of truth. Such renunciation means an expansion into the Universal, a union with the Supreme. It is the renunciation of the cocoon for the freedom of the living wings. So that the ideal hermitage of ancient India was not a theatre where the spirit should wrestle with the flesh, or where the monastic order should try conclusions with the social order,—it was to establish a harmony between all our energies and the eternal reality. That is why the relations of Indian humanity with beast and bird and tree had attained an intimacy which may seem strange to people of other lands. Our poets have told us that the *tapovana* is *shantarasaspadam,*—that the emotional quality peculiar to the forest-retreat is Peace, the peace which is the emotional counterpart of perfection. Just as the mingling of the colours of the spectrum gives us white light, so when the faculties of our mind, instead of being scattered, flow in a united stream, in harmony with the universal purpose, then does peace result—the peace which pervaded India's forest retreats, where man was not separate from, and had no quarrel with, the rest of his surroundings.

The two hermitages, which we have in the drama of Shakuntala, serve to give a magnitude to her joy and sorrow. One of these hermitages was on earth, the other on the border of the abode of immortals. In the first, we see the daughter of the hermitage watching in delight the union of the sweet flowering creeper with the mango tree round which it has twined; or busy rearing motherless young deer with handfuls of grass-seed, and picking the spear-grass out from their tender mouths, soothing the pricks with healing oil. This hermitage serves to make simple, natural and beautiful the love of the king for the hermit girl. The other hermitage was on the great cloud-like massive Hemakuta peak, standing like Shiva, with his locks of forest-growths and tangled creepers, lost in meditation, its gaze fixed on the sun. In this, Marichi, the revered preceptor of both Gods and Titans, together with his wife, was engaged in the pursuit of self-realization. There, when the young hermit boys would playfully snatch from the lioness her suckling cub, its distress would greatly exercise the tāpasa Mother. The second hermitage, in turn, serves to mellow with a great peace and purity the sorrow and insult which had driven Shakuntala there.

It has to be realized, that the former is of the earth, the region of the mortals, the latter of heaven, the region of the immortals. In other words, the one represents, 'what is,' the other 'what should be.' The unceasing movement of 'what is' is towards 'what should be.' It finds its true freedom in that movement. The first is Sati—the Real—the last Shiva, the Good. In the life of Shakuntala, likewise, the 'what is' had to find its fulfilment in the 'what should be.' What was of the earth had to come, through the path of sorrow, to the border of heaven.

Those who have followed the evolution of the principal idea in this drama,—its seed-life in the soil of passion, its deliverance of harvest in the sunlight of the purity of self-abnegation,—will understand the great poet Goethe's criticism of Shakuntala, so tersely expressed in a single verse:

> Wouldst thou the flower of the spring and fruit of the mature year,
> Wouldst thou what charms and enraptures and what feeds and nourishes,
> Wouldst thou heaven and earth in one name entwined,
> I name thee, O Shakuntala, and all is said.

For in Shakuntala the reconciliation is given, through the penance of pain and sacrifice, to the pair of contraries, that which attracts and that which gives freedom, the limitation of self and the dedication of self to the Eternal. Goethe's own drama Faust, in its first and in its second part, tries to show the same separation and then reconciliation between the Real and the Good, between Sati and Shiva.

However, my point is this, that the scene of such reconciliation is depicted, both in *Shakuntala* and in *Kumara-Sambhava*, upon the background of the *tapovana,* showing whence the spring of the ideal harmony welled forth, the harmony between Nature and man, between the life in the individual and life in the All.

In the Ramayana, Rama and his companions, in their banishment, had to traverse forest after forest; they had to live in leaf-thatched huts, to sleep on the bare ground. But as their hearts felt their kinship with woodland, hill and stream, they were not in exile amidst these. Poets, brought up in an atmosphere of different ideals, would have taken this opportunity of depicting in dismal colours the hardship of the forest-life in order to bring out the martyrdom of Ramachandra in the strong emphasis of contrast. But, in the Ramayana, we are led to realize the greatness of the hero, not in an inimical struggle with nature, but in sympathy with it.

Sita, the daughter-in-law of a great kingly house, goes along the forest paths.

एकैकं पादपं गुल्मं लतां वा पुष्पशालिनीम्
अदृष्ठरूपां पश्यन्तौ रामं पप्रच्छ सावला ।
रमणीयान् बहुविधान् पादपान् कुसुमोत्करान्
सीतावचनसंरब्ध आनयामास लक्ष्मणः ।
विचित्रवालुकाजलां हंससारसनादिताम्
रेमे जनकराजस्य सुता प्रेक्षा तदा नदीम् ॥

She asks Rama about the flowering trees and shrubs and creepers which she has not seen before. At her request, Lakshmana gathers and brings her plants of all kinds exuberant with flowers, and it delights her heart to see the forest rivers, variegated with their streams and sandy bank, resounding with the calls of heron and duck.

सुरभ्यमासाद्य तु चित्रकूटम्
मदीञ्च तां मालयवतीं सुतीर्थाम्

ननन्द दृष्टो मृगपक्षिजुष्टाम्
अहो च दुःखं पुरविप्रवासात् ॥

When Rama first took his abode in the Chitrakuta peak, that delightful *Chitrakuta,* by the *Malyavati* river, with its easy slopes for landing, he forgot all the pain of leaving his home in the capital at the sight of these woodlands, alive with beast and bird.

दीर्घकालोषितस्तस्मिनौ गिरी गिरिवनप्रियः having lived on that hill for long, Rama, who was गरिवनप्रिय, lover of the mountain and the forest, said one day to Sita:

न राजामंशमं भद्रे न कुचदिंभर्विनाभवः
मनो मे बाधते दष्टा रमणीयमिमं गिरिम्

When I look upon the beauties of this hill, the loss of my kingdom troubles me no longer, no does the separation from my friends cause me any pang.

When they went over to the Dandaka forest, they saw there a hermitage with a halo round it caused by the sacrificial fires blazing like the sun itself. This ashram was शरण्यम् सर्व्वभूतानाम् the refuge of all creatures; it was enfolded by *Brahmi Lakshmi*, the Spirit of the Infinite.

Thus passed Ramachandra's exile, now in woodland, now in hermitage scenes. The love which Rama and Sita bore each other united them, not only to each other, but to the Universe of life. That is why, when Sita was taken away, the loss seemed to be very great to the forest itself. The extinction of a star is doubtless a mighty event in the world of stars; and we would know, if we had pure vision, that any infliction of injury in the heart of a true lover gives rise to suffering which belongs to all the world. Sita's abduction robbed the forest of the most beautiful of its blossoms, the ineffable tenderness of human love,—that which imparted the mystery of a spiritual depth to all its sounds and forms.

Strangely enough, in Shakespeare's dramas, like those of Kalidasa, we find a secret vein of complaint against the artificial life of the king's court, the life of ungrateful treachery and falsehood. And almost everywhere, in his dramas, forest scenes have been introduced in connection with some working of the life of unscrupulous ambition. It is perfectly obvious in 'Timon of Athens'—but there Nature offers no message or balm to the injured soul of man. In 'Cymbeline' the mountainous forest and the cave appear in their aspect of obstruction to life's opportunities—which only seem tolerable in comparison with the vicissitudes of fortune in the artificial court life, as expressed by Belarius:

'Did you but know the city's usuries,
And felt them knowingly, the art o the court,
As hard to leave as keep; whose top to climb
Is certain falling, or so slippery that
The fear's as bad as falling:'

In 'As You Like It' the Forest of Arden is didactic in its lessons,—It does not bring peace, but it preaches when it says:

Hath not old custom made this life more sweet
Than that of painted pomp? Are not these woods
More free from peril than the envious court?

In the 'Tempest' in Prospero's treatment of Ariel and Caliban we realize man's struggle with nature and his longing to sever connection with her. In 'Macbeth,' as a prelude to a bloody crime of treachery and treason, we are introduced to a scene of barren heath where the three witches appear as the personification of Nature's malignant forces; and in 'King Lear,' it is the fury of a father's love turned into curses by the ingratitude born of the unnatural life of the court, that finds its symbol in the storm in the heath. The extreme tragic intensity of 'Hamlet' and 'Othello' is unrelieved by any touch of Nature's eternity. Excepting in a passing glimpse of a moonlight night in the love scene in the 'Merchant of Venice' Nature has not been allowed in other dramas of this series, including 'Romeo and Juliet' and 'Antony and Cleopatra,' to contribute her own music to the music of man's love. In 'The Winter's Tale' the suspicious cruelty of a king's love stands bare in its relentlessness, and Nature cowers before it offering no consolation. I hope it is needless for me to say that these observations of mine are not for criticizing Shakespeare's great power as a dramatic poet, but to show in his works the gulf between nature and human nature owing to the tradition of his race and time. It cannot be said that beauty of nature is ignored in his writings; only he fails to recognize in them the truth of the interpenetration of human life and the cosmic life of the world. When literature takes for its object the exhibition of the explosiveness of a human passion, then necessarily that passion is made detached from its great context of the universe and is shown in its extreme violence generated by the instability of equilibrium. And this is what we find in Elizabethan dramas,—the clash of passions in their fury of self-assertion. We observe a sudden and a completely different attitude of mind in the later English poets, like Wordsworth and Shelley, which can only be attributed to the great mental change in Europe, at that particular period, through the influence of the newly-discovered philosophy of India which stirred the soul of Germany and strongly roused the attention of other Western countries.

In Milton's 'Paradise Lost,' the very subject,—Man dwelling in the garden of Paradise,—seems to afford a special opportunity for bringing out the true greatness of man's relationship with Nature. But though the poet has described to us the beauties of the garden, though he has shown us the animals living there in amity and peace among themselves, there is no reality of kinship between them and man. They were created for man's enjoyment; man was their lord and master. We find no trace of the love of the first man and woman surpassing themselves and over-flowing the rest of creation, such as we find in the love scenes in *Kumara-Sambhava* and *Shakuntala* and in our Vaishnava lyrics, where love finds its symbols in the beauty of all natural objects. But in the seclusion of the bower, where the first man and woman rested in the garden of paradise,

Bird, beast, insect or worm
Durst enter none, such was their awe of man.

At the bottom of this gulf between man and Nature there is the lack of the message,—ईशावास्यमिदम् सर्व्वम् 'know all that is, as enveloped by God'. According to this epic of the West, God remains aloof to receive glorification from his creatures. The same idea persists in the case of man's relation to the rest of creation.

Not that India denied the superiority of man, but the test of that superiority lies, according to her, in the comprehensiveness of sympathy,—not in the aloofness of absolute distinction.

The love of Rama and Sita, in the *Uttara Rama Charita* has permeated the surrounding earth, water and sky with its exuberance. When Rama, for the second time, finds himself on the banks of the Godavari, he exclaims: यत्र द्रुमा अपि मृगा अपि बान्धवो मे 'this is the place even whose deer and whose trees are my friends'. When after Sita's exile he comes across some former haunt of theirs, he laments that his heart, even though turned to stone, melts when he sees the trees and the deer and the birds which Sita's own hands used to nourish with water, seed and grass.

In the *Meghaduta,* the exiled Yaksha is not shut up within himself in his grief. The very agony of his separation from his loved one serves to scatter his heart over the woods and streams, enriched by the prodigality of the rains. And so the casual longing of a love-sick individual has become part of the symphony of the universe. And this is the outcome of the spirit of teaching which springs from the ancient forest.

India holds sacred, and counts as places of pilgrimage, all spots which display a special beauty or splendour of nature. These had no original attraction, or account of any special fitness to be cultivated, or lived upon. Here, man is free, not to look upon nature as a source of supply of his necessities but to realize his soul beyond himself. The Himalayas of India are sacred and the Vindhya Hills. Her majestic rivers are sacred. Like Manasa and the confluence of the Ganges and the Jamuna are sacred. India has saturated with her love and worship the great nature with which her children are surround, whose light fills their eyes with gladness, whose water cleanses them, whose food gives them life, and from whose majestic mystery come forth constant messages of the infinite in music, scent, and colour, bringing awakening to their souls. India has gained the world through worship,—through communion of soul. And this is her heritage from her forest sanctuary.

Learning does not depend on the school alone. Much more does it depend upon the receptive mind of the pupil. There are scholars who win diplomas, but fail to learn. So do many of us frequent-places of pilgrimage, but come away from the door of the invisible shrine, where dwells the Eternal spirit of the place. They imagine that the mere journey to a place held sacred is sanctifying, that some peculiar virtues reside in particular soils and waters. Their minds do not shrink at the unspeakable pollution of the water and the air of those places, the pollution to which they themselves contribute, and the moral filth which they allow to accumulate there. The salutation of worship to the all-pervading divinity in the fire, water and plants, in all creation, has been bequeathed to us by our ancestors in the following immortal verse:

> यो देवोऽग्नो योऽप्सु यो विश्वम् भुवनमाविवेश
> य ओषधिषु यो वनस्यतिषु तस्मै देवाय नमो नमः ।

But we seem to have forgotten that all worship has also its duty of service, and in order truly to realize and approach the divine presence in the water and the air we have reverently to keep them clean and pure and healthful. The more our country has lost its powers of soul, the more elaborate have become its outward practices. The inner illumination of consciousness which is not only the object, but also the means of all true worship has, in our case, given place to the grossness of the senses and deadness of mere repetition of habits. But, even in these days of our spiritual sluggishness, I am unwilling to accept these mechanical practices as a permanent feature of India. It is absurd to believe as well-founded the idea, that a bath in a particular stream procures for the bather and millions of his ancestors a more favourable circumstance and desirable accommodation in the after life. Nor am I able to respect such a belief as something admirable. But my reverence goes out to the man, who when taking an immersion, can receive the water upon his body, and into his mind as well, in a devout spirit;—

for him the grimy touch of habit has not been able to tarnish the everlasting mystery which is in fire and earth, water and food; he has overcome, by the sensitiveness of his soul, the gross materialism,—the spirit of contempt, of the average man, which impels the latter to look upon water as mere liquid matter.

So long as man was unable to realize an all-pervading law in the material world, his knowledge remained petty and unfruitful. But the modern man feels himself united to the universe by physical laws governing all. This is Science's great achievement.

The quest which India set to herself was to realize the same unity in the realm of the spirit, that is to say, in its completeness. Such union enables us to see Him in all who is above all else. And the wisdom, which grew up in the quiet of the forest shade, came out of the realization of this Greater-than-all in the heart of the all.

Let no one think that I desire to extol this achievement, as the one and the only consummation. I would rather insist on the inexhaustible variety of the human race, which does not grow straight up, like a Palmyra tree, on a single stem, but like a banian tree spreads itself in ever-new trunks and branches. Man's history is organic, and deep-seated life-forces work towards its growth. It is hopeless to cater to some clamorous demand of the moment, by endeavouring to fashion the history of one people on the model of another,—however flourishing the latter may be. A small foot may be the sign of aristocratic descent, but the Chinese woman's artificial attempt has only resulted in cramped feet. For India to force herself along European lines of growth would not make her Europe, but only a distorted India.

That is why we must be careful to-day to try to find out the principles, by means of which India will be able for certain to realize herself. That principle is neither commercialism, nor nationalism. It is universalism. It is not merely self-determination, but self-conquest and self-dedication. This was recognized and followed in India's forests of old; its truth was declared in the Upanishad and expounded in the Gita; the Lord Buddha renounced the world that he might make this truth a household word for all mankind; Kabir, Nanak and other great spirits of India continued to proclaim its message. India's grand achievement, which is still stored deep within her heart, is waiting, to unite within itself Hindu, Moslem, Buddhist, and Christian, not by force, not by the apathy of resignation, but in the harmony of active co-operation.

An almost impossible task has been set to India by her Providence, a task given to no other great countries in the world. Among her children and her guests differences in race and language, religion and social ideals are as numerous as great, and she has to achieve the difficult unity which has to be true in spite of the separateness that is real. The best and the greatest of her sons have called us in immortal words to realize the unity of souls in all human beings and thus fulfil the highest mission of our history; but we have merely played with their words, and we have rigidly kept apart man from man, and class from class, setting up permanent barriers of indignity between them. We remained unconscious of the suicidal consequence of such divisions, so long as we lay stationary in the torpor of centuries, but when the alien world suddenly broke upon our sleep and dragged us on in its impetus of movement, our disjointed heterogeneity set up in its lumbering unwieldiness an internal clash and crush and unrhythmic stagger which is both ludicrous and tragic at the same moment. So long as we disregard or misread the message of our ancient forest, the message of all-pervading truth in humanity, the message of all-comprehensive union of souls which rises above all differences and goes deeper than mere expediency, we shall have to go on suffering sorrow after sorrow and endless humiliation, and in all things futility.

1919

Construction Versus Creation

Construction is for a purpose, it expresses our wants; but creation is for itself, it expresses our very being. We make a vessel because water has to be fetched. It must answer the question why. But when we take infinite trouble to give it a beautiful form, no reason has to be assigned. It is something which is ultimate; it is for the realization of our own spirit which is free, which is glad. If, in the works of our life, needs make themselves too domineering, purposes too obtrusive, if something of our complete humanity is not expressed at the same time, then these works become ugly and unspiritual.

In love, in goodness, man himself is revealed; these express no want in him; they show the fulness of his nature which flows out of himself and therefore they are purely creative. They are ultimate—therefore, in our judgment of man's civilization, they give us the true criterion of perfection.

Creation is the revelation of truth through the rhythm of forms. It has a dualism consisting of the expression and the material. Of these two wedded companions the material must keep in the background and continually offer itself as a sacrifice to its absolute loyalty to the expression. And this is true of all things, whether in our individual life or in our society.

When the material makes itself too aggressive and furiously multiplies itself into unmeaning voluminousness, then the harmony of creation is disturbed and truth is obscured. If the lamp takes a perverse pride in displaying its oil, then the light remains unrevealed. The material must know that it has no idea of completeness in itself, that it must not hold out temptations to decoy men under its destination away from their creative activities.

The laws of grammar are necessary for the construction of a poem, but the readers must not be made conscious of their constant dictatorship. In classical India we have a Sanskrit poem in which all the complex grammatical rules are deliberately illustrated. This gives continual shocks of delight to a class of readers who, even in a work of art, seek some tangible proof of power almost physical in its manifestation. This proves that by special cultivation a kind of mentality can be produced which is strangely capable of taking delight in contemplating the mere spectacle of power manipulating materials, forgetting that materials are not the truth. And these people of an athletic habit of mind encourage artists to sacrifice art to the vanity of performance, simplicity of truth to the antics of cleverness.

What is the truth of the world? Its truth is not the mass of materials, but their universal relatedness. A drop of water is not a particular assortment of elements, it is their mutuality. In fact matter, as a mass, is an abstraction to us; we know it by a betrayal of secret through science. We do not directly perceive it. We see a flower, but not matter. Matter in a laboratory has its use but no expression. This expression alone is creation; it is an end in itself. So also does our civilization find its completeness when it expresses humanity, not when it displays its power to amass materials.

I have said that the truth of this world is in its law of relatedness, that is to say, the law of keeping step together. For the world is a movement, and this movement must not be retarded in any of its parts by a break of cadence. The world of men is suffering the agony of pain, because its movements are not in harmony with one another, because the relationship of races has not yet been established in a balance of beauty and goodness. This balance cannot be maintained by external regulation. It is a dance which must have music to regulate it. This great music is lacking in the historical meeting of man which has taken place in the present age, and all its movements in their discongruity are creating complexities of pain.

We know of an instance in our own history of India when a great personality[1] struck up in his life and voice the key-note of the solemn music of man-love for all creatures. And that music crossed the sea and the mountain and the desert, and races belonging to different climes and habits and languages were

1. Gautama Buddha.

drawn together, not in a clash of arms or in the conflict of exploitation but in co-operation of life, in amity and peace. This was a creation. The great rhythm of this symphony was in the very heart of the world. This rhythm is what metre is to a poem, not a mere enclosure for keeping ideas from running off in disorder, but a vitalizing force, making them indivisible in a unity of creation.

When humanity lacks this music of soul, then society becomes a mechanical arrangement of compartments, of political and social classifications. Such a machine is a mere aping of creation, and not having unity at its heart it enforces it in its outer structure for mere convenience. In it the life that grows and feels is hurt, and either is crushed into insensibility or breaks out in constant convulsions.

The vital harmony is lacking to-day in unity of man, for the formalness of law and regulation has displaced the living ideal of personality from human affairs, and science has taken the office of religion in man's greatest creative work, his civilization.

The diversion of man's energy to the outside is producing an enormous quantity of materials which may give rise in us to the pride of power but not the joy of life. The hugeness of things is every day overawing the greatness of man, and the gap between matter and life is growing wider. For when things become too many, they refuse to be completely assimilated to life, thus becoming its most dangerous rival, as is an excessively large pile of fuel to the fire.

Expression belongs to a different plane from that of its material. Our physical body has its elaborate mechanism for its various vital needs. Yet the wholeness of our body, where it is an expression, where it is one with our personality, is absolutely different in its aspect and meaning from the muscular, vascular or nervous system, and it keeps its veil strictly drawn. The physiological mechanism as an organ of efficiency carefully exacts from its means and methods their full equivalents in results. But the body is more than this mechanism, it is divine. An exhaustive list of all its functions fails to give us its definiteness. It is a creation and not a mere construction, rising far above its purposes and composition. Creation is infinitely in excess of all measurements, it is the immaterial in matter.

In all art every display of power is vulgar, and a true artist is humble in his creation. He despises making a show of material in his work and a parade of the difficulties of its process. For the power which accumulates things and manipulates them is fundamentally different from the power which transmutes them into the perfection of a creative unity.

And God is humble in His creation. He does not keep His muscles bared, nor does He go out of His way to attract our attention to His store of things or account-book of their cost. He gives out Himself in the abundance of His nature.

It is the final object of man to prove his similarity of nature with God by his fulness of truth, by his creativeness. Whatever he does solely in obedience to natural law, goaded by hunger or other compulsions, he feels at heart to be alien to his own nature. He somehow feels a shame about their evidence in his life and tries to put a cover over it, some cover fashioned by his own creative mind.

For instance, in his necessity for eating there is no difference between man and other creatures, yet he seems unwilling fully to acknowledge this and consequently tries to hide away the hunger element from his meals till it is almost lost to sight. He takes endless care to make his food ornamental and likewise the vessel out of which he takes it. And so, with regulations and designs of his own make, he sets up an elaborate pretension that he is not busy satisfying any legitimate need of the physiological nature.

This is the process by which the unnecessary has assumed an enormously greater proportion than the necessary in our civilization. In its own turn it begets the danger of burdening us with fixed necessities of habit which have not the sanction of nature nor that of our creative freedom but get merely piled up into a refuse heap of conventionality.

It may be said that as life is a growth it cannot have a completeness of expression and, therefore, its only true expression is vigour. As intensity of passion leading to a variety of emotional experiences, and adventures of mind giving rise to a wealth of power and production, constitute what they call living, vigour of feeling and intellect is no doubt a great asset of life. But life, merely taken as a force, is elemental, it is not human. It has its use like steam and electricity, but there is no ideal of perfection in it. Those who make such life an object of their worship lose all pity for the personal man and have no compunction in sacrificing individuals to their blind infatuation for power and experiences. And I repeat it once again that life can only become an end in itself when it is a creation, just as the elements that go to the composition of a flower are fulfilled only when they are a flower.

Growth there must be in life. But growth does not mean an enlargement through additions. Things, such as masonry-structure, which have to be constructed by a gradual building up of materials, do not show their perfection until they are completed. But living things start with their wholeness from the beginning of their growth. Life is a continual process of synthesis. A child is complete in itself; it does not wait for the perfection of its lovability till it has come to the end of its childhood. The enjoyment of a song begins from the beginning of the singing and continually follows its course to the end. But the man whose sole concern is the acquisition of power or material deals with a task which is cursed with eternal incompleteness. For things find no meaning in themselves when their magnitude consists solely of accumulated bulk. They acquire truth only when they are assimilated to a living idea. This assimilation becomes impossible so long as the passion for acquisition occupies all our mind, when there is no large leisure for life force to pursue its own great work of self-creation.

There was a time when commerce was restricted to a narrow circle in society, and was meek enough to acknowledge its limitations. In spite of its usefulness men treated it with condescension, even with disrespect. This was because man tried to maintain an imperious aloofness from all exacting needs, and, while accepting their services, he refused to do homage to them. I believe and hope that in the range of all literature and art there is no single instance of a monied man being glorified for the mere sake of his money. Our Laxmi[1] is not the goodness of the cash balance in the bank: she is the symbol of that ideal plenitude which is never dissociated from goodness and beauty.

But in recent centuries has come a devastating change in our mentality with regard to the acquisition of money. We not only pursue it but bend our knees to it. For us its call has become the loudest of all voices, reaching even the sanctuaries of our temples. That it should be allowed a sufficiently large place in society there can be no question, but it becomes an outrage when it occupies those seats which are specially reserved for the immortals, by bribing us, by tampering with our moral pride, by recruiting the best strength of society on its side in a traitor's campaign against human ideals, disguising with the help of pageantry and pomp its innate insignificance.

Such a state has come to pass because, with the help of science, the possibility of profit has suddenly become immoderate. The whole of human society throughout its length and breadth has felt the gravitational pull of a giant planet of greed with its concentric rings of innumerable satellites. It has carried to our society a distinct deviation from its moral orbit, its mental balance being upset and its aspirations brought down to the dust. This is why never before in our history have our best instincts and endeavours been so openly flouted as a sickness of a rickety sentimentalism. And what is becoming a constant source of disaster for humanity is the incessant hypnotism of money and its secret action upon the mind. It manufactures opinions, it navigates newspapers through tortuous channels of suppression of truth and exaggeration, it pulls most of the strings of politics, it secretly maintains all kinds of slavery under all varieties of masks. In former times the intellectual and spiritual powers of this earth upheld their dignity of independence, but to-day, as in the fatal stage of disease, the influence of money has got into our brain and affected our heart.

Any impetuosity of passion that tends to overwhelm social equilibrium not only produces moral callousness but destroys

1. The Hindu goddess of abundance and fortune, wife of Vishnu.

our reverence for beauty. The truth of this was made evident to us when I set out from Calcutta on my voyage to Japan. The first thing that shocked me with a sense of personal injury was the sight of the ruthless intrusion of factories on both banks of the Ganges, where they are most unbecoming in their brazier-faced effrontery. The blow which it gave to me was owing to the precious memory of the days of my boyhood when the scenery of this river was the only great thing near my birthplace reminding me of the existence of a world made by God's own hands. You all know that Calcutta is an upstart town with no depth of sentiment in her face or in her manners. It may truly be said about its genesis, that in the beginning there was the spirit of the shop which uttered through its megaphone, 'Let there be the office,' and there was Calcutta. She brought with her no dowry of distinctions, no majesty of a noble or romantic origin. She never gathered round her any great historical associations, annals of brave sufferings or memory of mighty deeds done. The only thing which gave her the sacred baptism of beauty was the river, which carried the voice of the Genius of our race from an immortal past singing of its aspiration of the boundless. I was fortunate enough to be born before the smoke-belching Iron Dragon had devoured the greater part of the life on its banks; when the landing stairs descending into its water, caressed by its tide, appeared to me like the loving arms of the villages clinging to it.

I am afraid my complaint will evoke a feeling of pitying amusement in the minds of all sober people when these words reach them. To condemn the impairing of the beauty of a river bank and to overlook the substantial fact of the production of a prodigious quantity of gunny bags will sound too exquisitely unpractical to be able to cause any serious harm!

But as an instance of the contrast of the different ideal of a different age as incarnated in the form of a town, the memory of my last visit to Benares comes to my mind. What impressed me most deeply while I was there was the mother-call of the river Ganges which ever filled the atmosphere with an 'unheard melody,' attracting the whole population to its bosom every hour of the day. I am proud of the fact that India has felt a most profound love for this river which nourished her civilization on its banks, guiding its course from the majestic silence of the Himalayas to the sea with its myriad voices of solitude. This feeling of love is different in a great measure from the modern sentiment of patriotism. It is not too definitely associated with a particular geography or a limited series of political events. It represents the subconscious memory of a whole country, of her ages of endeavour after spiritual emancipation.

But what about our gunny bags? Sentiments are fine, but gunny bags are indispensable. I admit it, and am willing to allow them a place in society (but in strictly modest moderation), if my opponent will only admit that even gunny bags should have their limits and acknowledge the full worth of man who needs leisure and space for his joy and worship. But if this concession to humanity be denied or curtailed, and if profit and production are allowed to run amuck, they play havoc with our love of beauty, of truth, of justice and with our love for our fellow-beings. That man is brave, that he is social, that he is religious, that he is the seeker of the unknown—these have some aspect of the complete in them; but that he is a manufacturer of gunny bags and other articles has not in itself any idea of an organic wholeness. Therefore utility should never forget its subordinate position in human affairs: it must not be permitted to occupy more than its legitimate place and powers in society, nor to have the liberty to desecrate the poetry of life, or to deaden our sensitiveness to ideals, bragging of our coarseness as a sign of virility and bespattering with the mud of mockery our spiritual nature. That would be like allowing a rugged boulder to sneer at and browbeat the living perfection of a flower.

We have our out-offices in the back yard of our houses. And because they disturb the unity of the idea which is our home, we keep a line of separateness between the outside help bought with money and services of kinship, between necessity and sentiment. But the home gives way to the office if the necessity becomes overwhelming. This has made our modern civilization all out-offices, to which home is an adjunct. Modern civilization has become Shudra[1] in its character.

1. Servile caste whose duty is to serve the three higher castes according to the Hindu code of Manu.

For the name Shudra symbolizes one who is merely useful, in whom the man who is above usefulness is not recognized. The word Shudra denotes a classification which includes all named machines who have lost the decency of humanity, be their works manual of intellectual. They are like a walking stomach, or brain, and we feel, in pity, urged to call on God to make them into a man. When man adopted his ideals he did not give success a place of distinction; and even in war he held the ideal of honour above that of success. But success which is Shudra, and whose dwelling is in the office, has arrogantly come into the front. And if through its incessant touch of defilement we contract the ugly habit of deriding sentiments in favour of materials, then the slave dynasty will be confirmed for ever.

This is the root of the struggle of the present age. Man is refusing to accept for good his position as Shudra, and our civilization is feeling ashamed of the degradation imposed upon it by the lust of power and money.

In the old time when commerce was a member of the normal life of man, there ruled the spirit of Laxmi, who with her divine touch of humanity saved wealth from the unseemliness of rampant individualism, mean both in motive and method. Venice had very little that was deformed and discordant; Samarkand and Bokhara had in them the richness of human associations. We can imagine what Delhi and Agra must have been in the time to which they belonged. They manifested in their development some creatively human aspect of a great empire. Whatever might have been its character, even in their decay they still retain their magnificence which was the true product of the self-respect of man.

Then think of Calcutta, which on one side has its squalid congeries of clerks clinging to the meagre and precarious livelihood short of all margin for beauty and joy accorded to them in a niggardly spirit of utilitarianism, and on the other its pompously formal rows of buildings sheltering a nomadic swarm of money-mongers—with no human link between them, with no common sharing of social amenities. This is the hideousness of modern commerce—it does not stimulate men into a healthy and normal activity of production but organizes and makes use of them by mixing and mangling their minds; it is shabbily parsimonious in all that is connected with human life and extravagant in all that tends to the multiplying of market wares.

I do not for a moment mean to imply that in any particular period of their history men were free from the disturbances of their lower passions. Selfishness ever had its share in their government and trade. Yet there was a struggle for maintaining a balance of forces in our society, and our passions with their rude strength cherished no delusions about their own rank and value, and contrived no clever devices to hoodwink our moral nature. For in those days our intellect was not so tempted to put its weight into the balance on the side of over-greed.

But now our passion for power and money has no equal in the field. It has not only science for its ally, but also other forces that have some semblance of religion, such as nation-worship and the idealizing of self-interest.

Science is producing a habit of mind which is ever weakening in us this spiritual standpoint of truth that has its foundation in our sense of a person as the ultimate and innermost reality of existence. Science has its true sphere in analysing this world as a construction just as a grammarian has his legitimate mission in analysing the syntax of a poem. But the world as a creation is not a construction; it is also more than its syntax. It is a poem, which we are apt to forget when, by exclusive attention, grammar takes complete possession of our mind.

Upon the loss of the sense of religion, the reign of the machine and of method has been firmly established. It is the simplification of man by jettisoning a great part of his treasure; spiritually speaking, he has been made a homeless tramp, getting a freedom which is negative because superficial. Its concentrated hurt had been felt by all the world in the late war. Freed from the bond of spiritual relationship as the medium of the brotherhood of man, the different sections of society are continually being resolved into their elemental character of forces. Labour is a force, and also capital; so are the Government and the people, the man and the woman. It is said that when the forces lying latent even in a handful of dust are liberated from their bond of unity, which is their bond of creation, they can lift St. Paul's Cathedral to the height of a mountain. Such disfranchised forces roving as irresponsible freebooters may be useful to us for certain purposes, but St. Paul's Cathedral is, generally speaking, better for us standing secure on its foundation than shattered into pieces and scattered in the void. To own the secret of mastering these forces is a proud fact for us, but the power of self-control and self-sacrifice within is a truer subject of exultation for mankind. The genii of the *Arabian Nights* may have their lure and fascination for us, but God is infinitely more precious for imparting to our society its spiritual power of creation. But these genii are abroad everywhere; and even after their death-dance in the late war, incantations addressed to them are secretly being muttered, and their red-robed devotees are still getting ready to play tricks upon humanity by suddenly spiriting it away to some hill-top of desolation. The thunder-clouds of revolution which are ominously gathering and flashing their angry teeth and growling, are the outcome of a long process of separation of human personality from human power, reducing man into a ghost of abstraction.

Modern science has outwardly brought all mankind close together. The situation requires the spiritual realization of some great truth of relationship to save human societies from constant conflict of interest and friction of pride. The people who are mere forces, when not organically united, must prove their humanity by some creative transfusion. This is not a mere problem of construction, and therefore does not chiefly fall within the province of science, which deals merely with discovery and invention and not with creation. The outer bonds of telegraph wires and railway lines have helped men all the more efficiently to tear one another to pieces and to rob their weaker fellow-beings of food, of freedom, and of self-respect. Must the sword continue to rule for ever and not the sceptre, and must science after her great achievement of mastering the geography of the earth remain at the head of the administration? Can she establish peace and unity in this world of diverse races? Has it not been sufficiently proved that her material law of ruthless skilfulness can only commandeer the genii of power for her agents but cannot conjure up that spirit of creation which is the love of God and man? And yet science does not show any sign of vacating her seat in favour of humanity or submit to any curtailment of her jurisdiction after her own proper work has been finished. The powerful races who have the scientific mind and method and machinery have taken upon themselves the immense responsibility of the present age. We complain not of their law and government, which are scientifically efficient, but of the desolating deadliness of their machine domination. These people in their dealings with subject races all over the world forget that science and law are not a perfect medium for human communication. They refuse to acknowledge what an ordeal it can be for human beings meekly to have to receive gifts from animated pigeon-holes or condescension from a steam-engine of the latest type. We feel the withering fierceness of the spirit of modern civilization all the more because it beats directly against our human sensibility; and it is we of the Eastern hemisphere who have the right to say that those who represent this great age of great opportunities are furiously building their doom by their renouncement of the divine ideal of personality; for the ultimate truth in man is not in his intellect or in his material wealth; it is in his imagination of sympathy, in his illumination of heart, in his activities of self-sacrifice, in his capacity for extending love far and wide across all barriers of caste and colour, in his realizing this world not as a storehouse of mechanical power but as a habitation of man's soul with its eternal music of beauty and its inner light of a divine presence.

1920

A Cry for Peace

The world is crying for peace. The West is desiring the restoration of peace through a League of Powers. But can Powers find their equilibrium in themselves? Power cannot be made secure only against power, it must also be made secure against the weak; for there lies the peril of its losing balance. The weak are as great a danger for the strong, as quicksands for an elephant. They do not assist progress, because they do not resist, they only drag down. The people who grow accustomed to wield absolute power over others are apt to forget, that by doing it they generate an unseen disruptive force, which some day rends that power into pieces. The dumb fury of the down-trodden finds its awful support from the universal law of moral balance. The air which is thin and weak gives birth to storms that nothing can resist. This has been proved in history over and over again; and stormy forces arising from the heart of insulted humanity are openly gathering in the air even in the present day. Yet the psychology of athletic might stubbornly refuses its lessons and despises to take count of the terribleness of the weak. This is the gross stupidity, that, like an unsuspected worm, burrows at the bottom of the muscular bulk of the prosperous and the proud. Have we never read of the gorgeousness of a power, supinely secure in its arrogance, in a moment dissolving in the air at the explosion of the outraged weak? Politicians calculate upon the number of mailed hands that are on the sword-hilts; they do not possess the third eye to see the great invisible hand, that clasps in silence the hand of the helpless and waits its time. The strong form their League by combination of Powers, driving the weak to form their league alone with their God. I know I am crying in the wilderness, when I raise my voice of warning; and while the West is busy in its organization for building its machine-made peace, it will still continue to nourish, with its iniquities, underground forces of earthquake in the vast bosom of the Eastern Continent. The West seems unconscious that Science, by providing it with more and more power, is tempting it to suicide, encouraging it to accept the challenge of the disarmed, not knowing that this challenge comes from a higher source.

Two prophecies about the world's salvation are cherished in the hearts of the two great religions of the world. They represent the highest expectation of man, thereby indicating his faith in a truth, which he instinctively considers as ultimate,—the truth of love. These prophecies have not for their vision the fettering of the world into tameness with a closely linked power forged in the factory of a political steel trust. One of these religions has, for its meditation, the image of Buddha who is to come, Maitreya, the Buddha of love. And he is to bring peace. The other religion waits for the coming of Christ. For Christ preached peace when he preached love, when he preached Oneness of the Father among brothers who are many. And this was the truth of peace. Christ never held that peace was the best policy. For policy is not truth. The calculation of self-interest can never successfully fight the irrational force of passion—the passion which is perversion of love, and which can only be set aright by the truth of love. So long as the Powers build a League on the foundation of their desire for safety, and for securest enjoyment of gains,—for consolidation of past injustice, for putting off reparation of wrongs, while their fingers still wriggle for grabbing and still reek of blood,—rifts will appear in their union, and conflicts in future will take greater force and magnitude. It is the national and commercial egoism, which is the evil harbinger of war; by different combinations it changes its shape and dimensions, but not its nature. This egoism is still held almost as sacred as religion; and such religion, by its mere change of temple and of committee of priests, will never save men. We must know that, as, through science and commerce, the realization of the unity of the material world gives us power, so the realization of the great spiritual unity of man only can give us peace.

1919

The Call of Truth

Parasites have to pay for their readymade victuals by losing the power of assimilating food in its natural form. In the history of man this same sin of laziness has always entailed degeneracy. Man becomes parasitical, not only when he fattens on others' toil, but also when he becomes rooted to a particular set of outside conditions and allows himself helplessly to drift along the stream of things as they are; for the outside is alien to the inner self, and if the former be made indispensable by sheer habit, man acquires parasitical characteristics, and becomes unable to perform his true function of converting the impossible into the possible.

In this sense all the lower animals are parasites. They are carried along by their environment; they live or die by natural selection; they progress or retrogress as nature may dictate. Their mind has lost the power of growth. The bees, for millions of years, have been unable to get beyond the pattern of their hive. For that reason, the form of their cell has attained a certain perfection, but their mentality is confined to the age-long habits of their hive-life and cannot soar out of its limitations. Nature has developed a cautious timidity in the case of her lower types of life; she keeps them tied to her apron strings and has stunted their minds, lest they should stray into dangerous experiments.

But Providence displayed a sudden accession of creative courage when it came to man; for his inner nature has not been tied down, though outwardly the poor human creature has been left naked, weak and defenceless. In spite of these disabilities, man in the joy of his inward freedom has stood up and declared; 'I shall achieve the impossible.' That is to say, he has consistently refused to submit to the rule of things as they always have been, but is determined to bring about happenings that have never been before. So when, in the beginning of his history, man's lot was thrown in with monstrous creatures, tusked and taloned, he did not, like the deer, simply take refuge in flight, nor, like the tortoise, take refuge in hiding, but set to work with flints to make even more efficient weapons. These, moreover, being the creation of his own inner faculties, were not dependent on natural selection, as were those of the other animals, for their development. And so man's instruments progressed from flint to steel. This shows that man's mind has never been helplessly attached to his environment. What came to his hand was brought under his thumb. Not content with the flint on the surface, he delved for the iron beneath. Not satisfied with the easier process of chipping flints, he proceeded to melt iron ore and hammer it into shape. That which resisted more stubbornly was converted into a better ally. Man's inner nature not only finds success in its activity, but there it also has its joy. He insists on penetrating further and further into the depths, from the obvious to the hidden, from the easy to the difficult, from parasitism to self-determination, from the slavery of his passions to the mastery of himself. That is how he has won.

But if any section of mankind should say, 'The flint was the weapon of our revered forefathers; by departing from it we destroy the spirit of the race,' then they may succeed in preserving what they call their race, but they strike at the root of the glorious tradition of humanity which was theirs also. And we find that those, who have steadfastly stuck to their flints, may indeed have kept safe their pristine purity to their own satisfaction, but they have been outcasted by the rest of mankind, and so have to pass their lives slinking away in jungle and cave. They are, as I say, reduced to a parasitic dependence on outside nature, driven along blindfold by the force of things as they are. They have not achieved Swaraj in their inner nature, and so are deprived of Swaraj in the outside world as well. They have ceased to be even aware, that it is man's true function to make the impossible into the possible by dint of his own powers; that it is not for him to be confined merely to what has happened before; that he must progress towards what ought to be by rousing all his inner powers by means of the force of his soul.

Thirty years ago I used to edit the Sādhanā magazine, and there I tried to say this same thing. Then English-educated India was frightfully busy begging for its rights. And I repeatedly endeavoured to impress on my countrymen, that man is not under any necessity to beg for rights from others, but must create them for himself; because man lives mainly by his inner nature, and there he is the master. By dependence on acquisition from the outside, man's inner nature suffers loss. And it was my contention, that man is not so hard oppressed by being deprived of his outward rights as he is by the constant bearing of the burden of prayers and petitions.

Then, when the Bangadarshan magazine came into my hands, Bengal was beside herself at the sound of sharpening of the knives for her partition. The boycott of Manchester, which was the outcome of her distress, had raised the profits of the Bombay mill-owners to a super-foreign degree. And I had then to say, 'This will not do, either; for it is also of the outside. Your main motive is hatred of the foreigner, not love of country.' It was then really necessary for our countrymen to be made conscious of the distinction, that the Englishman's presence is an external accident,—mere *māyā*—but that the presence of our country is an internal fact which is also an eternal truth. *Māyā* looms with an exaggerated importance, only when we fix our attention exclusively upon it, by reason of some infatuation—be it of love, or of hate. Whether in our passion we rush to embrace it, or attack it; whether we yearn for it, or spurn it; it equally fills the whole field of our blood-shot vision.

Māyā is like the darkness. No steed, however swift, can carry us beyond it; no amount of water can wash it away. Truth is like a lamp; even as it is lit *māyā* vanishes. Our Shastras tell us that Truth, even when it is small, can rescue us from the terror which is great. Fear is the atheism of the heart. It cannot be overcome from the side of negation. If one of its heads be struck off, it breeds, like the monster of the fable, a hundred others. Truth is positive: it is the affirmation of the soul. If even a little of it be roused, it attacks negation at the very heart and overpowers it wholly.

Alien government in India is a veritable chameleon. Today it comes in the guise of the Englishman; to-morrow perhaps as some other foreigner; the next day, without abating a jot of its virulence, it may take the shape of our own countrymen. However determinedly we may try to hunt this monster of foreign dependence with outside lethal weapons, it will always elude our pursuit by changing its skin, or its colour. But if we can gain within us the truth called our country, all outward *māyā* will vanish of itself. The declaration of faith that my country it there, to be realized, has to be attained by each one of us. The idea that our country is ours, merely because we have been born in it, can only be held by those who are fastened, in a parasitic existence, upon the outside world. But the true nature of man is his inner nature, with its inherent powers. Therefore that only can be a man's true country, which he can help to create by his wisdom and with his love and his actions. So in 1905, I called upon my countrymen to *create* their own country by putting forth their own powers from within. For the act of creation itself is the realization of truth.

The Creator gains Himself in His universe. To gain one's own country means to realize one's own soul more fully expanded within it. This can only be done when we are engaged in building it up with our service, our ideas and our activities. Man's country being the creation of his own inner nature, when his soul thus expands within it, it is more truly expressed, more fully realized. In my paper called 'Swadeshi Samaj', written in 1905, I discussed at length the ways and means by which we could make the country of our birth more fully our own. Whatever may have been the shortcomings of my words then uttered, I did not fail to lay emphasis on the truth, that we must win our country, not from some foreigner, but from our own inertia, our own indifference. Whatever be the nature of the boons we may be seeking for our country at the door of the foreign Government, the result is always the same,—it only makes our inertia more densely inert. Any public benefit done by the alien Government goes to their credit, not to ours. So whatever outside advantage such public benefit might mean for us, our country will only get more and more completely lost to us thereby. That is to say, we shall have to pay out in soul value for what we purchase as material advantage. The Rishi has said: 'Then son is dear, not because we desire a son, but because we desire to realize our own soul in him.' It is the same with our country. It is dear to us, because it is the expression of our own soul. When we realize this, it will become impossible for us to allow our service of our country to wait on the pleasure of others.

These truths, which I then tried to press on my countrymen, were not particularly new, nor was there anything therein which need have grated on their ears; but, whether anyone else remembers it or not, I at least am not likely to forget the storm of indignation which I roused. I am not merely referring to the hooligans of journalism whom it pays to be scurrilous. But even men of credit and courtesy were unable to speak of me in restrained language.

There were two root causes of this. One was anger, the second was greed.

Giving free vent to angry feelings is a species of self-indulgence. In those days there was practically nothing to stand in the way of the spirit of destructive revel, which spread all over the country. We went about picketing, burning, placing thorns in the path of those whose way was not ours, acknowledging no restraints in language or behaviour,—all in the frenzy of our wrath. Shortly after it was all over, a Japanese friend asked me: 'How is it you people cannot carry on your work with calm and deep determination? This wasting of energy can hardly be of assistance to your object.' I had no help but to reply: 'When we have the gaining of the object clearly before our minds, we can be restrained, and concentrate our energies to serve it; but when it is a case of venting our anger, our excitement rises and rises till it drowns the object, and then we are spend-thrift to the point of bankruptcy.' However that may be, there were my countrymen encountering, for the time being, no check to the overflow of their outraged feelings. It was like a strange dream. Everything seemed possible. Then all of a sudden it was my misfortune to appear on the scene with my doubts and my attempts to divert the current into the path of self-determination. My only success was in diverting their wrath on to my own devoted head.

Then there was our greed. In history, all people have won valuable things by pursuing difficult paths. We had hit upon the device of getting them cheap, not even through the painful indignity of supplication with folded hands, but by proudly conducting our beggary in threatening tones. The country was in ecstasy at the ingenuity of the trick. It felt like being at a reduced price sale. Everything worth having in the political market was ticketed at half-price. Shabby-genteel mentality is so taken up with low prices that it has no attention to spare for quality, and feels inclined to attack anybody who has the hardihood to express doubts in that regard. It is like the man of worldly piety who believes that the judicious expenditure of coin can secure, by favour of the priest, a direct passage to heaven. The dare-devil who ventures to suggest that not heaven but dreamland is likely to be his destination must beware of a violent end.

Anyhow, it was the outside *māyā* I which was our dream and our ideal in those days. It was a favourite phrase of one of the leaders of the time that we must keep one hand at the feet and the other at the throat of the Englishman,—that is to say, with no hand left free for the country! We have since perhaps got rid of this ambiguous attitude. Now we have one party that has both hands raised to the foreigner's throat, and another party which has both hands down at his feet; but whichever attitude it may be, these methods still appertain to the outside *māyā*. Our unfortunate minds keep revolving round and round the British Government, now to the left, now to the right; our affirmations and denials alike are concerned with the foreigner.

In those days, the stimulus from every side was directed towards the heart of Bengal. But emotion by itself, like fire, only consumes its fuel and reduces it to ashes; it has no creative power. The intellect of man must by itself, with patience, with skill, with foresight, in using this fire to melt that which is hard and difficult into the object of its desire. We neglected to rouse our intellectual forces, and so were unable to make use of this surging emotion of ours to create any organization of permanent value. The reason of our failure, therefore, was not in anything outside, but rather within us. For a long time past we have been in the habit, in our life and endeavour, of setting apart one place for our emotions and another for our practices. Our intellect has all the time remained dormant, because we have not dared to allow it scope. That is why, when we have to rouse ourselves to action, it is our emotion which has to be requisitioned, and our intellect has to be kept from interfering by the hypnotism of some magical formula,—that is to say we hasten to create a situation absolutely inimical to the free play of our intellect.

The loss which is incurred by this continual deadening of our mind cannot be made good by any other contrivance. In our desperate attempts to do so we have to invoke the magic of *māyā* and our impotence jumps for joy at the prospect of getting hold of Aladin's lamp. Of course everyone has to admit that there is nothing to beat Aladin's lamp, its only inconvenience being that it beats one to get hold of. The unfortunate part of it is that the person, whose greed is great, but whose powers are feeble, and who has lost all confidence in his own intellect, simply will not allow himself to dwell on the difficulties of bespeaking the services of some of the lamp. He can only be brought to exert himself at all by holding out the speedy prospect of getting at the wonderful lamp. If any one attempts to point out the futility of his hopes, he fills the air with wailing and imprecation, as at a robber making away with his all.

In the heat of the enthusiasm of the partition days, a band of youths attempted to bring about the millennium through political revolution. Their offer of themselves as the first sacrifice to the fire which they had lighted makes not only their own country, but other countries as well, bare the head to them in reverence. Their physical failure shines forth as the effulgence of spiritual glory. In the midst of their supreme travail, they realized at length that the way of bloody revolution is not the true way; that where there is no politics, a political revolution is like taking a short cut to nothing; that the wrong way may appear shorter, but it does not reach the goal, and only grievously hurts the feet. The refusal to pay the full price for a thing leads to the loss of the price without the gain of the thing. These impetuous youths offered their lives as the price of their country's deliverance; to them it meant the loss of their all, but alas! the price offered on behalf of the country was insufficient. I feel sure that those of them who still survive must have realized by now, that the country must be the creation of all its people, not of one section alone. It must be the expression of all their forces of heart, mind and will.

The creation can only be the fruit of that *yoga,* which gives outward form to the inner faculties. Mere political or economical *yoga* is not enough; for that all the human powers must unite.

When we turn our gaze upon the history of other countries, the political steed comes prominently into view; on it seems to depend wholly the progress of the carriage. We forget that the carriage also must be in a fit condition to move; its wheels must be in agreement with one another and its parts well fitted together; with which not only have fire and hammer and chisel been busy but much thought and skill and energy have also been spent in the process. We have seen some countries which are externally free and independent; when, however, the political carriage is in motion, the noise which it makes arouses the whole neighbourhood from slumber and the jolting produces aches and pains in the limbs of the helpless passengers. It comes to pieces in the middle of the road, and it takes the whole day to put it together again with the help of ropes and strings. Yet however loose the screws and however crooked the wheels, still it is a vehicle of some sort after all. But for such a thing as is our country,—a mere collection of jointed logs, that not only have no wholeness amongst themselves, but are contrary to one another,—for this, to be dragged along a few paces by the temporary pull of some common greed or anger, can never be called by the name of political progress. Therefore, is it not, in our case, wiser to keep for the moment our horse in the stable and begin to manufacture a real carriage?

From the writings of the young men, who have come back out of the valley of the shadow of death, I feel sure some such thoughts must have occurred to them. And so they must be realizing the necessity of the practice of *yoga* as of primary importance;—that form which is the union in a common endeavour of all the human faculties. This cannot be attained by any outside blind obedience, but only by the realization of self in the light of intellect. That which fails to illumine the intellect, and only keeps it in the obsession of some delusion, is its greatest obstacle.

The call to make the country our own by dint of our own creative power, is a great call. It is not merely inducing the people to take up some external mechanical exercise; for man's life is not in making cells of uniform pattern like the bee, nor in incessant weaving of webs like the spider; his greatest powers are within, and on these are his chief reliance. If by offering some allurement we can induce man to cease from thinking so that he may go on and on with some mechanical piece of world, this will only result in prolonging the sway of *Māyā,* under which our country has all along been languishing. So far, we have been content with surrendering our greatest right—the right to reason and to judge for ourselves—to the blind forces of shastric injunctions and social conventions. We have refused to cross the seas, because Manu has told us not to do so. We refuse to eat with the Mussulman, because prescribed usage is against it. In other words, we have systematically pursued a course of blind routine and habit, in which the mind of man has no place. We have thus been reduced to the helpless condition of the master who is altogether dependent on his servant. The real master, as I have said, is the internal man; and he gets into endless trouble, when he becomes his own servant's slave—a mere automaton, manufactured in the factory of servitude. He can then only rescue himself from one master by surrendering himself to another. Similarly, he who glorifies inertia by attributing to it a fanciful purity, becomes, like it, dependent on outside impulses, both for rest and motion. The inertness of mind, which is the basis of all slavery, cannot be got rid of by a docile submission to being hoodwinked, nor by going through the motions of a wound up mechanical doll.

The movement, which has now succeeded the Swadeshi agitation, is ever so much greater and has moreover extended its influence all over India. Previously, the vision of our political leaders had never reached beyond the English-knowing classes, because the country meant for them only that bookish aspect of it which is to be found in the pages of the Englishman's history.

Such a country was merely a mirage born of vapourings in the English language, in which flitted about thin shades of Burke and Gladstone, Mazzini and Garibaldi. Nothing resembling self-sacrifice or true feeling for their countrymen was visible. At this juncture, Mahatma Gandhi came and stood at the cottage door of the destitute millions, clad as one of themselves, and talking to them in their own language. Here was the truth at last, not a mere quotation out of a book. So the name of Mahatma, which was given to him, is his true name. Who else has felt so many men of India to be of his own flesh and blood? At the touch of Truth the pent-up forces of the soul are set free. As soon as true love stood at India's door, it flew open: all hesitation and holding back vanished. Truth awakened truth.

Stratagem in politics is a barren policy,—this was a lesson of which we were sorely in need. All honour to the Mahatma, who made visible to us the power of Truth. But reliance on tactics is so ingrained in the cowardly and the weak, that, in order to eradicate it, the very skin must be sloughed off. Even today, our worldly-wise men cannot get rid of the idea of utilizing the Mahatma as a secret and more ingenious move in their political gamble. With their minds corroded by untruth, they cannot understand what an important thing it is that the Mahatma's supreme love should have drawn forth the country's love. The thing that has happened is nothing less than the birth of freedom. It is the gain by the country of itself. In it there is no room for any thought, as to where the Englishman is, or is not. This love is self-expression. It is pure affirmation. It does not argue with negation; it has no need for argument.

Some notes of the music of this wonderful awakening of India by love, floated over to me across the seas. It was a great joy to me to think that the call of this festivity of awakening would come to each one of us; and that the true *shakti* of India's spirit, in all its multifarious variety, would at last find expression. This thought came to me because I have always believed that in such a way India would find its freedom. When Lord Buddha voiced forth the truth of compassion for all living creatures, which he had obtained as the fruit of his own self-discipline, the manhood of India was roused and poured itself forth in science and art and wealth of every kind. True, in the matter of political unification the repeated attempts that were then made as often failed; nevertheless India's mind had awakened into freedom from its submergence in sleep, and its overwhelming force would brook no confinement within the petty limits of country. It overflowed across ocean and desert, scattering its wealth of the spirit over every land that it touched. No commercial or military exploiter, to-day, has ever been able to do anything like it. Whatever land these exploiters have touched has been agonized with sorrow and insult, and the fair face of the world has been scarred and disfigured. Why? Because not greed but love is true. When love gives freedom it does so at the very centre of our life. When greed seeks unfettered power, it is forcefully impatient. We saw this during the partition agitation. We then compelled the poor to make sacrifices, not always out of the inwardness of love, but often by outward pressure. That was because greed is always seeking for a particular result within a definite time. But the fruit which love seeks is not of to-day of tomorrow, nor for a time only: it is sufficient unto itself.

So, in the expectation of breathing the buoyant breezes of this new found freedom, I came home rejoicing. But what I found in Calcutta when I arrived depressed me. An oppressive atmosphere seemed to burden the land. Some outside compulsion seemed to be urging one and all to talk in the same strain, to work at the same mill. When I wanted to inquire, to discuss, my well-wishers clapped their hands over my lips, saying: 'Not now, not now. To-day, in the atmosphere of the country, there is a spirit of persecution, which is not that of armed force, but something, still more alarming, because it is invisible.' I found, further, that those who had their doubts as to the present activities, if they happened to whisper them out, however cautiously, however guardedly, felt some admonishing hand clutching them within. There was a newspaper which one day had the temerity to disapprove, in a feeble way, of the burning of cloth. The very next day the editor was shaken out of his balance by the agitation of his readers. How long would it take for the fire which was burning cloth to reduce his paper to ashes? The sight that met my eye was, on the one hand, people immensely busy; on the other, intensely afraid. What I heard on every side was, that reason, and culture as well, must be closured. It was only necessary to cling to an unquestioning obedience. Obedience to whom? To some *mantra*, some unreasoned creed!

And why this obedience? Here again comes that same greed, our spiritual enemy. There dangles before the country the bait of getting a thing of inestimable value, dirt cheap and in double-quick time. It is like the faqir with his goldmaking trick. With such a lure men cast so readily to the winds their independent judgment and wax so mightily wroth with those who will not do likewise. So easy is it to overpower, in the name of outside freedom, the inner freedom of man. The most deplorable part of it is that so many do not even honestly believe in the hope that they swear by. 'It will serve to make our countrymen, do what is necessary'—say they. Evidently, according to them, the India which once declared: 'In truth is Victory, not in untruth'—that India would not have been fit for *Swaraj*.

Another mischief is that the gain, with the promise of which obedience is claimed, is indicated by name, but is not defined. Just as when fear is vague it becomes all the more strong, so the vagueness of the lure makes it all the more tempting; inasmuch as ample room is left for each one's imagination to shape, it to his taste. Moreover there is no driving it into a corner because it can always shift from one shelter to another. In short, the object of the temptation has been magnified through its indefiniteness, while the time and method of its attainment have been made too narrowly definite. When the reason of man has been overcome in this way, he easily consents to give up all legitimate questions and blindly follows the path of obedience. But can we really afford to forget so easily that delusion is at the root of all slavery—that all freedom means freedom from *māyā*? What if the bulk of our people have unquestioningly accepted the creed, that by means of sundry practices *swaraj* will come to them on a particular date in the near future, and are also ready to use their clubs to put down all further argument,—that is to say, they have surrendered the freedom of their own minds and are prepared to deprive other minds of their freedom likewise,—is not this by itself a reason for profound misgiving? We were seeking the exorciser to drive out this very ghost; but if the ghost itself comes in the guise of exorciser then the danger is only heightened.

The Mahatma has won the heart of India with his love; for that we have all acknowledged his sovereignty. He has given us a vision of the *shakti* of truth; for that our gratitude to him is unbounded. We read about truth in books: we talk about it: but it is indeed a red-letter day, when we see it face to face. Rare is the moment, in many a long year, when such good fortune happens. We can make and break Congresses every other day. It is at any time possible for us to stump the country preaching politics in English. But the golden rod which can awaken our country in Truth and Love is not a thing which can be manufactured by the nearest goldsmith. To the wielder of that rod our profound salutation! But if, having seen truth, our belief in it is not confirmed, what is the good of it all? Our mind must acknowledge the truth of the intellect, just as our heart does the truth of love. No Congress or other outside institution succeeded in touching the heart of India. It was roused only the touch of love. Having had such a clear vision of this wonderful power of Truth, are we to cease to believe in it, just where the attainment of *Swaraj* is concerned? Has the truth, which was needed in the process of awakenment, to be got rid of in the process of achievement?

Let me give an illustration. I am in search of a Vina player. I have tried East and I have tried West, but have not found the man of my quest. They are all experts, they can make the strings resound to a degree, they command high prices, but for all their wonderful execution they can strike no chord in my heart. At last I come across one whose very first notes melt away the sense of oppression within. In him is the fire of the *shakti* of joy which can light up all other hearts by its touch. His appeal to me is instant, and I hail him as Master. I then want a Vina made. For this, of course, are required all kinds of material and a different kind of science. If, finding me to be lacking in the means, my master should be moved to pity and say: 'Never mind, my son, do not go to the expense in workmanship and time which a Vina will require. Take rather this simple string tightened across a piece of wood and practice on it. In a short time you will find it to be as good as a Vina.' Would that do? I am afraid not. It would, in fact, be a mistaken kindness for the master thus to take pity on my circumstances. Far better if he were to tell me plainly that such things cannot be had cheaply. It is he who should teach me that merely one string will not serve for a true Vina; that the materials required are many and various; that the lines of its moulding must be shapely and precise; that if there be anything faulty, it will fail to make good music, so that all laws of science and technique of art must be rigorously and intelligently followed. In short, the true function of the master player should be to evoke a response from the depths of our heart, so that we may gain the strength to wait and work till the true end is achieved.

From our master, the Mahatma,—may our devotion to him never grow less!—we must learn the truth of love in all its purity, but the science and art of building up *Swaraj* is a vast subject. Its pathways are difficult to traverse and take time. For this task, aspiration and emotion must be there, but no less must study and thought be there likewise. For it, the economist must think, the mechanic must labour, the educationist and statesman must teach and contrive. In a word, the mind of the country must exert itself in all directions. Above all, the spirit of Inquiry throughout the whole country, must be kept intact and untrammeled, its mind not made timid or inactive by compulsion, open or secret.

We know from past experience that it is not any and every call to which the Country responds. It is because no one has yet been able to unite in *Yoga* all the forces of the country in the work of its creation, that so much time has been lost over and over again. And we have been kept waiting and waiting for him who has the right and the power to make the call upon us. In the old forests of India, our *Gurus,* in the fulness of their vision of the Truth had sent forth such a call saying: 'As the rivers flow on their downward course, as the months flow on to the year, so let all seekers after truth come from all sides.' The initiation into

Truth of that day has borne fruit, undying to this day, and the voice of its message still rings in the ears of the world.

Why should not our *Guru* of to-day, who would lead us on the paths of *Karma,* send forth such a call? Why should he not say: 'Come yet from all sides and be welcome. Let all the forces of the land he brought into action, for then alone shall the country awake. Freedom is in complete awakening, in full self-expression.' God has given the Mahatma the voice that can call, for in him there is the Truth. Why should this not be our long-awaited opportunity?

But his call came to one narrow field alone. To one and all he simply says: Spin and weave, spin and weave. Is this the call: 'Let all seekers after truth come from all sides'? Is this the call of the New Age to new creation? When nature called to the Bee to take refuge in the narrow life of the hive, millions of bees responded to it for the sake of efficiency, and accepted the loss of sex in consequence. But this sacrifice by way of self-atrophy led to the opposite of freedom. Any country, the people of which can agree to become neuters for the sake of some temptation, or command, carries within itself its own prison-house. To spin is easy, therefore for all men it is an imposition hard to bear. The call to the ease of mere efficiency is well enough for the Bee. The wealth of power, that is Man's can only become manifest when his utmost is claimed.

Sparta tried to gain strength by narrowing herself down to a particular purpose, but she did not win. Athens sought to attain perfection by opening herself out in all her fulness,—and she did win. Her flag of victory still flies at the masthead of man's civilization. It is admitted that European military camps and factories are stunting man, that their greed is cutting man down to the measure of their own narrow purpose, that for these reasons joylessness darkly lowers over the West. But if man be stunted by big machines, the danger of his being stunted by small machines must not be lost sight of. The *charka* in its proper place can do no harm, but will rather do much good. But where, by reason of failure to acknowledge the differences in man's temperament, it is in the wrong place, there thread can only be spun at the cost of a great deal of the mind itself. Mind is no less valuable than cotton thread.

Some are objecting: 'We do not propose to curb our minds for ever, but only for a time.' But why should it be even for a time? Is it because within a short time spinning will give us Swaraj? But where is the argument for this? Swaraj is not concerned with our apparel only—it cannot be established on cheap clothing; its foundation is in the mind, which, with its diverse powers and its confidence in those powers, goes on all the time creating Swaraj for itself. In no country in the world is the building up of Swaraj completed. In some part or other of every nation, some lurking greed or illusion still perpetuates bondage. And the root of such bondage is always within the mind. Where then, I ask again, is the argument, that in our country Swaraj can be brought about by everyone engaging for a time in spinning? A mere statement, in lieu of argument, will surely never do. If once we consent to receive fate's oracle from human lips, that will add one more to the torments of our slavery, and not the least one either. If nothing but oracles will serve to move us, oracles will have to be manufactured, morning, noon and night, for the sake of urgent needs, and all other voices would be defeated. Those for whom authority is needed in place of reason, will invariably accept despotism in place of freedom. It is like cutting at the root of a tree while pouring water on the top. This is not a new thing, I know. We have enough of magic in the country,—magical revelation, magical healing, and all kinds of divine intervention in mundane affairs. That is exactly why I am so anxious to re-instate reason on its throne. As I have said before, God himself has given the mind sovereignty in the material world. And I say to-day, that only those will be able to get and keep Swaraj in the material world who have realized the dignity of self-reliance and self-mastery in the spiritual world, those whom no temptation, no delusion, can induce to surrender the dignity of intellect into the keeping of others.

Consider the burning of cloth, heaped up before the very eyes of our motherland shivering and ashamed in her nakedness. What is the nature of the call to do this? Is it not another instance of a magical formula? The question of using or refusing cloth of a particular manufacture belongs mainly to economic science. The discussion of the matter by our countrymen should have been in the language of economics. If the country has really come to such a habit of mind that precise thinking has become impossible for it, then our very first fight should be against such a fatal habit, to the temporary exclusion of all else if need be. Such a habit would clearly be the original sin from which all our ills are flowing. But far from this, we take the course of confirming ourselves in it by relying on the magical formula that foreign cloth is 'impure'. Thus economics is bundled out and a fictitious moral dictum dragged into its place.

Untruth is impure in any circumstances, not merely because it may cause us material loss, but even when it does not; for it makes our inner nature unclean. This is a moral law and belongs to a higher plane. But if there be anything wrong in wearing a particular kind of cloth, that would be an offence against economics, or hygiene, or aesthetics, but certainly not against morality. Some urge that any mistake which brings sorrow to body or mind is a moral wrong. To which I reply that sorrow follows in the train of every mistake. A mistake in geometry may make a road too long, or a foundation weak, or a bridge dangerous. But mathematical mistakes cannot be cured by moral maxims. If a student makes a mistake in his geometry problem and his exercise book is torn up in consequence the problem will nevertheless remain unsolved until attacked by geometrical methods. But what if the schoolmaster comes to the conclusion that unless the exercise books are condemned and destroyed, his boys will never realize the folly of their mistakes? If such conclusion be well-founded, then I can only repeat that the reformation of such moral weakness of these particular boys should take precedence over all other lessons, otherwise there is no hope of their becoming men in the future.

The command to burn our foreign clothes has been laid on us. I, for one, am unable to obey it. Firstly, because I conceive it to be my very first duty to put up a valiant fight against this terrible habit of blindly obeying orders, and this fight can never be carried on by our people being driven from one injunction to another. Secondly, I feel that the clothes to be burnt are not mine, but belong to those who most sorely need them. If those who are going naked should have given us the mandate to burn, it would, at least, have been a case of self-immolation and the crime of incendiarism would not lie at our door. But how can we expiate the sin of the forcible destruction of clothes which might have gone to women whose nakedness is actually keeping them prisoners, unable to stir out of the privacy of their homes?

I have said repeatedly and must repeat once more that we cannot afford to lose our mind for the sake of any external gain. Where Mahatma Gandhi has declared war against the tyranny of the machine which is oppressing the whole world, we are all enrolled under his banner. But we must refuse to accept as our ally the illusion-haunted magic-ridden slave-mentality that is at the root of all the poverty and insult under which our country groans. Here is the enemy itself, on whose defeat alone Swaraj within and without can come to us.

The time, moreover, has arrived when we must think of one thing more, and that is this. The awakening of India is a part of the awakening of the world. The door of the New Age has been flung open at the trumpet blast of a great war. We have read in the Mahabharata how the day of self-revelation had to be preceded by a year of retirement. The same has happened in the world today. Nations had attained nearness to each other without being aware of it, that is to say, the outside fact was there, but it had not penetrated into the mind. At the shock of the war, the truth of it stood revealed to mankind. The foundation of modern, that is Western, civilization was shaken; and it has become evident that the convulsion is neither local nor temporary, but has traversed the whole earth and will last until the shocks between man and man, which have extended from continent to continent, can be brought to rest, and a harmony be established.

From now onward, any nation which takes an isolated view of its own country will run counter to the spirit of the New Age, and know no peace. From now onward, the anxiety that each country has for its own safety must embrace the welfare of the world. For some time the working of the new spirit has occasionally shown itself even in the Government of India, which has had to make attempts to deal with its own problems in the light of the world problem. The war has torn away a veil from before our minds. What is harmful to the world, is harmful to each one of us. This was a maxim which we used to read in books. Now mankind has seen it at work and has understood that wherever there is injustice, even if the external right of possession is there, the true right is wanting. So that it is worth while even to sacrifice some outward right in order to gain the reality. This immense change, which is coming over the spirit of man raising it from the petty to the great, is already at work even in Indian politics. There will doubtless be imperfections and obstacles without number. Self-interest is sure to attack enlightened interest at every step. Nevertheless it would be wrong to come to the decision that the working of self-interest alone is honest, and the larger-hearted striving is hypocritical.

After sixty years of self-experience, I have found that out and out hypocrisy is an almost impossible achievement, so that the pure hypocrite is a rarity indeed. The fact is, that the character of man has always more or less of duality in it. But our logical faculty, the trap-door of our mind, is unable to admit opposites together. So when we find the good with the bad, the former is promptly rejected as spurious. In the universal movement, as it becomes manifest in different parts of the world, this duality of man's character cannot but show itself. And whenever it does, if we pass judgment from past experience, we are sure to pronounce the selfish part of it to be the real thing; for the spirit of division and exclusion did in fact belong to the past age. But if we come to our judgment in the light of future promise, then shall we understand the enlightened large-heartedness to be the reality, and the counsel which will unite each to each to be the true wisdom.

I have condemned, in unsparing terms, the present form and scope of the League of Nations and the Indian Reform Councils. I, therefore, fell certain that there will be no misunderstanding when I state that, even in these, I find signs of the Time Spirit, which is moving the heart of the West. Although the present form is unacceptable, yet there is revealed an aspiration, which is towards the truth, and this aspiration must not be condemned. In this morning of the world's awakening, if in only our own national striving there is no response to its universal aspiration, that will betoken the poverty of our spirit. I do not say for a moment that we should belittle the work immediately to hand. But when the bird is roused by the dawn, all its awakening is not absorbed in its search for food. Its wings respond unweariedly to the call of the sky, its throat pours forth songs for joy of the new light. Universal humanity has sent us its call to-day. Let our mind respond in its own language; for response is the only true sign of life. When of old we were immersed in the politics of dependence on others, our chief business was the compilation of others' shortcomings. Now that we have decided to dissociate our politics from dependence, are we still to establish and maintain it on the same recital of others' sins? The state of mind so engendered will only raise the dust of angry passion, obscuring the greater world from our vision, and urge us more and more to take futile short cuts for the satisfaction of our passions. It is a sorry picture of India, which we shall display if we fail to realize for ourselves the greater India. This picture will have no light. It will have in the foreground only the business side of our aspiration. Mere business talent, however, has never created anything.

In the West, a real anxiety and effort of their higher mind to rise superior to business considerations, is beginning to be seen. I have come across many there whom this desire has imbued with the true spirit of the *Sannyasin,* making them renounce their home-world in order to achieve the unity of man, by destroying the bondage of nationalism; men who have within their own soul realized the *Advaita* of humanity. Many such have I seen in England who have accepted persecution and contumely from their fellow countrymen in their struggles to free other peoples from the oppression of their own country's pride of power. Some of them are amongst us here in India. I have seen *sannyasins* too in France—Romain Rolland for one, who is an outcast from his own people. I have also seen them in the minor countries of Europe. I have watched the faces of European students all a glow with the hope of a united mankind, prepared manfully to bear all the blows, cheerfully to submit to all the insults, of the present age for the glory of the age to come. And are we alone to be content with telling the beads of negation, harping on others faults and proceeding with the erection of *swaraj* on a foundation of quarrelsomeness? Shall it not be our first duty in the dawn to remember Him, who is One, who is without distinction of class or colour, and who with his varied *shakti* makes true provision for the inherent need of each and every class; and to pray to the Giver of Wisdom to unite us all in right understanding—

Yo ekōvarno vahudhā shakti yōgāt
Varnānanekān nihitārthodadhāti
Vichaiti chānte vishvamādau
Sa no buddhyā subhayā samyunaktu!

1921

The Union of Cultures

It cannot but be admitted that this is a day of victory for the people of the West. The world is theirs to draw upon as they please and their stores are overflowing. We are left standing at a distance, agape, watching our share growing less and less; and with the fire of our hunger blazes the fire of our wrath. We wish we could have the opportunity of getting hold of the man who has been eating our share of the food. But so far he has got hold of us, and the opportunity still remains in his hands, and has not reached us at all.

But why does, the chance not come to us? Why is the enjoyment of the earth's plenty for them alone? Surely because of some underlying truth. It is not a case of banding ourselves together in a particular way so as to be able to deprive them and provide for ourselves. The matter is not quite so simple as that. It is mere folly to expect to get the locomotive under control by hitting the driver on the head: for it is not the man but his science which makes the engine go. So the fire of our wrath will not serve the purpose; we must acquire the requisite science, if we covet the boon which Truth has in her gift.

It is like a father with two sons. The father drives his own motor car and has promised it to the son who learns first how to drive. One of the sons is alert and full of curiosity. His eye is always on the driving to see how it is done. The other one is excessively good natured. His reverent gaze is always on his father's face. He pays no regard to what the hands are doing with lever and wheel. The clever one soon picks up the science of motor driving, and one fine day he drives off all by himself, with exultant toots of the horn. So absorbed does he become in the joy of his new acquisition that he forgets even the existence of his father. But the father does not punish him for the liberty he is taking, nor take the car away from him; for he is pleased that his son should succeed. The other son, when he sees his brother careering madly over his fields, playing havoc with his corn, dare not stand in the way to protest, even in the name of their father; for that would mean certain death. So he keeps his gaze fixed on his father's face, saying that this is all in all to him.

But whoever contemns the useful, saying he has no use for it, simply courts suffering. Every utility has its rightful claim, the ignoring of which entails a permanent slavery in the way of payment of interest until its dues are fully met. The only way to get rid of the school master's importunity is to do one's lessons properly.

There is an outside aspect of the world where it is simply an immense machine. In this aspect, its laws are fixed and do not yield by a hair's breadth either this way or that. This mechanical world gets in our way at every step; and he who, through laziness or folly, tries to evade its laws, does not succeed in cheating the machine, but only himself. On the other hand, he who has taught himself its working is able not only to avoid its obstruction, but to gain it for an ally, and so is enabled to ride swiftly over the paths of the material world. He reaches the place of his quest first, and has his fill of the good things there. But those who have lagged behind, jogging along unaided arrive late to find very little left over for themselves.

Since these are the facts, merely to revile the science by which Westerners have gained their victory in the modern world, will not tend to relieve our sufferings, but will rather add to the burden of our sins. For this science which the West has mastered is true. If you say, it is not their science, but their satanic abuse of it to which you object, that point need not disturb us; for we may be certain that the satanic part of it will be the death of them, because Satan's way is not true.

The beasts live if they get food, and die if they get hurt. They accept what comes, without question. But one of the greatest traits of man is his habit of protesting. Unlike the beast, he is a rebel by nature. Man has achieved his glorious position in the history of the world because he has never been able to accept as final what has been imposed upon him without his concurrence or co-operation. In short, man is by no means a mild creature only; he is ever in revolt. From the beginning of his career, man has sworn to sway the world of events. How? By conquering it, or else coming to an understanding with the forces of which it is the resultant. He will never be content to be merely a fact; he needs must be a factor. He began with magical practices, because at first it seemed to him that whatever was happening was due to some wonderful magic at work behind the scenes. He felt that he also could take a hand in it, if he could but master the art. The activities which began as magic ended in science, but the motive in both cases has been the refusal to be subservient to the blind forces of nature. Those, whose efforts were successful, attained the mastery over the material world, and were no longer its slaves.

The belief in universal, immutable laws, is the basis of science, and loyalty to this belief has led to victory. Secure in this loyalty, the people of the West are winning their way through the obstructions and difficulties of the material world. But those who have held on to a lingering faith in magic have failed to acquire control over the world's mechanism, and are being defeated at every turn. At a time when we were still busy invoking the exorciser against ill and the fortune-teller against poverty and misfortune, while we were content to seek protection against small-pox from Sitala Devi, and relied on charms and spells for the destruction of our enemies, in Europe a woman asked Voltaire, whether it was true that incantations could kill a flock of sheep. She got the reply that doubtless they could, provided there was enough arsenic. I do not mean that there is no belief in magic in any corner of Europe today; but certainly belief in the efficacy of arsenic is universal. That is why they can kill when they want to, and we have to die even when we do not.

It is a platitude to be saying today that the phenomenal world is only a manifestation of universal law, and that, through the law of reason, we realise the laws of the material world. It is because we know such power to be inherent in us, that we can take our ultimate stand on our own selves. But he who, in his commerce with the universe, cannot get rid of the habit of looking to accidental interventions, tends to rely on anything and everything except himself. One who doubts that his intelligence will avail, ceases to question, or to experiment. He casts about for some external master, and as a result is exploited, right and left, beginning from police officers and ending with malaria-breeding mosquitoes. Cowardliness of intellect is a fertile source of feebleness of power.

From what period did political liberty begin to evolve in the West? In other words, when did the people of the West begin to realize, that political power was not the privilege of special individuals or classes, but depended on their own consent? It was from the time that their pursuit of science freed them from nameless fears, and they discovered that only those laws were true which could not be distorted or diverted by anyone's whim or fancy.

Giant Russia was so long the slave of her Czars, because her people relied in every matter on Providence and not in their own powers. Even now, when her Czar is gone that power which has taken his place is but dragging her through a sea of blood to the barren shore of starvation. The reason is that self-rule cannot be established through outside agency, but must be based on that self-reliance which is born of trust in one's own intellect.

I was once engaged in trying to improve one of our Bengal villages. There had been a fire and I asked the villagers how it was they had not been able to save a single homestead? "It was our fate!" they exclaimed. "Not fate," said I, "but the lack of wells. Why not make wells?" "That will be as the master pleases," was the reply. So it comes to pass that the people, whose homesteads are gutted by fate and whose wells await the master's pleasure, may lack all else but never a master.

From the very beginning God has given us Swarajya in His universe. That is to say He has given us for ourselves universal laws independent of Himself. We cannot be prevented from bringing these under our control by anyone or anything except our own folly. So the Upanishat has it, that God has given us laws for our own material provisions, immutable for all time. That is to say those laws hold good for all people and all period, and all occasions. Had this not been so, man would have remained weakly dependent on God at every step, all his energies exhausted in propitiating, now this intermediary, now the other, in a chronic state of abject fear. But our God-given Magna Charta of Swaraj sets us for ever free from the wiles of all pretending intermediaries,—with our freedom firmly based on well-ordered and enduring laws. In the glowing letters of sun, moon and stars, God gives us His message: "You have no need of my help at every turn in the material world. I stand aside. On the one hand, you have the laws of matter; on the other, the laws of your mind. Use them together, and grow in greatness. The empire of the universe is yours; yours its wealth, yours its armoury of forces. May yours be the victory!"

He who accepts this charter of material Swaraj has the opportunity to achieve all other kinds of Swaraj and also to keep them when achieved. But those, who surrender their intellect to the slave-driver have no help but to be slaves in politics as well. Those who insist on invoking masters, where God Himself has refrained from asserting. His own mastery, those who court insult where God has granted them dignity,—their self-rule will certainly mean rule after rule, the only doubt being as to that little prefix "self".

The science of material existence is in the keeping of the professors of the West. This is the science which gives us food and clothing, health and longevity and preserves us from the attacks of matter, brute and barbarian. This is the science of the unchangeable laws of matter and self-rule can only be achieved when these are brought into harmony with the laws of our mind. There is no other way.

Let us consider the case of a departure from this truth. Take the idea that, if a Mussalman draws water from the well of a Hindu, the water becomes impure. This is a confusion indeed! For, water belongs to the world of matter, and impurity to the realm of the spirit. Had it been said, that if the Hindu contemns the Mussalman, this shows the impurity of his mind, the proposition would have been intelligible, it would be wholly a spiritual question. But when impurity is imputed to the Mussalman's vessel, then that which belongs to the category of the material is taken entirely outside the scope of material laws. The intellect is defrauded of its legitimate scope. The Hindu disciple of the West will urge that this imputation of impurity is only a religious way of promulgating a sanitary doctrine. Sanitation, however, takes no account of moral purity. The answer is given us: "But it is only put thus in order to induce people, who have no faith in Science, to obey its laws." This is not a right reply. For if external compulsion be once brought in, it comes to stay. Those for whom it is made necessary, lose all initiative of their own and get into the habit of depending on injunctions. Furthermore, if truth has to be bolstered up by untruth, it ends by getting smothered. By using the phrase 'morally impure', where 'physically unclean' is meant, truth is made difficult of apprehension. Whether a thing is unclean or not can be proved. And if uncleanliness be the charge, a comparative inquiry into the vessels and wells of Hindu and Moslem should be made, and we should find out if there is anything less sanitary in the Moslem water arrangements than in those of the Hindu. Uncleanliness itself being an external fault, it can be remedied by external means. But an allegation of impurity takes the question out of the jurisdiction of the ordinary mind, and makes it a matter of religion. Is that a sound method of achieving the desired object? To keep the intellect in a state of delusion cannot be the way to attain high moral excellence. Untruth from the teacher, together with blindness in the pupil, will never create a spiritually healthy society.

So if we call Western Science 'impure', merely because it was discovered in the West, we shall not only be unable to master it, but shall also be placing in a bad light that Eastern Science which teaches of moral purity.

Here I am apprehensive of another argument. Many will ask, whether when the West was still savage, clothed in skins and living by hunting, we in the East had not been able to feed and clothe ourselves? When they fared forth merely for plunder, had we not evolved a political commonwealth? Certainly, we were then far more advanced than the West. But the reason was that, in those days, we in the East had a superior knowledge of Science and its laws. We had then the knowledge of cultivation and weaving. That scientific knowledge went far further than mere skill in hunting which the West then possessed. It requires more science to conduct a stable government than to hunt wild beasts. How then did the parts become reversed? It was not by any trick of fate. It was by no luck or magic. Rather it was due to the West learning the same Science which the East had learnt before, and to a still more useful purpose. Therefore, it is not by looking to some external force that we can now compete with the West. We can resist their onslaught only if we make their Science our own. To say this implies that the greatest of our problems in India is the problem of Education.

But at this point in the argument, I have to answer the further question, whether I have found satisfaction in that aspect of power, which the West is now presenting to mankind. My answer would be, 'No'. What I saw did not satisfy me. The picture was that of self-aggrandizement, not that of happiness. For seven months at a stretch I have lived in the giant's Castle of Wealth, in America. Through my hotel window sky-scrapers frowned on me. They only made me think of the difference between Lakshmi, the Goddess of grace, who transmutes wealth into well-being, and the ugly god Mammon, who represents the spirit of insensate accumulation. The process of piling up has no ultimate end in view. Twice two are four, twice four are eight, twice eight are sixteen, the figures leap frog-like over increasing spans. He who is obsessed by their stride becomes intoxicated by it and revels in the glory of mere multiplication. But, what oppressiveness it produces in the mind of an onlooker, I can best explain by an analogy.

Once I was in a house-boat on the brimming autumn river, seated at the window on the eve of the full moon. Not far off, moored alongside the bank, there was an up country cargo boat, whose crew were enthusiastically engaged in entertaining themselves. Some of them had tom-toms, others had cymbals; none of them had a voice; but all of them had muscles beyond any possibility of question! And the beats of their clanging sped on from double-quick to quadruple-quick time, with the stimulus of its own frenzy. Ten o'clock passed, eleven o'clock passed; it was well on towards midnight, yet they would not stop. Why should they? Had there been a song, there would have been some natural pause. Anarchic rhythm, on the other hand, has movement, but no rest: excitement, but no satisfaction. Those rhythm-maniacs on the cargo boat had no doubt that they were scaling the topmost heights of enjoyment. But what of poor me?

I was much in the same plight over there on the other side of the Atlantic. The *crescendo* of their rhythmic advance like a wilderness of bricks and mortar was obvious. But where was the song? That was the burdening question. And standing before the forbidding might of their towering opulence, the son of indigent downtrodden India was left cold, murmuring—"What then?"

I am not for emptiness, in the garb of renunciation. External restraint is true, only when it is the expression of internal fulness,—just as time and tune are kept properly regulated because the artist is full of his song. Unmitigated noise has no occasion for disciplined restraint. If there be the truth called Love, at the heart, enjoyment must be restrained, service must be true, that is to say, such a process of realization needs the spirit of charity to help it. The renunciation, which is in the chastity of love, is the true renunciation. The union of the Goddess of Plenitude with the God who needs no wealth is the true union.

When I was in Japan, the spirit of old Japan gave me a profound pleasure. Old Japan had found Beauty reigning on the lotus throne of her heart. In her dress and ornament, in her dwellings and furniture, in her work and play, in her rites and ceremonials, she expressed in various forms the One who is beauty. Utter penury is as unmeaning as lavish represented neither, but rather the fulness of perfection. Such fulness makes man's heart hospitable,—its passion is for welcome and not for rejection. Side by side with the old I have also seen the modern Japan. Here the spirit of the rhythm-maniac has assumed control, and its din mocks the moonlight.

By all this, I do not mean that railways and telegraphs are not needed. They gave their use, but not their message. Where man has needs, he must furnish himself with materials; but where he has fulness, there is manifest his immortality; Man's envy and hatred are in the region of his material needs, the region where he is in want. Here he erects his barricades and maintains his guards. Here he is for self-aggrandizement and for the exclusion of others. But where he is immortal he displays, not things, but his soul. He invites all to enter. His distribution does not mean diminution; and so peace reigns.

When Europe was opening out the mystery chambers of the Universe with the keys of Science, she found at every step fixed laws. And their constant presence in her field of vision ever since has caused her to forget that there is something more behind these laws, which has its harmony of delight in accord with our complete humanity. By the help of natural laws we achieve success, but man aspires to gain something greater than success. The laws which the tea-garden manager imposes on his coolies, if well-devised, tend to increase his output. But where the manager's friends are concerned, he does not dream of efficient laws. In dealing with his friends he does not increase his output; he spends his tea in entertainment. It is well to believe in the laws which make for efficiency. But if ever it is believed, that the truth of friendship is not a part of an infinite truth, then that belief tends to destroy our humanity itself. We cannot make friends with a machine. Therefore, if we cease to be aware of anything beyond mechanism, then our personality which is ever seeking its own affinity in other persons finds no permanent refuge. The West, in its one-sided pursuit of Science has been steadily thrusting personality further and further into the background till hardly any room has been left for it. If our own one-sided spiritual tendency of mind has made us lose our way and left us stranded in the quagmire of weakness and poverty, the limping gait of the West has taken it no nearer, from its own side, to humanity's goal.

True, it is difficult to cope with those who consistently keep to the tea-garden-manager outlook on the universe; for they have enlisted the services of the genie of efficiency. The good natured man invariably gets caught by their recruiters, and once in their net, there is no escape. He has no conception of the value of fixed laws of the world. He insists on pinning his faith just where he should not, whether it be on the unluckiness of Thursday, the virtue of talismans, the trustworthiness of touts, or the honesty of tea-garden recruiters. But even the most helplessly good natured man has a place, beyond the reach of laws, where he can take his stand and say: "God grant I may never be born, despite my trials and troubles, to be a tea-garden manager!"

And yet the tea-garden manager also has his own methods of benevolence. He makes sanitary dwellings for his coolies, soundly and symmetrically built, and his arrangements for their supplies are admirable. But this non-human benevolence is but an appendage of efficiency. It helps to increase the profits; it bestows a kind of benefit upon the human tools. But from that springs not even a fraction of true happiness.

Let no one imagine that I am referring to the relations between the Western masters and their Eastern servants only. The undue stress laid on the mechanical side of the world, both in external and internal relations, has similarly created a split in the polity of the West. If the mechanical bonds of association be made into a fetish, the living bonds of voluntary fellowship slacken. And this, in spite of the fact that these mechanical bonds make for extraordinary mechanical efficiency. Commodities multiply, markets spread, tall buildings pierce the sky. Not only so, but in education, healing and the amenities of life, man also gains real success. That is because the machine has its own truth. But this very success makes the man, who is obsessed by its mechanism, hanker for more and more mechanism. And as his greed continually increases, he has less and less compunction in lowering man's true value to the level of his own machine.

Greed is not an ideal—it is a passion. Passion cannot create. So when any civilization gives the first place to greed, the soul relation between man and man is severed; and the more luxurious such a civilization grows in pomp and power, the poorer it becomes in truth of soul. A picture is a creation, because it is the harmony of many lines, related to one another. An engineer's plan is not a picture, because the lines there are bound to each other by some external necessity. When greed of success is the main nexus between man and man. Society becomes a huge plan and ceases to be a picture of the ideal. Man's spiritual relations are lost sight of; money becomes the prime mover; the capitalist the driver; and the rest of mankind merely the fuel for the running of the machine. It is possible to measure the value of such civilization in terms of the speed of its progress. But man, at the bottom of his heart, does not worship Mammon, and so has no real happiness in the triumphal progress of his car. Because his faith in Mammon is wanting, the cords, by which man is bound to Mammon's service, are not bonds of loyalty, but shackles. And man ever revolts when he feels himself shackled. The dark clouds of this social revolt lower only too dismally over the West. There the union, devised for exploitation, has ended in disruption. In India the union, imposed by customary rule has resulted in emasculation. Because traditional customs and professional dealings are not ideals, therefore they make their arrangements by keeping man's soul out of the account.

What is the ideal? Jesus Christ said: "I and my father are one." Here is one ideal. "My unity with my father," is a true unity. But the unity of the coolie with the manager is not true. Again a great ideal has been given utterance to in the Isha Upanishat. "All that moves in this moving world is enveloped by God. Therefore enjoy by renunciation; never covet others' possessions." I have already referred in terms of condemnation to the greed which has become the dominant motive in the West. Why do we condemn it? The Rishi tells us the reason,—"Do not covet." Why should we not covet? Because truth cannot be obtained through greed. But if I say, "I want my enjoyment rather than truth." Well, the Rishi also says, "Enjoy." But there can be no enjoyment outside truth. What then is the truth? It is this: "All that moves in this moving world is enveloped by God." "Had all that moves in the world" been itself the ultimate truth, then to keep piling up would have been the best thing to do; and greed would have been the most efficient of man's virtues. But the truth being this, that God is there, enveloping all things, we have to enjoy this truth with our soul, and for such enjoyment renunciation is needed, not greed. During my seven months' stay in America, the land mountain-high piles of lucre, I have watched this striving in the reverse direction. There, "all that moves in this moving world" has become prominent. God, who "envelops all things" has become obscured in the thick dust of dollars. Therefore, in America, the injunction to enjoy is not observed with the help of truth, but with the help of money. Truth gives us Unity. Money sets up separation. Furthermore, it keeps our soul empty. Therefore, it causes in us a hankering to fill that emptiness from outside, and we pursue the path of multiplying numbers in hot haste. While our desire runs at a break-neck pace, jumping from one figure to another in the multiplication table, we grow dizzy and forget that whatever else we may have been acquiring, it is not happiness.

Our Rishis have told us that satisfaction is only to be found in the One. Apples fall one after another. The truth about their falling cannot be arrived at by counting them: arithmetical progression marches on indefinitely and the mind turns away unsatisfied from each fresh enumeration, saying: "What does it all mean?" But when innumerable falls find their unity in the principle of gravitation, the intellect at last finds satisfaction and can say: "Enough, I have found the truth."

And what of the truth of Man. It is not in the Census Report, not in an interminable series of figures. Man is expressed, says the Upanishat, when he realises all creation in himself and himself in all creation. Otherwise his truth is obscured. There is a telling example of this in our history. When the Lord Buddha realised humanity in a grand synthesis of unity, his message went forth to China as a draught from the fountain of immortality. But when the modern empire-seeking merchant, moved by his greed, refused allegiance to this truth of unity, he had no qualms in sending to China the deadly opium poison, nay, in thrusting it down her throat at the cannon's mouth. What could be a better illustration of how the soul of man is revealed, and how it is obscured?

Many at the present moment will exclaim: "That is just what we were saying. How can we possibly maintain relations with those, who only know how to divide, whose rapacious maw continually opens wider and wider? They know nothing of the spirit of the Infinite which is all in all to us. They follow the cult of the finite. Must we not keep at arm's length their pernicious teaching and culture?"

But this attitude is also one of division, while it has not even the merit of worldly prudence behind it. India's ancient teaching was not this. Manu says: "Restraint cannot be practised so well by leaving the world, as by remaining in it purified by wisdom." That is because the responsibility of the material world is also on us and cannot be shirked, if we would do justice to the responsibilities of the world of the spirit. So the Upanishat says: "Rescue yourself from death by the cult of the finite, and then by the cult of the infinite you shall attain immortality." Shukra, the preceptor of the Titans, was master of the art of material existence; and in his school Kacha, the emissary of the Gods, had to gain admission in order to learn the secret of immortality.

One of the first steps in the culture of the Soul is to free it from the tyranny of matter. This is the basic effort which must be made to start with; and unless the foundation be thus well and truly laid the powers of the majority of men will be exhausted in their struggles to stave off sheer physical starvation. It is quite true, that the West has kept its head bent to the ground and become so absorbed in the spade work that no time has been left to lift its head upwards. Nevertheless, it will not do for those, who aspire to live in the light and air of the upper storey to despise the spade work itself. In the region of the spirit, our seers have told us ignorance is bondage, knowledge is freedom. The same is true in the material world. Those who do not know its laws are its slaves those who do are emancipated. The bondage of external forces is an illusion which science alone can dispel.

Anyhow, the Western continents have been striving for liberation from the *maya* of matter, striking hard whenever they encounter any of the roots of that ignorance which breeds hunger and thirst, disease and want, or other ills of mundane life. In a word, they have been engaged in securing for man protection against physical death. On the other hand the striving of the Eastern peoples has been to win for man his spiritual kingdom, to lead him to immortality. By their present separateness, East and West alike are now in danger of losing the fruits of their age-long labours. That is why the Upanishat, from the beginning, has enunciated the principle, which yet may serve to unite them. "Gain protection," it says, "from death by the cult of the finite, and then by the cult of the infinite you shall attain immortality." "All that moves in the moving world" is the province of Science. "God envelops all this" is the province of the philosophy of the Infinite. When the Rishi enjoins us to combine them both, then that implies the union of the East and the West. For want of that union, the East is suffering from poverty and inertia and the West from lack of peace and happiness.

There is a danger of my being misunderstood as to what I mean by Union. I should like to make that point quite plain to my readers. Uniformity is not unity. Those who destroy the independence of other races, destroy the unity of all races of humanity. Modern Imperialism is that idea of Unity, which the python has in swallowing other live creatures. I have said before that if the spiritual altogether swallows up the material interest of man that cannot be called harmony. But when the spiritual and the material keep separate, in their own respective provinces, then they can find their unity. In like manner, when we respect the true individuality of men, then we can discover their true unity.

While Europe, after the great war, has been yearning for peace, the smaller nations have been more and more insistent in claiming self-determination. If a new era is really to be ushered in, it must be signalised by the overthrow of the monster, Wealth, and the monster, Empire, and also of the enormity of organizations. The true unity must be established upon true units. Those who co-operate with the New Age must cultivate their own individuality in order to attain successfully the spirit that shall unite. They must remember that Freedom (which is the great quest) is not of this or that nation, but of universal man.

The truth that 'the man who knows others as himself is truly revealed' is not only to be found in the pages of man's scriptures. Its working can be seen throughout human history. In the beginning, we see man gathered into separate groups within barriers of mountain and ocean. As soon as man came into touch with man, the problem of his truth as a member of the human race demanded attention. Whenever men came together, but were unable to unite, they lost their truth. Those of them, who, having come into contact, hit out wildly against one another, none trusting the other, each trying to gain the advantage, have all disappeared from the face of the earth. And those, who have tried to realize the one Soul in the souls of all, have developed into great peoples.

Thanks to Science, so many vehicles of communication are speeding overland and water and even through the air, that today there are no longer any geographical barriers. Now, not only individual men, but whole nations have come into contact, and the problem has become acute. Those whom Science has brought together how shall man put asunder? If the conjunction of man is a real union, then all goes well, otherwise nearness produces conflict. Such an age of universal conflict has come. The outward forces which are bringing men together are running at a great speed; the inner forces which make men united are lagging behind. It is as if a locomotive were to rush on with its train, the driver left behind wringing his hands in despair, while a cheering crowd of onlookers are lost in admiration at its headlong speed, crying 'This is progress indeed!' And we, the mild men of the East, who are in the habit of trudging along on foot, how can we possibly bear the brunt of the collision? Things which are near us and yet keep aloof, if they have their movement, always give us shocks. Such a conjunction of shocks may not be comfortable, but, in certain circumstances, it may be wholesome.

However that may be, nothing is more obvious than the fact, that nations have come together, but yet are not united. The agony of this presses on the whole world. Why is it, that, in spite of its torture, the world can find no solution? Because even those, who had mastered the art of uniting within their own boundaries, have not yet learnt the secret of uniting outside them. The barrier, by limiting truth, makes truth itself at first easier of comprehension; so man is apt to give the credit to the barrier and not to the truth; he worships the priest to the exclusion of the divinity, and fears the policemen more than the king.

Nations have risen on the strength of truth, but it was not their Nationalism which was true. And yet human sacrifices are being offered to this barrier-god. So long as the victims were of alien race no question arose; but all of a sudden, in 1914, the votaries developed a mania for sacrificing one another. Then the doubt arose: 'Is this after all the right kind of household god, who fails to distinguish between kindred and stranger?' While he was fastening his fangs on the limbs of the offerings from the East, sucking out their substance, the festivity of the sacrificial rites waxed fast and furious, for stimulants were not lacking either. Today some of them are to be seen with bowed heads, oppressed with the misgiving, that perhaps this kind of riotous worship might not be altogether healthy. While the war was at its height, there was some hope that the orgy of Nationalism might soon be brought to an end. But the war, which disappeared in one aspect came back wearing the mask of peace. The thinkers of the West are bemoaning the tragic fact, that, the infatuation from which this disaster has been caused, is still as vigorous as ever. This infatuation is Nationalism, the collective Egotism of the whole nation. It is a passion whose tendency is against the ideal of Unity. Its pull is towards itself.

The people have come together. This great truth cannot be crushed beneath the triumphal car of any imperialistic ambition. Then we must establish relations with this truth. Otherwise there will be no end to these wars of annihilation. Since it is essential that education should fit in with the spirit of the time, the high priests of Nationalism will avail themselves of every pretext and opportunity to inculcate by means of education the doctrine of national pride in the growing generation. When Germany frankly made her Universities the servitors of her political ambitions, other European nations condemned her. But which of the greater European nations has not followed suit? The only difference has been that Germany being the greater master of scientific method, carried on the nationalistic propaganda more thoroughly. She made her education into a scientific incubator for hatching the eggs of Nationalism, and the chickens produced have been more vigorous than those of the neighbouring nations. The same has become the function of the press,—the unremitting circulation of plausible national untruths.

An Education which can free the nations from this ungodly fetish of Nationalism is what is chiefly needed today. Tomorrow is to begin the chapter of the federation of races. Any evil tendencies of thought and sinful habits, which militate against the spirit of federation will unfit us to take our part in the history of tomorrow. I hope I can claim to be duly conscious of the glories of my own country, but my fervent prayer is that such consciousness may never make me forgetful of the earliest message of our seers, the message of unity, in which the forces of disruption have no place.

I can hear, from over the seas the wailing of men questioning themselves: 'Wherein was our sin,—in what part of our thoughts, of our education,—that this terrible suffering is ours today?' May the reply of our Rishis reach them: 'There can be no blindness and sorrow, where all beings are known as oneself and the Unity is realized.' I can hear, from over the seas, the cry for Peace. We must give them the message of our great forefathers: 'Peace is where the Good is; the Good is where there is Unity.'

Shantam, Shivam, Advaitam.
Unity is peace; for Unity is the Good.

I am fully conscious of the glories of my motherland, so it shames me even to think, that now, on the eve of the new age, when the command of Rudra, the Terrible, has gone forth to sweep away the rubbish of decayed ages, this same rubbish should be piled up into an altar for her worship. He who is Peace, who is Good, is the One Universal Refuge of all the different Nations of men. Cannot the chanting of the *mantra,*—Shantam, Shivam, Advaitam,—with the first fresh glow of the dawning era, rouse in us once more our ancient love of truth?

It is the dream of my heart, that the culture-centre of our country should also be the meeting ground of the East and West. In the field of business, antagonism still prevails; it struggles hard against reconcilement. In the field of culture, there is no such obstacle. The householder, who is exclusively occupied with his domestic concerns and is chary of his hospitality, is poor in spirit. No great country can afford to be confined to its kitchen, it must have its reception room where it can do honour to itself by inviting the world.

India has only government institutions, or their prototypes, for her education. By far the greater part of it consists begging for the crumbs of other people attaining. When begging becomes a habit the lack of hospitality ceases to cause shame. So the Indian Universities have no compunction in proclaiming themselves mendicants with nothing to offer in return for what they receive. It is not true that nothing is expected from them. I have often been confronted in Europe with the question: 'Where is India's voice.' But when the enquirer from the West comes to India, and listens at her door he says: 'The words which we hear are only the feeble echoes of our own words the mere parodies of things preached by us.' To me, it has always seemed that when the Indian disciple of Max Muller boasts in strident tones of his Aryan descent, there is heard all the blatant noise of the Western brass band; and also when in a frenzy of condemnation he rejects the West, there is heard only the most discordant sounds of the Western tunes.

It is my prayer that India should, in the name of all the East, establish a centre for the culture of Truth to which all may be invited. I know she lacks material wealth, but she has no lack of spiritual wisdom. On the strength of the latter she may invite the world, and be invited into every part of the world, not to hang round the threshold, but to take the seat prepared for her in the inmost chamber. But even that honour may be left out of sight. The real object of our endeavour should be to realize truth in our inner nature and then to manifest it in the outer world,—not for the sake of expediency: not for gaining honour, but for emancipating man's spirit from its obscurity. The ideal revelation of soul must be expressed, through all our education and through all our work, and then by honouring all men we shall ourselves be honoured, and by welcoming the new age we shall ourselves be freed from the burden of senility. The mantra of that education is this:

'He, who realizes all creatures in himself and himself in all creatures, is never obscured.'

1921

A Vision of India's History

When individual communities, who come to dwell in the same neighbourhood, differ from each other in race and culture the first attempts at unity become too obviously mechanical in their classified compartments. Some system of adjustment is needed in all kinds of Society, but in order that a system should be successful it most completely submit itself to the principle of life and become the organ for the vital functions.

The history of India has been the history of the struggle between the constructive spirit of the machine, which seeks the cadence of order and conformity in social organization, and the creative spirit of man, which seeks freedom and love for its self-expression. We have to watch and see if the latter is still living in India; and also whether the former offers its service and hospitality to life, through which its system can be vitalized.

We know not who were the heroes of the day when the racial strife between Aryan and non-Aryan was at its height. The significant fact is that the names of such conquering heroes have not been sung in Indian epic. It may be that an episode of that race war in India lies enshrouded in the mythical version of King Janamejaya's ruthless serpent sacrifice—the attempted extermination of the entire Nāga race. There is, however, no special glorification of that king on this account. But he who strove to bring about the reconciliation between Aryan and non-Aryan is worshipped to this day as an Avatar.

As the leading figures of the grand movement of that age, which sought to embrace both Aryan and non-Aryan in a larger synthesis, we find the names of three Kshatriyas standing out in the story of the Rāmāyaṇa. There Janaka, Visvāmitra and Rāmachandra are not merely related by bonds of kinship or affection, but through oneness of ideal. What if it be possible that Janaka, Visvāmitra and Rāma may not have been contemporaries as a matter of historical fact? That does not take away from their nearness to one another in the plane of idea. Viewed from the standpoint of intervening space, the distance between the earth and the moon may loom large, and tend to obscure the fact of their relationship. There are many double stars in the firmament of history, whose distance from each other does not affect the truth of their brotherhood. We know, from the suggestion thrown out by the poet of Rāmāyana, that Janaka, Visvāmitra and Rāma, even if actually separated by time, were nevertheless members of such a triple system.

In the history of idea, as distinguished from the history of fact, a hero often comes to mean, for his race, the *ideal;* and ceases to be an individual. In Aryan history, Janaka and Visvāmitra as well as Rāma have become historical symbols. They are composite pictures of numerous personalities having a common purpose. Just as King Arthur, from the Christendom of the Dark Ages, represents the Christian Knight, the valiant champion of the faith against all challengers, so in India we get glimpses of the Kshātra ideal gathering round its champions for a determined and prolonged crusade against its opponents. Proofs are not wanting that often these opponents were the Brahmins.

The idea, which was behind the neo-Kshatriya movement of old, cannot be known to-day in its full meaning, but still it is possible to make out the lines along which the divergence of Brahmin and Kshatriya had occurred.

The four-headed god Brahmā represents the four Vedas with all their hymns and regulations of sacrifice. The Brahmin Bhrigu, one of the most renowned priests of the ancient days, is said to have sprung from the heart of Brahmā, thereby showing that he occupied a prominent part in the cult of Vedic ceremonialism. It is said in the Bhāgavata Purāṇa that the Kshatriya king, Kārtavīrya, stole a sacrificial cow from Yamadagni, a priest of the same Bhrigu clan, which was the cause of the class-war led by Parasu-rāma, the son of Yamadagni, against the whole Kshatriya community. Unless the stealing of the sacrificial cow stands for an idea, such a crusade of the Brahmin against the entire Kshatriya class misses its meaning. It really indicates that among a great body of Kshatriyas there arose a spirit of resistance against sacrificial rites, and this gave rise to a fierce conflict between the two communities.

It has to be noted that the series of battles begun by Parasu-rāma, the descendant of Bhrigu, at last came to their end with his defeat at the hands of Rāma-chandra. This Kshatriya hero, as we all know, is accepted and adored as an incarnation of Vishnu, the deity of the monotheistic sect of Bhāgavatas. It certainly means that this fight was a fight of ideals, which terminated in the triumph of the religion in which, at a later date, Rāma-chandra occupied a central place.

It is well known that Rāma had an intimate relationship with the great king Janaka, which also we consider to be a relationship of ideals. Janaka has won from the people of India the title of Rājarshi, the kingly prophet. It has been said about him in the Bhagavad-Gitā:

कर्मणैव हि संसिद्धि आस्थिता जनकादय:।[1]

Janaka and others of his kind have attained their fulfilment through the performance of duty. This means that Janaka, and others who had the same faith as he, followed the path of moral action for attaining spiritual perfection. This was specially mentioned because it was not the path of the orthodox religion, which laid stress on ceremonials performed for the sake of averting injuries or acquiring merit or wealth. It was evidently a revolutionary movement, one of whose leaders was Janaka, and Rāma-chandra obtained his inspiration from him. Therefore, when we find that it was the Kshatriya Rāma-chandra who defeated the Brahmin Parasu-rāma, we feel certain that the battle which was fought was the battle of two differing ideals.

Those institutions which are static in their nature raise their fixed walls of division. This is why, in the history of religions, priesthood has everywhere hindered the freedom of man and maintained dissensions. The moving principle of life unites. It deals with the varied, and seeks unity in order to be able to deal truly. The Brahmins, who had the static ideals of Society in their charge, spun into elaboration the different forms of ritualism

1. The *Bhagavad-Gītā,* 3/20.

and set up sectarian barriers between clans and classes. Of the two original deities of the Indo-Aryan tribe, the Sun and Fire, the latter specially represented the cult of Brahmins. Round it different forms of sacrifice gathered and grew in number, accompanied by strict rules of incantation; with it came to be intimately associated the pluralism of divinity, since fire had always been made the vehicle of oblation to numerous gods.

The Kshatriyas, on the other hand, as they sallied forth in their endeavour against all obstacles, natural and human, developed in their life the principle which was for expansion and inclusion. Born and bred amidst the clash of forces, hostile and favourable, in the field of life's strenuous conflict, the superfine complexities of the external forms of religious worship could have no special significance for them. With them the Sun-god seems to have a special connection. From him, Manu, the law giver who was a Kshatriya, and also the great kingly line of Raghu, to which belonged Rāma-chandra, are said too have sprung. This Sun-god, in course of time, developed into the personal god Vishnu, the god of the Bhāgavata sect, the god who principally belonged to the Kshatriyas.

From Brahmā's four mouths had issued the four Vedas, revealed for all time, jealously sealed against outsiders, as unchanging as the passive features of Brahmā himself rapt in meditation. This was the symbol of Brahmanism, placid and immutable, profoundly filled with the mystery of knowledge. But the four active arms of Vishnu were busy, proclaiming the sway of the Good; expanding the cycle of unity; maintaining the reign of law; supporting the spirit of beauty and plenitude. All the symbols carried by Vishnu have the different aspects of Kshatriya life for their significance.

Brahma-vidyā, the knowledge of Supreme Truth, had its origin in the seclusion of the primeval forest of India, where the human mind could intensely concentrate itself in the depth of things and the reality of spiritual existence. The world must acknowledge its debt to the contemplative Indo-Aryan for this profound vision of truth which he has revealed to man. This Brahma-vidyā in India has followed two different courses. In the one, the Supreme Soul is viewed as monistic, absolutely negating the phenomenal world; in the other as dualistic in creative imagination, yet one in essence. Unless duality is admitted there can be no worship; but, if at the same time, fundamental unity be not recognized, the worship cannot be intimate and loving.

The original gods of the Vedas were separate from man; they received worship which consisted only of external ceremony, not the homage of love. When the relationship between God and man came to be known as based on their spiritual unity, then only the worship of love became possible. That is how the mystic Brahma-vidyā brought in its train the Religion of Love, of which the god was Vishnu. There is no doubt that the religion of love had its origin, or at least its principal support, among Kshatriyas whose freedom of movement had the effect of liberating their minds from the coils of established forms of sacrifice.

That, naturally, there was a period of struggle between the cult of ritualism supported by the Brahmins, and the religion of love, is evident. The mark of the Brahmin Bhrigu's kick, which Vishnu carries on his breast, is a myth-relic of the original conflict. In the fact that Krishna, a Kshatriya, was not only at the head of the Vaishnava cult, but the object of its worship, that in his teaching, as inculcated in the Bhagavad-Gītā, there are hints of detraction against Vedic verses, we find a proof that this cult was developed by the Kshatriyas. Another proof is found in the fact that the two non-mythical human avatars of Vishnu, Krishna and Rāma-chandra, were both Kshatriyas, and the Vaishnava religion of love was spread by the teaching of the one and the life of the other.

The ideal, which was supported by the Kshatriya opponents of the priesthood, is represented by the Bhagavad-Gītā. It was spoken to the Kshatriya hero Arjuna, by the Kshatriya prophet Krishna. The doctrine of Yoga which it advocates—the doctrine of the disinterested concentration of life, with all its thoughts and deeds, in the Supreme Being—had its tradition, according to Krishna, along the line of the Rājarshis, the kingly prophets. He says:

एवं परम्पराप्राप्तमिमं राजर्षयो विदुः ।
स कालेनेह महता योगो नष्टः परन्तप ।।[1]

This, handed on down the line, the king-sages knew. This Yoga, by great efflux of time, decayed in the world, O Parantapa.

That this religion of Yoga, as revived by Krishna and inculcated in the Bhagavad-Gītā, was not in harmony with Vedic scriptures is directly affirmed by the Master in his teaching to his disciple Arjuna when he says:

श्रुतिविप्रतिपन्ना ते यदा स्थास्यति निष्चला ।
समाधावचला बुद्धिस्तदा योगमवास्यसि ।।[2]

When thy mind, bewildered by the scriptures, shall stand immovable in contemplation, then shalt thou attain unto Yoga.

Krishna undoubtedly takes his stand against the traditional cult of sacrificial ceremonies, which according to him distracts our minds from the unity of realization when he speaks thus:

यामिमां पुष्पितां वाचं प्रवदन्स्यविपष्चितः ।
वेदवादरताः पार्थ नान्यदस्तीतिवादिनः ।।
कामात्मानः स्वर्गपरा जन्मकर्मफलप्रदाम् ।
क्रियाविशेषबहुलां भोगैश्वर्यगतिं प्रति ।।
भोगैश्वर्यप्रसक्तानां तयानहृतचेतसाम् ।
व्यवसायात्मिका बुद्धिः समाधौ न विधीयते ।।[3]

The flowery speech that the unwise utter, O Partha, clinging to the word of the Veda, saying there is nothing else, ensouled by desire and longing after heaven, the speech that offereth only rebirth as the ultimate fruit of action, that is full of recommendations to various rites for the sake of gaining enjoyments and sovereignty—the thoughts of those misled by that speech cleaving to pleasures and lordship, not being inspired with resolution, is not engaged in contemplation.

1. The *Bhagavad-Gītā,* 4/2.
2. The *Bhagavad-Gītā,* 2/53.
3. The *Bhagavad-Gītā,* 2/42-44.

These words are evidently of him, who in his teachings has for his opponents the orthodox multitude, the believers in Vedic texts.

The Kurukshetra war, described in the Mahābhārata, was a war between two parties, one of which had rejected Krishna, the other consisting of his followers, guided by him in the war. The motive of this conflict, which had attracted all the great ruling powers of that age into one or other of the two opposing parties, could not have been a mere scramble for land between cousins. In this latter version of the epic the fact is suppressed that it was an unorthodox religious movement, acknowledging Krishna to be its prophet, that gave rise to the most desperate fight in the ancient ages in India. The very fact that Krishna was the charioteer of Arjuna is proof enough that it was a war of rival creeds; and for that very reason the battleground of Kurukshetra has ever remained a sacred spot of pilgrimage.

It is significant to note that the lives of great Brahmins of the olden times, like that of Yājñavalkya, have the association of intellectual profundity and spiritual achievement, while those of great Kshatriyas represent ethical magnanimity which has love for its guiding principle. It is also significant that the people of India, though entertaining deep veneration for the Brahmin sages, instinctively ascribe divine inspiration to the Kshatriya heroes who actively realized high moral ideals in their personalities. Parasu-rāma, the only historical personage belonging to the Brahmin caste who has been given a place in the list of avatars, has never found a seat in the hearts of the people. This shows that, according to India, the mission of divine power in this country is to bring reconciliation, through moral influence, between races that are different—never to acquire dominance over others through physical prowess and military skill.

The most important aspect of Rāma-chandra's life, which has made the Vaishnava accept him as the incarnation of divine love, has been missed by the current version of the Rāmāyaṇa. There he is depicted merely as an ideal son, brother and husband, a paragon of the domestic virtues, a king who holds that cultivation of popularity is a duty higher than doing justice in the teeth of clamorous disapprobation. I have no doubt that the real story of his life, which has become dim in the course of time and with the growth of conventionalism, is concerned with his sympathy for the despised races, his love for the lowly; and that this made him the ideal of the primitive people whose totem was Hanumān.

The religion represented by the third human avatar of Vishnu, who is Buddha, has in it the same moral quality which we find in the life and teaching of Rāma and Krishna. It clearly shows the tendency of the Kshātra ideal with its freedom and courage of intellect, and above all its heart, comprehensive in sympathy, generous in self-sacrifice.

Foreign critics are too often ready to misread the conservative spirit of India, putting it down as the trade artifice of an interested priestcraft. But they forget that there was no racial difference between Brahmin and Kshatriya. These merely represented two different natural functions of the body politic, which, though from the outside presenting the appearance of antagonism, have as a matter of fact co-operated in the evolution of Indian history. Sowing seed in one's own land and reaping the harvest for distant markets are apparently contradictory. The seed-sowers naturally cling to the soil which they cultivate, while the distributors of the harvest develop a different mentality, being always on the move. The Brahmins were the guardians of the seed of culture in ancient India and the Kshatriyas strove to put into wide use the harvest of wisdom. The principle of stability and the principle of movement, though they depend upon each other for their truth, are, in human affairs, apt to lose their balance and come into fierce conflict. Yet these conflicts, as meteorology tells us in the physical plane, have the effect of purifying the atmosphere and restoring its equilibrium. In fact, perfect balance in these opposing forces would lead to deadlock in creation. Life moves in the cadence of constant adjustment of opposites; it is a perpetual process of reconciliation of contradictions.

The divergence of ideals between the Brahmins, dwellers in the forest, and the Kshatriyas, founders of cities, often led to prolonged fights, a fact which is revealed by the story of the struggle between Vasishtha and Visvāmitra. The Brahmins were not all on one side, nor the Kshatriyas all on the other. Many Kshatriyas espoused the Brahmin cause. We are told how the Brahmanic *Vidyās* as personified in the form of three maidens outraged by Visvāmitra were sore distressed, and how the chivalrous Kshatriya King, Harischandra, came to their rescue, losing his all for their sake. Then again, Krishna in the course of his endeavour to liberate the Kshatriya victims from a dread ceremonial, slew King Jarāsandha with the help of the Pāṇḍava braves. This Jarāsandha, himself a Kshatriya, was on the other side and had defeated and imprisoned many Kshatriya kings. Krishna and the Pāṇḍavas had to disguise themselves as Brahmins in order to gain entrance within the walls of his stronghold. Many other legends bear this out. The spiritual movement started by Krishna had something in it which went against the orthodox forms of worship. This is further hinted at by the legend, belonging to a later period, of his taking the part of the Abhiras against their persecution by Indra, the king of the Vedic gods, and preventing the devastation of the pasture land, Govardhana, held by that tribe.

Anyhow, it is abundantly clear that the ideals represented by Krishna had divided the Aryan community into two rival camps. When King Yudhishthira, as overlord, summoned a Rājasūya Yagña in order to heal those dissensions, King Sisupāla tried to wreck the proceedings by publicly insulting Krishna, the acknowledgment of whose precedence over all assembled Brahmins and Kshatriyas was the object of that great conclave. The main motive behind the devastating Kurukshetra war was this very internal strife within the community—the party which opposed Krishna being generalled by Drona, the famous Brahmin warrior, with his kinsmen Kripa and Asvatthāmā. It is a notable fact that Drona himself was a disciple of Parsu-rāma; and Karna, one of the most important fighters who stood against Krishna's party, also had Parasu-rāma for his teacher.

There can be no doubt that the period of history covered by the main incidents related in the Rāmāyaṇa, and that of the Kurukshetra war, are widely apart in time. Therefore, we have no other alternative but to admit that Parasu-rāma, who takes part in both the narratives, represents a long continued Brahmin movement, anti-Kshatriya in character; and Rāma and Krishna, who come out victorious in this conflict, have some common ideal, which also had a long period of struggle for its manifestation and development.

Any number of such stories show that the two epics of India were concerned with this same social revolution, that is to say, with the conflict of the new and the old within the Aryan community. We have its analogy in comparatively modern days when the Bengali epic, Kavikankan Chandī, was written. In this poem is also described the conflict of religious ideals, with the god Siva on one side and the goddess Chandī on the other. It represented the tragedy of the downfall of a higher principle of religion which had its devotees in the cultured classes, and the usurpation of its altar by the vindictive deity Chandī, patron of wild animals, who was worshipped by the aboriginal Vyādha tribes, as is described in the poem.

In the age of which the Rāmāyaṇa tells, Rāma-chandra was the champion of the new party. Rāma was born in the orthodox creed at the head of which was Vasishtha, the priest of the royal house. But from his boyhood he was won over by Visvāmitra, the implacable antagonist of Vasishtha. From this Kshatriya sage the Kshatriya prince received his initiation into a path of adventure, which evidently had behind it a mighty movement led by the great personalities of the age. It appears to me that Rāma's banishment had its cause in some conflict of ideals between Vasishtha, who stood as the symbol of the Brahmanic tradition, and Visvāmitra, who had fought against it and had wrenched Rāma-chandra away from the clasp of the unwilling royal household.

When later, for sectarian reasons, the story of the great movement was retold as the Rāmāyaṇa—a dynastic history—the absurd reason was invented about the weak old king yielding to a favourite wife, who took advantage of a vague promise which could fit itself to any demand of hers, however preposterous. This story merely reveals the later degeneracy of mind, when form assumed a greater value than spirit, and some casual words uttered in a moment of infatuation could be deemed more sacred than the truth which is based upon justice and perfect knowledge.

Janaka is considered to be an embodiment of the kingly virtues of an ideal Kshatriya. In the history of the colonization of India by the Aryans, his life must have served a great purpose. We can guess from his own position in the story of the Rāmāyaṇa that he was the principal inspiration in an enterprise which had a large meaning, and that Rama accepted his mission of life from Janaka. If we pierce through the mist which has gathered round the original narrative, we shall see that there is a general challenge to all Kshatriyas of that time in the story of Sītā's wedding.

Sītā is said to have been no ordinary mortal. She came out of the soil itself when King Janaka was employed in ploughing, as was his wont. 'Furrow-line' is the meaning which the name 'Sītā' bears. This daughter of the soil he promised to give in marriage to him who could break the bow of Siva. Rāma was led to this trial by Visvāmitra, and he succeeded first in bending the bow and then breaking it, thereupon being declared worthy of receiving Sītā from the hand of Janaka. A great fact of history, which very probably occupied a large expanse of time and was borne along by several generations of heroes, appears to have been condensed in this story. Janaka was one of those sublime figures who could focus in himself all the significance of an epoch-making endeavour, scattered through time and space.

The fact that Janaka's personality comprehended in its inner realization the Brahma-vidyā, and in its outer activity the cultivation of the soil, indicates that the Kshatriya kings developed the art of agriculture, on which the civilization of the Aryans of India was established. Originally the tending of flocks had been the main occupation of the Aryan tribes. This pastoral life likewise suited the forest tracts of India, and Brahmins in their forest retreats continued to regard the cow as their principal wealth. But though tending cattle was fit for the nomad life or for that of small groups of individuals living in forests, the concentration of large bodies of men in cities required the organized production of food. Naturally, the necessity of such organization was more keenly felt by Kshatriyas, who were founders of cities, than by the others. Therefore in the life of Janaka, the ideal king of ancient India, are seen, side by side, Brahma-vidyā—the philosophy which, if truly accepted, could be the spiritual support of the unity of races—and Agriculture which could be the material support of the economic union effected by the large communities. And just as the European colonists in America, while cutting down its forests, had to contest every step with the aborigines who depended on the chase for their living, so also in India the pioneers of agriculture encountered the opposition of the non-Aryans living in its wildernesses, whose fierce onslaughts made their task far from easy.

It is interesting to note in this connection that Zarathushtra, the great spiritual master of ancient Iran, had, like Janaka himself, an ideal which combined spiritual wisdom with a faith in agricultural civilization. And it also became his mission to save agriculture from the depredation of nomadic hordes.

Let me quote from 'Zarathushtra in Gathas,' translated from Dr Geiger's book on the subject, a passage which bears strong analogy to the aspect of the old Aryan history in India as revealed by the legend of Janaka. He says:

> The Iranian people of the Gathic period were, in fact, subdivided into husbandmen and nomads, and in the sharp opposition which obtained between the two, the prophet Zarathushtra played a prominent part. In a number of Gathic passages we see him standing as an advocate of the settled husbandmen. He admonishes them not to be tired of their good work, to cultivate diligently the fields and to devote to their cattle that fostering care which they deserve. And far and wide spreads the dominion of husbandmen and the settlements of the pious people increase, in spite of all molestations, all persecutions and violence, which they have to suffer from the nomads who attack their settlements in order to desolate their son fields and to deprive them of their herds.

King Janaka reigned over Mithila, which shows that the Aryan colonies had extended along the North to the easternmost natural boundary of India. But the Vindhya hills were then inaccessible, and the forest regions to their South remained intact. Here the Dravidian culture had reached its height, proving a formidable rival to that of the Aryans, and here the puissant Rāvaṇa had established the Dravidian god, Siva, defeating Indra and other Vedic deities.

The question which then arose in the Aryan community as to who should be the champion of their civilization, proving his competency to carry his standard forward by success in the preliminary trial of the breaking of *Haradhanu,* Siva's bow, is to be read in the same light. He who could break the strong resistance of the Siva-worshippers and carry into the South the civilization which had Brahma-Vidyā for its spirit, and for its body Agriculture, would verily win, for his spouse, Janaka's earth-born daughter Sītā.

When Rāma-chandra set out under his master Visvāmitra on what became his life-mission he started, even at that early age, by emerging triumphant through three severe tests. First, he slew the foremost of the obstructive barbarians in the vicinity. Next, at his skilled touch, the desert soil which had lain for long years bound in the hardness of stone—becoming Ahalyā, not fit for ploughing—resumed the bloom of life. It was the self-same soil which Rishi Gautama, the foremost of the early Aryan pioneers who had striven to drive the plough southwards, had found treacherous and had abandoned in despair. Thirdly, to the prowess and wisdom of this disciple of the Kshatriya sage was due the subduing of the virulence of the anti-Kshatriya movement personified in the Brahmin Parasu-rāma.

Both in the Rāmāyaṇa and Mahābhārata, the wedding of the principal heroes is connected with the story of a preliminary trial. This is not a mere chance coincidence. It is the crystallization, in the memory of the race, of a great fact which had an epoch-making character. In both cases, it was the acknowledgment of a difficult ideal which involved the heroic responsibility of upholding it in the teeth of desperate opposition. In both cases the bride was not a mortal woman, but a great mission. The trial described in the Mahābhārata is the piercing of a disc in the sky, difficult to discern, fixed in the centre of a revolving wheel, which has to be reached by concentrating one's attention on its shadow reflected in a vessel of water. This trial is obviously of a spiritual nature. The fixed centre of Truth in the heart of the revolving wheel of the World (*Samsāra*) is reflected in the depth of our own being, which can be reached by the one-pointed concentration of Yoga. Is not this the doctrine of the Gītā in the language of a picture? The symbolism of the piercing of the target is well known to us, as it is used in the Upanishad:

प्रणवोधनुः शरो ह्यात्माब्रह्म तत् लक्ष्यमुच्यते ।[1]

The bow is omkāra,—the utterance of the sound Om, which helps mental concentration,—the soul is the arrow, and the Infinite the target.

Though it was Arjuna who originally won the maiden whose name was Krishṇā, she was accepted in marriage by all the brothers. It is ridiculous to try to establish, on the strength of this fact, that the Pāṇḍava clan came from the Himalayan regions, where polyandry is tolerated. As a matter of fact, it was a sacred rite of ideal polyandry which came to be shared by all the brothers. Krishnā is the impersonation of the truth taught by Krishna himself, which had some association with the Sun-worship which was the original meaning of Vishnu-worship. It is related in the epic that in the vessel carried by Krishṇā food would become inexhaustible when she invoked the sun to help her. This must refer to the unlimited spiritual food ready for all guests who chose to come and enjoy it.

Evidently, the Pāñchāla kingdom was one of the great centres of this unorthodox religion led by the Kshatriyas. It is to be noted that it was in Pāñchāla that the Brahmin student, Svetaketu, went to the Kshatriya King, Pravāhana Jaibāli, for instruction in the mystic philosophy consisting in the doctrine that the creative process going on in the world of stars, in sky and earth, and in man himself, is a perpetual ceremony of sacrifice, for which the sacrificial fire appears in different aspects and forms. We know the story of how the Brahmin

1. The *Mundakopanishad,* 2/2/36.

Drona had a grudge against the King of Pāñchāla owing to the latter not recognizing the right of his Brahmin comrade to an equal share in his kingly wealth and power. It is not unlikely that in this legend lies hidden the history of the conflict between the power of the priesthood and that of the religious movement started by the Kshatriyas.

It can be surmised that it was from the province of Pāñchāla, in the close neighbourhood of Mathurā, that the Pāṇḍava brothers received the new creed preached by Krishna. It is significant that the Brahmin Drona, who originated the quarrel, was the first general on the side of the Kurus. Krishṇā was insulted by the Kuru brothers, as was Sītā by Rāvaṇa, and she was rescued from her humiliation by Krishna. It was proved to those who tried to expose her to indignities that her veil of honour, was of unlimited length, just as the food in her vessel was inexhaustible. It was proved, in like manner, that Rāvaṇa had not the power to defile Sītā, though, for a time, she was under his dominance, for ideal truth is inviolable ever though it may remain for a time in obscurity. That the hero of the Rāmāyaṇa, the rescuer of Sītā, and the hero of the Mahābhārata, the friend of Krishṇā, both occupied the same exalted position in the later Vaishnava religion, is not a mere accident. This fact itself gives us the clue that the original narration in the case of both the epics had for its motive the great fight for the ideal, which ushered in a new age with its new outlook upon life.

It is evident that the sun, which is the one source of light and life to us, had led the thoughts of the Indo-Aryan sages towards the monotheistic ideal of worship. The following prayer addressed to the sun, with which the Ishopanishad is concluded, is full of the mystic yearning of the soul:

हिरण्मयेन पात्रेण सत्यस्यापिहितं मुखम् ।
तत्त्वं पूषन्नपावृणु सत्यधर्माय दृष्टये ।।[1]

O Sun, nourisher of the world, Truth's face lies hidden in thy golden vessel. Take away thy cover for his eyes, who is a devotee of Truth.

1. The *Ishopanishad*, 15.

According to the Chāndogya Upanishad, the teacher Ghora, after having explained to his disciple Krishna, who had become *apipāsa,* free from desire, the consecration ceremony which leads to giving oneself a new spiritual birth, and in which *austerity, almsgiving, harmlessness, truthfulness* are one's gifts for the priests, winds up his teaching with these words: 'In the final hour one should take refuge in these three thoughts: *You are the Indestructible; you are the Unshaken, you are the very Essence of Life.*' On this point there are these two Rig verses:

आदित् प्रत्नस्य रेतसो
ज्योतिष्पश्यन्ति वासरम्
परो यदिध्यते दिवि।
उदवयं तमसस्परि
ज्योतिष्पश्यन्त उत्तरम्-
स्वः पश्यन्त उत्तरम्-
देव देवत्रा सूर्यम्
अगन्म ज्योतिरुत्तममिति
-ज्योतिरुत्तममिति ॥[1]

Proceeding from primeval seed,
The early morning light they see,
That gleameth higher than the heaven,
From out of darkness all around,
We, gazing on the higher light—
Yea, gazing on the higher light—
To Surya, god among the gods,
We have attained the highest light!
—Yea, the highest light![2]

We find a hint here of the teaching which was developed by Krishna into a great religious movement which preached freedom from desire and absolute devotion to God, and which spiritualized the meaning of ceremonies. That this religion had some

1. Quoted in the *Chhāndogya Upanishad* 3/17/7 from the *Rigveda* (8/6/30 and 1/50/10) with slight changes.
2. *The Thirteen Principal Upanishads,* translated by R.E. Hume, 1921, pp. 212-13.

association with the sun can be inferred from the legend of Krishnā finding an inexhaustible store of food in her vessel after her worship of the sun, and also the one about the piercing of the target of the disc by Arjuna, which very likely was the mystic disc of the sun, the golden vessel that holds Truth hidden in it, the Truth which has to be attained by piercing the cover.

It is interesting to see how in the history of religion the sun has also had a strong monotheistic suggestion in civilizations other than the Aryan. The great Egyptian King, Akhenaten, belonging to the 14th century BC, struggled against the congregated might of the priestly polytheistic ceremonials, substituting for them the purer form of worship of 'the radiant energy of the sun'. Here also we find the significant analogy of a religious revolution, initiated by one belonging to the kingly caste, against the opposition of the orthodox priestly sect of the land. This Egyptian King, like other prophets of his type, speaks of the truth coming to him as a personal revelation when he sings:

Thou art in my heart, there is none
Who knoweth thee excepting thy son;
Thou causest that he should have understanding,
In thy ways and in thy might.

'In ethics a great change also marks this age,' says Prof. Flinders Petrie. 'The motto "Living in Truth" is constantly put forward as the keynote to the king's character, and to his changes in various lines.'[1] Thus we find that History is a plagiarist that steals its own ideals over and over again.

In connection with this we have to note that the spiritual religion which Krishna preached must have ignored the exclusiveness of priestly creeds and extended its invitation to peoples of all classes, Aryans and non-Aryans alike. The legend of his intimate relationship with the shepherd tribes supports this view, and we still find the religion, of which Krishna is the centre, to be the great refuge of the lower castes and outcastes of the present Indian population. The most significant fact of

2. W.M. Flinders Petrie, *A History of Egypt*, p. 218.

Indian history is that all the human avatars of Vishnu had, by their life and teaching, broken the barriers of priestcraft by acknowledging the relation of fellowship between the privileged classes and those that were despised.

There came the day when Rāma-chandra, the Kshatriya of royal descent, embraced as his friend and comrade the lowest of the low, the untouchable *chandāla,* Guhaka—an incident in his career which to this day is cited as proof of the largeness of his soul. During the succeeding period of conservative reaction, an attempt was made to suppress this evidence of Rāma-chandra's liberality of heart in a supplemental canto of the epic, which is an evident interpolation; and in order to fit it with the later ideal, its votaries did not hesitate to insult his memory by having it in their rendering of the episode that Rāma beheaded with his own hands an ambitious Sudra for presuming to claim equal status in the attainment of spiritual excellence. It is like the ministers of the Christian religion, in the late war, taking Christ's name for justifying the massacre of men.

However that may be, India has never forgotten that Rāma-chandra was the beloved comrade of a *chandāla;* that he appeared as divine to the primitive tribes, some of whom had the totem of monkey, some that of bear. His name is remembered with reverence because he won over his antagonists as his allies and built the bridge of love between Aryan and non-Aryan.

This is the picture we see of one swing of the pendulum in the Aryan times. We shall never know India truly unless we study the manner in which she reacted to the pull of the two opposite principles, that of self-preservation represented by the Brahmin, and that of self-expansion represented by the Kshatriya.

When the first overtures towards social union were being made, it became necessary for the Aryans to come to an understanding with the non-Aryan religion as well. In the beginning, as we have seen, there was a state of war between the followers of Siva and the worshippers of the Vedic gods. The fortune of arms favoured sometimes one side, sometimes the other. Even Krishna's valiant comrade, Arjuna, had once to acknowledge defeat at the hands of Siva of the *Kirātas,* a hunter tribe. Then there is the well known record of a refusal to give Siva place in a great Vedic sacrifice, which led to the breaking up of the ceremony by the non-Aryans. At last, by the identification of Siva with the Vedic Rudra, an attempt had to be made to bring this constant religious antagonism to an end. And yet in the Mahābhārata we find the later story of a battle between Rudra and Vishnu, which ended in the former acknowledging the latter's superiority. Even in Krishna worship we find the same struggle, and therefore in the popular recitation of Krishna legends we often hear of Brahmā's attempt at ignoring Krishna, till at last the ancestor god of the Aryans is compelled to pay homage to the later divinity of the populace. These stories reveal the persisting self-consciousness of the newcomers even after they had been admitted to the privileges of the old-established pantheon.

The advent of the two great Kshatriya founders of religion, Buddha and Mahāvīra, in the same eastern part of India where once Janaka had his seat, brought into being a spirit of simplification. They exercised all their force against the confusing maze of religions and doctrines, which had beset the bewildered country and through which it could not find its goal. Amidst the ceremonial intricacies on the one hand, and the subtleties of metaphysical speculation on the other, the simple truth was overlooked that creeds and rites have no value in themselves; that human welfare is the one object towards which religious enthusiasm has to be directed. These two Kshatriya *sannyāsins* refused to admit that any distinctions between man and man were inherent and perpetual; according to their teaching, man could only be saved by realizing truth, and not by social conformity or non-ethical practice. It was wonderful how the triumph of these Kshatriya teachers rapidly overcame all obstacles of tradition and habit, and swept over the whole country.

Long before the full flood of the Buddhistic influence had subsided, most of the protecting walls had been broken down, and the banks of the discipline through which the forces of unification had been flowing in a regulated stream had been obliterated. In fact, in departing, Buddhism left all the numerous aboriginal diversities of India to rear their heads unchecked, because one of the two guiding forces of Indian history had been enfeebled, which with its spirit of resistance had been helping the process of assimilation.

In the midst of the Buddhistic revolution only the Brahmins were able to keep themselves intact, because the maintaining of exclusiveness had all along been their function. But the Kshatriyas had become merged into the rest of the people, and so in the succeeding age we find that most of the kings had ceased to belong to Kshatriya dynasties. Then there were the Sakas and the Hunas whose repeated hordes flowed into India and got mixed with the elder inhabitants. The Aryan civilization, thus stricken to the quick, put forth all its life force in a supreme attempt at recovery, and its first effort was directed to regaining its race consciousness, which had been overwhelmed.

During the long period of this social and religious revolution, which had the effect of rubbing out the individual features of the traditional Aryan culture, the question 'What am I?' came to the forefront. The rescue of the racial personality from beneath the prevailing chaos became the chief endeavour. Aroused by the powerful shock of a destructive opposition, it was then, for the first time, that India sought to define her individuality. When she now tried to know and name herself, she called to mind the empire of Bhārata, a legendary suzerain of by-gone days, and defining her boundaries accordingly, she called herself Bhāratavarsha. She tried to pick up the lost threads of her earlier achievements in order to restore the fabric of her original civilization. Thus collection and compilation, not new creation, were characteristics of this age. The great sage of this epoch, Vyāsa, who is reported to have performed this function, may not have been one real person, but he was, at any rate, the personification of the spirit of the times.

The movement began with the compilation of the Vedas. Now that it had become necessary to have some common unifying agent, the Vedas, as the oldest part of Aryan lore, had to be put on a pedestal for the purpose, in order to serve as a fixed centre of reference round which the distracted community could rally.

Another task undertaken by this age was the gathering and arranging of historical material. In this process, spread over a long period of time, all the scattered myths and legends were brought together, and not only these but also the beliefs and discussions of every kind which still lingered in the racial memory. And thus a great literacy image of the Aryan India of old was formed which was called the Mahābhārata—the great Bhārata. The very name shows the awakened consciousness of the unity of the people struggling to find its expression and permanent record.

The eager effort to gather all the drifting fragments from the wreck resulted in the overloading with indiscriminate miscellanies of the central narrative of the epic. The natural desire of the artist to impart an aesthetic relevancy to the story was swamped by the exigency of the time. The most important need of the age was for an immortal epic, a majestic ship fit to cross the sea of time, to serve the purpose of carrying various materials for the building of a permanent shelter for the race mind.

Therefore, though the Mahābhārata may not be history in the modern western definition of the term, it is, nevertheless, a receptacle of the historical records which had left their impress upon the living memory of the people for ages. Had any competent person attempted to sift and sort and analyse this material into an ordered array of facts, we should have lost the changing picture of Aryan society which they present, a picture in which the lines are vivid or dim, connected or confusedly conflicting, according to the lapses of memory, changes of ideal, and variations of light and shade incident to time's perspective. Self-recording annals of history, as they are imprinted on the living tablet of ages, are bared before our sight in this great work.

The genius of that extraordinary age did not stop short at the discovery of the thread of unity on which were strung the variegated materials scattered through its history; it also searched out the unity of a spiritual philosophy running through all contradictions that are to be found in the metaphysical speculations of the Vedas. The outline presentation of this philosophy was made by the same Vyāsa, who had not only the industry to gather and piece together details, but also the power to visualize the whole in its completeness. His compilation is a creative synthesis.

One thing which remains significant is the fact that this age of compilation has insisted upon the sacredness of the Brahmins and Brahmanic lore by constant reiteration in exaggerated language. It proves that there was a militant spirit fighting against odds, and that a complete loss of faith in the freedom of intellect and conscience of the people had come about. Its analogy can be found in the occasional distrust of democracy which we observe among some modern intellectuals of Europe.

The main reason for this was that, during the period of alternating ascendancy of Brahmin and Kshatriya, the resulting synthesis had its unity of Aryan character, but when during the Buddhist period not only non-Aryans but also non-Indians from outside gained free access, it became difficult to maintain organic coherence. A strong undercurrent of race-mingling and religious compromise had set in, and as the mixed races and beliefs began to make themselves felt, the Aryan forces of self-preservation struggled to put up wall beyond wall in order to prevent successive further encroachments. Only those intrusions which could not be resisted found a place within extended barriers.

Let no one imagine, however, that the non-Aryan contributions were taken in by sheer force of circumstance only, and that they had no value of their own. As a matter of fact, the old Dravidian culture was by no means to be despised, and the result of its combination with the Aryan, which formed the Hindu civilization, was that the latter acquired both richness and depth under the influence of its Dravidian component. Dravidians might not be introspective or metaphysical, but they were artists, and they could sing, design and construct. The transcendental thought of the Aryan by its marriage with the emotional and creative art of the Dravidian gave birth to an offspring which was neither fully Aryan, nor Dravidian, but Hindu.

With its Hindu civilization, India attained the gift of being able to realize in the commonplaceness of life, the infinity of the Universal. But on the other hand, by reason of the mixed strain in its blood, whenever Hinduism has failed to take its stand on the reconciliation of opposites which is of its essence, it has fallen a prey to incongruous folly and blind superstition. This is the predicament in which Hindu India has been placed by its birthright. Where the harmony between the component differences has been organically effected, there beauty has blossomed; so long as it remains wanting, there is no end to deformities. Moreover, we must remember that not only the Dravidian civilization, but things appertaining to primitive non-Aryan tribes also, found entrance into the Aryan polity; and the torment of these unassimilable intrusions has been a darkly cruel legacy left to the succeeding Hindu society.

When the non-Aryan gods found place in the Aryan pantheon, their inclusion was symbolized by the Trinity, Brahmā, Vishnu and Siva—Brahmā standing for the ancient tradition, exclusive externalism; Vishnu for the transition when the original Vedic Sun-god became humanized and emerged from the rigid enclosure of scriptural texts into the world of the living human heart; and Siva for the period when the non-Aryan found entrance into the social organization of the Aryan. But though the Aryan and non-Aryan thus met, they did not merge completely. Like the Ganges and the Jamuna at their confluence, they flowed on together in two separately distinguishable streams.

In spite of Siva's entry amongst the Aryan gods, his Aryan and non-Aryan aspects remained different. In the former, he is the lord of ascetics, who, having conquered desire, is rapt in the bliss of *nirvāṇa,* as bare of raiment as of worldly ties. In the latter, he is terrible, clad in raw, bleeding elephant hide, intoxicated by the hemp decoction. In the former, he is the replica of Buddha, and as such has captured many a Buddhist shrine; in the latter, he is the overlord of demons, spirits and other dreadful beings, who haunt the places of the dead, and as such has appropriated to himself the worshippers of the phallus, and of snakes, trees and other totems. In the former, he is worshipped in the quietude of meditation; in the latter, in frenzied orgies of self-torture.

Similarly in the Vaishnava cult, Krishna, who became the mythological god of the non-Aryan religious legends, was not the same in character as the brave and sagacious ruler of Dvārakā who acted as the guide, philosopher and friend of the valiant Arjuna. Alongside the heights of the Song Celestial are ranged the popular religious stories of the cowherd tribes.

But in spite of all that was achieved, it was quite impossible, even for the Aryan genius, to bring into harmony with itself and assimilate each and every one of the practices, beliefs and myths of innumerable non-Aryan tribes. More and more of what was non-Aryan came to be not merely tolerated, but welcomed in spite of incongruities, as the non-Aryan element became increasingly predominant in the race mixture. This led to the formulation of the principle that any religion which should satisfy the capacity of a particular sect was enough for its salvation. But in consequence, the organizing force was reduced to the mere compulsion of some common customs, some repetition of external practices, which barely served loosely to hold together these heterogeneous elements. For the mind which has lost its vigour, all external habits become tyrannical. The result for India is that the tie of custom which is extraneous has become severely tight, hardly leaving any freedom of movement even in insignificant details of life. This has developed in the people an excessively strong sense of responsibility to the claims of the class tradition which divides, but not the conviction of that inner moral responsibility which unites.

We have seen how, after the decline of Buddhism, a path had to be cleared through the jungle of rank undergrowth which had been allowed to run wild during the prolonged inaction of the Brahmanic hierarchy. At the latter end of its career in India the mighty stream of Buddhism grew sluggish and lost itself in morasses of primitive superstitions and promiscuous creeds and practices, which had their root in non-Aryan crudities. It had lost its depth of philosophy and breadth of humanity, which had their origin in the Aryan mind.

Therefore the time came for the Brahmins to assert themselves and bring bark into the heart of all this incongruity some unity of ideal, which it had always been their function to maintain. It was now a difficult task for them because of the varied racial strains which had become part of the constitution of the Indian people. And so, in order to save their ideals from the attack of this wild exuberance of heterogeneous life, they fixed them in a permanent rigidity. This had the reactionary effect of making their own ideals inert, and unfit for adaptation to changes of time; while it left to all the living elements of the different races included in the people their freedom of growth, unguided by any dictates of reason. The result has been our huge medley of customs, ceremonials and creeds, some of which are the ruins of the old, and some merely the anomalies of the living outgrowths which continue clinging to them and smothering them in the process.

And yet the genius of India went on working, albeit through the tremendous obstacle of the shackled mind of the people. In the Vedic times, as we have seen, it was mainly the Kshatriyas who repeatedly brought storms of fresh thought into the atmosphere of the people's life whenever it showed signs of stagnation. In later ages, when the Kshatriyas had lost their individuality, the message of the spiritual freedom and unity of man mainly sprang from the obscure strata of the community, where belonged the castes that were despised. Though it has to be admitted that in the medieval age the Brahmin Rāmānanda was the first to give voice to the cry of unity, which is India's own, and in consequence lost his honoured privileges as a Brahmin guru, yet it is none the less true that most of our great saints of that time, who took up this cry in their life and teaching and songs, came from the lower classes, one of them being a Muhammadan weaver, one a cobbler, and several coming from ranks of society whose touch would pollute the drinking water of the respectable section of Hindus. And thus the living voice of India ever found its medium even in the darkest days of our downfall, the voice which proclaimed that he only knows Truth who knows the unity of all beings in the spirit.

The age in which we now live, we cannot see clearly in its true features, as from without. Yet we feel that the India of to-day has roused herself once more to search out her truth, her harmony, her oneness, not only among her own constituent elements, but with the great world. The current of her life, which had been dammed up in stagnation, has found some breach in the wall and can feel the pulse of the tidal waves of humanity outside. We shall learn that we can reach the great world of man, not through the effacement but through the expansion of our own individuality. We shall know for certain that just as it is futile mendicancy to covet the wealth of others in place of our own, so also to keep ourselves segregated and starved by refusing the gift which is the common heritage of man because it is brought to us by a foreign messenger, only makes for utter destitution.

Our western critics, whose own people, whenever confronted with non-western races in a close contact, never know any other solution of the problem but extermination or expulsion by physical force, and whose caste feeling against darker races is brutally aggressive and contemptuous, are ready to judge us with a sneering sense of superiority when comparing India's history with their own. They never take into consideration the enormous burden of difficulty which Indian civilization has taken upon itself from its commencement. India is the one country in the world where the Aryan colonizers had to make constant social adjustments with peoples who vastly outnumbered them, who were physically and mentally alien to their own race, and who were for the most part distinctly inferior to the invaders. Europe, on the other hand, is one in mind; her dress, custom, culture, and with small variations her habits, are one. Yet her inhabitants, although only politically divided, the perpetually making preparations for deadly combats, wherein entire populations indulge in orgies of wholesale destruction unparalleled in ferocity in the history of the barbarian. It is not merely such periodic irruptions of bloody feuds that are the worst characteristic of the relationship between the countries of Europe, even after centuries of close contact and intellectual co-operation, but there is also the intense feeling of mutual suspicion generating diplomatic deceitfulness and shameless moral obliquities.

India's problem has been far more complex than that of the West, and I admit that our rigid system of social regulation has not solved it. For, to bring order and peace at the cost of life is terribly wasteful, whether in the policy of government or of society. But all the same, I believe that we have cause to be proud of the fact that for a long series of centuries beset with vicissitudes of stupendous proportions, crowded with things that are incongruous and facts that are irrelevant, India still keeps alive the inner principle of her own civilization against the cyclonic fury of contradictions and the gravitational pull of the dust.

This has been the great function of the Brahmins of this land, to keep the lamp lighted when the storm has been raging on all sides. It has been their endeavour gradually to permeate the tremendous mass of obstructive material with some quickening ideal of their own that would transmute it into the life-stuff of a composite civilization; to discover some ultimate meaning in the inarticulate primitive forms struggling for expression, and to give it a voice. In a word, it was the mission of the Brahmin to comprehend by the light of his own mature understanding the undeveloped minds of the people.

It would be wrong for us, when we judge the historical career of India, to put all the stress upon the accumulated heap of refuse, gross and grotesque, that has not yet been assimilated in one consistent cultural body. Our great hope lies there, where we realize that something positively precious in our achievements still persists in spite of circumstances that are inclement. The best of us still have our aspiration for the supreme end of life, which is so often mocked at by the prosperous people who hold their sway over the present-day world. We still believe that the world has a deeper meaning than what is apparent, and that therein the human soul finds its ultimate harmony and peace. We still know that only in this spiritual wealth and welfare does civilization attain its end, and not in a prolific production of materials, not in the competition of intemperate power with power.

It has certainly been unfortunate for us that we have neglected the cult of *Anna Brahma,* the infinite as manifested in the material world of utility, and we are dearly paying for it. We have set our mind upon realizing the eternal in the intensity of spiritual consciousness so long, that we have overlooked the importance of realizing the infinite in the world of extension by ever pursuing a path which is endless. And in this great field of adventure the West has attained its success, for which humanity has to be immensely grateful to it.

But the true happiness and peace are awaiting the children of the West in the *tapasyā*, which is for realizing Brahma in spirit, for acquiring the luminous inner vision before which the sphere of immortality reveals itself. If ever that time comes, if the western world does not meet its catastrophic end under the trampling tread of contending commerce and politics, of monstrous greed and hatred, then the world will owe its gratitude to the Brahmins for the faith in the infinitude of the human spirit which they have upheld in the face of forces that spurned it, exultingly counting the skulls of their victims.

I love India, not because I cultivate the idolatry of geography, not because I have had the chance to be born in her soil, but because she has saved through tumultuous ages the living words that have issued from the illuminated consciousness of her great sons: *Satyam, Jñānam, Anantam Brahma,* Brahma is truth, Brahma is wisdom, Brahma is infinite; *Sāntam, Sivam, Advaitam,* peace is in Brahma, goodness is in Brahma, and the unity of all beings.

ब्रह्मनिष्ठोगृहस्थः स्यात् तत्त्वज्ञानपरायणः ।
यद्यत् कर्म प्रकुर्वीत तद्ब्रह्मणि समर्पयेत् ।।[1]

The householder shall have his life established in Brahma, shall pursue the deeper truth of all things and in all activities of life dedicate his works to the Eternal Being.

Thus we have come to know that what India truly seeks is not a peace which is in negation or in some mechanical adjustment, but that which is in *Sivam,* in goodness, which is in

1. The *Mahānirvāṇ Tantra,* 8/23.

Advaitam, in the truth of perfect union; that India does not enjoin her children to cease from *karma,* but to perform their *karma* in the presence of the Eternal, with the pure knowledge of the spiritual meaning of existence; that this is the true prayer of Mother India:

> य एकोऽवर्णोबहुधा शक्तियोगाद्
> वर्णाननेकान्निहितार्थोदधाति ।
> विचैति चान्ते विश्वमादौ सदेव:
> सनोबुद्धया शुभया संयुनक्तु ।।[1]

> He who is one, who is above all colour distinctions, who dispenses the inherent needs of men of all colours, who comprehends all things from their beginning to the end, let Him unite us to one another with the wisdom which is the wisdom of goodness.

1923

---

1. The *Svetāsvataropanishad,* 4/1.
All the translations of the verses from the *Bhagavad-Gītā* are in the words of Annie Besant.

The Way to Unity

Now that mutual intercourse has become easy, and the different peoples and nations of the world have come to know one another in various relations, one might have thought that the time had arrived to merge their differences in a common unity. But the significant thing is, that the more the doors are opening and the walls breaking down outwardly, the greater is the force which the consciousness of individual distinction is gaining within. There was a time when we believed that men were remaining separate, because of the obstacles between them; but the removal of these to the largest possible extent, is not seen to have the effect of doing away with the differences between diverse sections of mankind.

The smaller nations, who had been content to remain attached to one or other of the greater powers, have become restlessly anxious to be established on their own separate bases. Norway and Sweden have become divided from each other. Ireland has been struggling unweariedly through many a long year to achieve her separateness; her people, meanwhile, also being busy with the revival of their own literature. The Flemings have become enthusiastic about winning a distinct place for their original language and culture in Belgium, where so long French had reigned undisputed. The minor peoples who lived side by side within the Empire of Austria, have burst their bonds and are happy to have their separate existence. Russia in its frantic efforts to absorb Finland discovered that it was easier to swallow than to assimilate. For all the blood which flowed in Turkey, in her day of undisputed Empire, the differences of her subject races could not be washed away. For England, the desire to consolidate her overseas dominions into integral parts of a truly imperial body, has become an obsession; but none of the proposals for facilitating centralised control has met with favour in her colonies, who protest vigorously whenever any specific freedom of theirs is at stake.

The shibboleths, that unification means strength, or that bulk means greatness, do not hold today. Where there is a true distinction, its truth does not admit of being blindly overlooked for the sake of expediency, or in the hope of greater solidarity. Suppressed distinctions are dangerously explosive, and if allowed to remain suppressed may burst out in a revolution at the slightest shock. The true way to maintain a harmonious unity is by according due respect to the true distinctness of the different parts.

When man realises his own individuality, it stimulates his desire to grow greater. This growth of greatness for an individual can only become real by establishing wide relationship with a large number of other individuals. He who has no conscious regard for his own personality, lets go the helm of self and becomes merged in the crowd. In this he does not attain greatness, because one's relation to a crowd is a superficial relation of mere propinquity, with no scope for that ever-active voluntary adjustment which is living and creative. The differences of sleeping men are hardly perceptible, but these loudly assert themselves in the waking state. In the bud, the petals are compressed into oneness: only when each petal attains its separate distinctness, does it find its perfect unity in a flower and can help to attain the common object, which is fruition. Today the clash of the different parts of the world coming into contact, has brought about a general awakening, and under the law of manifestation each part is seeking its own self-unfoldment. No living thing, whose vital force is awake can feel itself any the greater by merging into something else, however large; it stakes its very life to be saved from being assimilated into something bigger, however superior that may be to itself.

What then is to be the end of such sectional movements? Nothing more or less than this, that the consciousness of the dignity of separate individuality will impel man to accept suffering for the sake of becoming greater; and true greatness can only be achieved by each section of mankind finding its field of self-realization in the great world of man. Only then can be attained real Unity, harmonious in structure, and therefore permanent. The artificial consolidation of the mangled in spirit, the crippled in life, the dependent and the hard-pressed, can only remain a jumble of incongruent parts.

At the period of the Swadeshi movement in Bengal, we experienced a desire to make the Moslems one with ourselves, but we did not succeed in doing so. Doubtless a coalition with them would have been very convenient for us, but it is not enough that a thing should be convenient for it to be feasible. If there are differences between Hindu and Moslem which are real, they cannot be spirited away by any jugglery. If, in our anxiety to secure some convenience, we ignore the facts, the facts will ignore our convenience. We failed because the invitation which we extended to the Moslems was for serving a purpose, not because it was inevitable, as is the invitation of mutual good feeling in common service.

True, in the immediate past, the consciousness of differences in the two communities was not obtrusively strong. Both of us then lived as neighbours under conditions which did not tend to bring out our divergence so acutely as to make us aware of it to the degree of active opposition. But, after all, the lack of consciousness, whether of differences or anything else, does not point to any superiority in our former circumstances; it merely shows that something then was wanting in ourselves, namely, vigour of life. Along with the arousing of our political aspiration, the movement of Hindu revivalism was started as a protest against the western influence on our life and mind. When, with the new age, the Hindu rose to a sense of the dignity of his Hinduism, if the Moslem had simply acquiesced therein, that would doubtless have suited us admirably; but the same causes likewise roused the Moslem to a sense of the dignity of Islam.

What is disconcerting in this circumstance is the fact that, while it lasts, peace between the two sections of the population can only be had either through apathy and forgetfulness, or through fear of foreign rule and common hatred against it. They may form an alliance for some such immediate object of mutual self-interest; but these alliances, like political alliances between countries which have traditions of antagonism, are not only transitory, but in constant danger of ending in violent re-action. For, the bond which depends upon some special expectation, either becomes a menace at the slightest sign of disappointment, or ceases to exist when that expectation is fulfilled. The most difficult problem for India is, that both Hindus and Mohamedan, when they reach the full consciousness of their individuality, become, in the natural course of things as they exist today, mutually exclusive and antagonistic.

There must be something radically wrong in our mental and social life when such can be the case. It must be the result of some narrowness of vision, some distrust of human nature in its universal aspect, which distracts our sympathy from the great course of its development that is to comprehend all humanity.

Individuality is precious, because only through it we can realize the universal. If it were a prison-house to shut us in for ever within a strictly circumscribed range of truth, devoid of movement or growth, then our existence itself would become an insult to us who have a living soul, just as a cage is to winged creatures. Unfortunately there are people who take enormous pride in magnifying their speciality and proclaiming to the world that they are fixed for ever on their pedestal of uniqueness. They forget that only discords are unique and therefore can claim their own separate place outside the universal world of music.

It should be the function of religion to provide us with this universal ideal of truth and maintain it in its purity. But men have often made perverse use of their religion, building with it permanent walls to ensure their own separateness. In the region of worldly interest, our individual boundaries, in spite of their strength, are adjustable; they are ever changing their lines of demarcation. A man who, in the natural course of things, is a stranger to me may establish intimate kinship with me tomorrow; one who has been my enemy may become my best friend in time. But if we use religion itself for the delimitation of our mutual relationships, then these boundaries become rigidly unalterable.

Religion must only deal with things that belong to the spiritual realm of the eternal, and with sentiments that are self-luminous, carrying their ultimate value in themselves. It should allow a great part of human existence to lie outside its direct interference, so that life may enjoy its freedom of growth guided by laws of reason, or rhythm of beauty. The guidance of reason constantly varies its course, in its perpetual process of adjustment with unforeseen circumstances; its scope is ever being widened by contact with new data. But if religion, which is to give us emancipation in the realm of the infinite, tries also to usurp the place of reason in the world of the finite, then it brings about utter stagnation and sterility.

There was a time in the middle age in Europe when religion acted like a wall surrounding the whole life of the people. We know how it tried to keep its sway over the western world through persecution, excommunication and even suppression of science. By the sheer vigour of their intellect the western people have broken through this imprisonment of their mind and have achieved in their life a freedom which makes it possible for them to approach and receive truth in its various phases and forms.

Intercourse between men is not merely external its deepest channel is through the freedom of mind. When religion instead of emancipating mind, fetters it within the narrow confinement of creeds and conventions, then it becomes the greatest barrier against a true meeting of races. Christianity, when it minimises its spiritual truth which is universal and emphasises its dogmatic side which is a mere accretion of time has the same effect of creating a mental obstruction which leads to the misunderstanding of people who are outside its pale. A great deal of the unmerited contempt and cruelty, which the non-western peoples have suffered in their political, commercial or other relations at the hands of the West, is owing to sectarian calumnies with which even the western children's textbooks are contaminated. Nevertheless this sectarian religion does not occupy the greater part of the western life and therefore in its heart still remains the possibility of a better human relationship than what prevails now between the races.

We have seen Europe cruelly unscrupulous in its politics and commerce, widely spreading slavery over the face of the earth in various names and forms. And yet, in this very same Europe, protest is always alive against its own iniquities. Martyrs are never absent whose lives of sacrifice are the penance for the wrongs done by their own kindred. The individuality which is western is not to be designated by any sect-name of a particular religion, but is distinguished by its eager attitude towards truth, in two of its aspects, scientific and humanistic. This openness of mind to Truth has also its moral value and so in the West it has often been noticed that, while those who are professedly pious have sided with tyrannical power, encouraging repression of freedom, the men of intellect, the sceptics, have bravely stood for justice and the rights of man.

I do not mean to say that those who seek truth always find truth, and we know that men in the West are apt to borrow the sanction of science under false pretences to give expression to their passions and prejudices. To many thinkers there has appeared a clear connection between Darwin's theories and the 'imperialism', Teutonic and other, which was so marked a feature during the 'sixties. We have also read western authors who, admirably mimicking scientific mannerism, assert that only the so-called Nordic race has the proper quality and therefore the right to rule the world, extolling its characteristic ruthlessness as giving it the claim to universal dominance. But we must not forget that such aberrations of science, padded with wrong or imperfect data, will be knocked down by science itself. The stream of water in a river does carry sand, but so long as the stream is fluent it will push away that sand from its own path. If the mental attitude is right we need not be afraid of mistakes. That is why the individual in the West has no unsurpassable barrier between himself and the rest of humanity. He may have his prejudices, but no irrational injunctions to keep him in internment away from the wide world of men.

A Mahomedan is defined by his religion. But a religion does not consist merely in its spiritual essence; a great deal of it is formal, the outcome of special historical circumstances. All things that constitute mere forms of religion are exclusive,—no man belonging to a different creed can claim them as his own. These are, therefore, fences that separate; and are, moreover, constant causes of conflict so long as they are more valued than the essential truths of religion. Therefore the people who are chiefly recognised by their religion, whose behaviour and intellect itself is dominated by the externals of that religion, must find it difficult to establish channels of intimate relationship with neighbours belonging to a different religion.

Men often are unreasonable, but their unreason is as fluid in character as life itself; it is constantly mitigated by experience and education. But when religion stands against reason in the region which by right belongs to the latter, then it becomes a fixed screen of darkness against all communication of light. Truth finds no permanent antagonism in our passion or stupidity, just as sunshine is not perpetually obstructed by mist. But when religion, with its own material and authority, builds a barricade against truth, then woe to the men who bend their knees to such a power, terrible because it is the power of light that has blinded itself.

On the other side, a Hindu also is known by his speciality, which is not so much his religion as his social conventions. A Mahomedan is comparatively free in matters of his personal life, as to his food, companionship or occupation. Therefore he has more freedom of opportunity in the choice of his vocation than an orthodox Hindu. A narrow range of vocation not only curtails for men their field of livelihood, but also limits their chance of coming into close touch with others in the active pursuit of common objects. Surrounded in his personal life by prohibitions of all kinds about the most insignificant details of his daily career, an orthodox Hindu lives insulated in the confinement of his conventional solitary cell. His is a world which has its one gate of entrance, the gate of birth, though those of departure are innumerable. The strict code of Hinduism is, in every way, inhospitable to the world at large, which cannot but re-act upon the mind of the orthodox Hindu by narrowing and deadening his human interest, detracting from his power of forming great combinations.

We have to realize this in India, and know that the religion, chiefly based upon a fixed code of custom, which we have allowed to fasten upon the entire region of our life, has been the one radical cause of the separateness of our races, and has made the cracks from which comes out the poisonous gas of degeneracy.

The problem of untouchability is merely one of the numerous symptoms of this fatal malady. By suppressing these through external means we do not cure the disease. The thorny bushes of evil are overspreading our social soil, made barren by the obsession of a religion that insults reason. Uprooting a few of these will not help us in improving the soil, the impoverishment of which is the real origin of our futility.

Civilization is that which gives individuals the best facility to deal with the greatest number of human beings in the noblest spirit of truth. Unfortunately for India, the latter development of Hinduism has been the product of a history of re-action. It represents the most powerfully organized effort of a people, not only to withdraw itself from contact with the larger world, but also to separate its own component parts so that they become out of touch with each other. The greater portion of the world is branded by it with impurity. Defilement is waiting for it at every turn, against which its only security is the strict system of segregation built up by itself. In order to build this effectively, it has not been content with forbidding its members to cross the sea, but has nearly obliterated from its annals and literature all mention of foreign contact. For, though from Greek, Tibetan, Chinese and other sources we find; materials for that great period of India's history when her influence transcended her geographical limits and spread civilization over peoples completely alien to her own children, we find no mention in the Indian scriptures about what those outside countries were to her. So much so, that all the records of the greatest of India's sons were banished for centuries from her memory, till they were brought back to her by foreigners. The mentality produced by such a contemptuous ignoring of the world outside her own immediate surroundings, still persists in the life and culture of India's people.

No doubt, in all parts of the world we have such restrictions of narrowness, under different names. Societies in all countries have their irrational conventions and traditions that have outlived their original meaning, clogging the path of human intercourse with incongruities. Everywhere such social holes and ditches are the breeding places of moral disease and callousness of heart. The spirit of nationalism itself in the West is another such confinement, which raises a barrier against the large human world and gives rise to degeneracy of soul. How, in the end, it becomes disastrous to its own cause, has been proved in the frank brutality of the late War, and perhaps more so in the sinister manoeuvres of the Peace conferences.

I know how reluctant it makes us feel to give any credit for humanity to the western civilization when we observe the brutalities into which this nationalism of theirs breaks out, instances of which are so numerous all the world over,—in the late war, in the lynching of Negroes, in cowardly outrages allowed to be committed by European soldiers upon helpless Indians, in the rapacity and vandalism practised in Peking during the Boxer war by the very people who are never tired of vulgarly applying the epithet of Hun to one section of their own confederates. But while I have never sought to gloss over or keep out of mind any of these ugly phenomena, I still aver that in the life of the West they have a large tract where their mind is free; whence the circulation of their thought currents can surround the world. This freedom of the mind's ventilation constantly bears in it the promise of righting the wrong and purifying the noxious accumulation within.

The latter-day orthodox Hinduism of our country, on the other hand, though free from militant aggressiveness, is even more fatal in its effects on its own votaries, for it has to kill the mind first in order to make it possible for human beings to accept such deprivation of freedom and outrage on dignity as are entailed by its prohibitions and exactions. Accustomed as we are to it, we may not feel the humiliation of such restriction of life and mind, or may even glorify it in our blind pride; but in these days, when we are talking about nation-building and the uniting of the different Indian races, we must know that Hindus and Mahomedans can never effect any real union until we can cast off the shackles of our non-essentials, and free our mind from the grip of unmeaning dead tradition.

To me the mere political necessity is unimportant; it is for the sake of our humanity, for the full growth of our soul, that we must turn our mind towards the ideal of the spiritual unity of man. We must use our social strength, not to guard ourselves against the touch of others, considering it as contamination, but generously to extend hospitality to the world, taking all its risks however numerous and grave. We must manfully accept the responsibility of moral freedom, which disdains to barricade itself within dead formulae of external regulation, timidly seeking its security in utter stagnation. For, men who live in dread of the spirit of enquiry and lack courage to launch out in the adventure of truth, can never achieve freedom in any department of life. Freedom is not for those who are not lovers of freedom and who only allow it standing space in the porter's vestibule for the sake of some temporary purpose, while worshipping, in the inner shrine of their life, the spirit of blind obedience.

In India what is needed more than anything else, is the broad mind which, only because it is conscious of its own vigorous individuality, is not afraid of accepting truth from all sources. Fortunately for us we know what such a mind has meant in an individual who belongs to modern India. I speak of Rammohun Roy. He was thoroughly oriental in his early training and did not study English till he was of mature age. He was a profound scholar of Sanskrit, Persian, Arabic and he learnt Hebrew in order to study the Old Testament in its original oriental setting. He knew more of Sanskrit scriptures and Indian philosophy than any contemporary pandit. His learning, because of its depth and comprehensiveness, did not merely furnish him with materials for scholarship, but trained his mind for the free acceptance of truth. Rammohun Roy developed the courage and capacity to discriminate between things that are essential and those that are non-essential in the culture which was his by inheritance. This helped him to realise that, truth can never be foreign, that money and material may exclusively belong to the particular country which produces them, but not knowledge, or ideas, or immortal forms of art.

The spirit of orthodox Hinduism is not modern, because it is fixed in the past,—the present age does not exist for it, and therefore it goes on missing its future. Rammohun Roy received from the storehouse of his country's past, things that were living. Therefore the future for him had its reality. For, life has its growth, which means that it perpetually carries its future in its own past and present; in other words, its present is a bridge between its past and its future. Rammohun was typically modern, because in his life and work he not only built such a bridge between the past and the future of his own country, but between India and the rest of the world.

The very magnitude of mind of such men becomes almost a grievance for smaller personalities, and Rammohun has been misunderstood by his own countrymen because he had in him this modern spirit of freedom and comprehensive grasp of truth. We must, however, never make the mistake that those great men who are belittled by their contemporary compatriots do not represent their countries; for, countries are not always true to themselves.

Giordano Bruno more truly represented the spirit of the intellectual probity of Europe than the Europe herself of that period which killed him. The Judea which held her god to be the god of a chosen people did not clearly know her own ideal; her truth was represented by the prophets who realized the Kingdom of God in the unbounded realm of humanity. The true life of India has been obscured by the night which overtook her and the slightest glimmer of light on her eastern horizon is more her own than the vast darkness which contradicts it. The India which keeps her religion shackled in chains of dead custom that refuse to be responsible to reason or to conscience, is *maya,*—she reveals her soul only there, where her seers have declared that religion recognises no external bond.

We have often seen in human history that at the very time and place where facts appear overwhelming in their congregated attack against the dignity of man, there appears the prophet who discovers some sovereign truth which raises its head above the rebellious turmoil. And because in India the heterogeneity of races is a most overbearing fact that has produced such incoherence of mind, such division in life, making our present problems seem well-nigh insoluble, there is a strong hope that in the India of to-day will be evolved some great spiritual guidance which will lead her to an enlightened future across irrational dogmas, or nationalistic cults. For, obstacles are like blocks of marble with which those who are artists amongst men fashion the best living images of truth.

In Rammohun Roy's life we find a concrete illustration of what India seeks, the true indication of her goal. Thoroughly steeped in the best culture of his country, he was capable of finding himself at home in the larger world. His culture was not for rejection of those cultures which came from foreign sources, on the contrary, it had an uncommon power of sympathy which could adjust itself to them with respectful receptiveness. His mind had a natural reverence for Saraswati, the goddess of knowledge,—for the Truth, whose dwelling is in the hundred-petalled lotus-heart of humanity. It is an utter lack of reverence for truth which, in the name of Patriotism, can ignore the grand quest of man for knowledge because, for the time being, its field of activity happens to be in the West. And I must strenuously maintain that such irreverence is not in harmony with the spirit of our land.

The ideal I have formed of the culture which should be universal in India, has become clear to me from the life of Rammohun Roy. I have come to feel that the mind, which has been matured in the atmosphere of a profound knowledge of its own country and of the perfect thoughts that have been produced in that land, is ready to accept and assimilate the cultures that come from foreign countries. He who has no wealth of his own can only beg, and those who are compelled to follow the profession of beggary at the gate of the intellectually rich may gain occasional scraps of mental food, but they are sure to lose the strength of their intellectual character and their minds are doomed to become timid in thought and in creative endeavour.

All this time we have been receiving education on purely western lines. When this first began, western culture was imbued with a supreme contempt for that of the East. And to this day, consequently, we have been brought up in this contempt. This speaks of internal dissensions within the temple of Mother Saraswati. Her eastern sons kept closed the door leading to the western side for fear of adulteration, and her western sons barred their eastern windows through want of respect. Meanwhile the system of education in India remained, and still remains, absurdly un-Indian, making no adequate provision for our own culture. We have, here, not even anything like the facility which the German student enjoys in Germany, for the study of the lore of Hindu and Moslem. And if we have become conscious of this vital deficiency in our education, that is because of the spirit of the times.

A certain number of us do not admit that our culture has any special features of value. These good people I leave out of account. But the number of those others is not few, who while admitting this value in theory, ignore it more or less in practice. Very often, the flourishing of the banner of this culture is not for the sake of the love of truth but for that of national vaingloriousness,—like brandishing a musical instrument in athletic display before one's own admiring family, instead of using it to make music.

This section of our people while never neglecting to make proud boast of their country's glory, have an absurdly narrow conception of the ideal in which that glory consists. Their indiscriminate reverence is for the actual, not for the eternal. The habits and customs of our decadence which have set up barriers between us and the world, splitting us into mutually exclusive sections, making us weak and bowing our heads in shame at every turn of our later history,—these are the idols of their special worship, which they endow with endless virtues of their own imagining. They consider it to be their sacred mission to retain in perpetuity the waste matter sloughed off by age, as the true insignia of our Hindu civilization; to extol the gleam of the will-o-the-wisp, born of the noxious miasma of decay, as more time-hallowed than the light of sun, moon and stars.

Up to now we have not been submitting our own scriptures to the same critical, historical and scientific tests to which we are accustomed in the case of western lore. As if, everywhere else in the world, the normality of universal law prevails, but the door is barred to it in India, whose history, forsooth, has no beginning and is altogether beyond the province of science! Some god is responsible for its grammar, another for its chemistry, a third for its science of medicine. Everything in this wonderland has been set going, once for all, by the co-operation of gods and sages. What critic can be allowed to pry too curiously into an arrangement of such perfection? That is why even our educated men do not feel any qualms in counting our miraculous myths as integral parts of our history.

Therefore it is reckoned as a sin to enquire into the why and wherefore of what we do as Hindus. The ordinary laws of cause and effect cannot be taken into consideration in the India of the Infallibles, where the injunctions of the *shastras* are the one cause of all action. So when we debate whether sea-voyage is good or bad, we have to look into our scriptures to find the reply; and if we want to know whether the presence of a particular person in the room will contaminate the water in our vessels, we must go to a pandit for the solution. If we dare to question why the caste, which may handle our milk or our molasses, may not come near our water, or why foreign food should destroy our caste while foreign strong drink apparently does not, our mouths may be stopped, in more senses than one, by a stoppage of all supplies.

It seems to me that one reason for the persistence of these absurdities, even in our educated circles, is, that we reserve western science and method only for our school hours, while the current traditions and beliefs are imbibed at other times when, with our school dress, we have likewise doffed the school habit of precise thinking. They are kept in separate compartments, and so never come to a mutual understanding. Thus it is no matter of difficulty for us to believe that only in our class lessons we need to be rational; for the rest, if we be but grammatical, that is enough.

In our greed for immediate political result, we are apt to ascribe the fact of our tendency towards separateness to accidental circumstances, refusing to see that a code of behaviour, which has not the sanction of reason, and yet has the support of religion, must result in the creation of irreconcilable divisions between men. In reason alone can we have our common meeting ground; for that which is against reason needs must be peculiar and exclusive, offering constant friction until worn away by the ever-active, rational mind of man. So when, for a body of men, popular custom is artificially protected by a religion which is allowed to usurp the entire range of human knowledge and conduct, it becomes a potent factor in maintaining an immense gap of aloofness and antagonism between closest neighbours.

The evolving Hindu social ideal has never been present to us as a whole, so that we have only a vague conception of what the Hindu has achieved in the past, or can attempt in the future. The partial view, before us at any moment, appears at the time to be the most important, so we can hardly bring ourselves to believe that it is this very aspect which, not only hides from us the true ideal, but tends to destroy it. And we have thus come to imagine a picture of the Hindu Samaj continually bathing, fasting and telling beads, emaciated with doing penance, shrinking into a corner away from the rest of the world.

We forget that Hindu civilization was once very much alive, crossing the seas, planting colonies, giving to and taking from all the world. It had its arts, its commerce, its vast and strenuous field of work. In its history, new ideas had their scope, social and religious revolutions their opportunity. Its women also, had their learning, their bravery, their place in the civic life. In every page of the Mahābhārata we shall find proofs that it was no rigid, cast-iron type of civilization. The men of those days did not, like marionettes, play the same set piece over and over again. They progressed through mistakes, made discoveries through experiment, and gained truth through striving. They belonged to a free and varied *samāj,* quick with life, driven into ever new enterprise by its active vigour.

This, however, was a society which orthodoxy to-day would hardly recognise as Hindu, because it was living and had a growth which was revealing its inner unity through outer changes. So the *dharma* of life which thinks and doubts, accepts and rejects, progresses, changes and evolves, cannot, according to orthodoxy, be a part of the Hindu Dharma. Man shows his mental feebleness when he loses his faith in life because it is difficult to govern, and is only willing to take the responsibility of the dead because they are content to lie still under an elaborately decorated tomb-stone of his own make. We must know that life carries its own weight, while the burden of the dead is heavy to bear,—an intolerable burden which has been pressing upon our country for ages. Can we really believe that with this incubus of social inertness on our bowed back we can cross the pathless wilderness and succeed in reaching the hill-top of political independence?

The fact stands out clearly to-day that the Divinity dwelling within the heart of man cannot be kept immured any longer in the darkness of particular temples. The day of the *Ratha-yātrā,* the Car Festival, has arrived when He shall come out on the highway of the world, into the thick of the joys and sorrows, the mutual commerce, of the throng of men. Each of us must set to work to build such car as we can, to take its place in the grand procession. The material of some may be of value, of others cheap. Some may break down on the way, others last till the end. But the day has come at last when all the cars must set out.

I feel proud that I have been born in this great age. I know that it must take time before we can adjust our minds to a condition which is not only new, but almost exactly the opposite of the old. Let us not imagine the death struggle of the doomed to be a sign of life. Let us announce to the world that the light of the morning has come, not for entrenching ourselves behind barriers, but for meeting in mutual understanding and trust on the common field of co-operation; never for nourishing a spirit of rejection, but for that glad acceptance which constantly carries in itself the giving out of the best that we have.

1923